PRAISE FOR *Awake*

"In our pursuit of happiness, this moving book should be a dog-eared, worn-out companion. . . . As you work through this elegant material, you will find yourself laughing a little longer, dancing a little more, and awakening to the beauty of what lies inside you and in those nearby."
—DACHER KELTNER, professor of psychology, UC Berkeley, and author of *Born to Be Good: The Science of a Meaningful Life*

"This book is an inspiring gift that will open your heart to the presence of love and joy in everyday life."
—FRANCES VAUGHAN, PH.D., psychologist, and author of *Shadows of the Sacred: Seeing Through Spiritual Illusions*

"This book should be read by every person who cares about making this a better world. It can enhance the joys of working to develop a wiser and more compassionate society, and help make us both happier and more effective in challenging times."
—DANIEL ELLSBERG, author of *Secrets: A Memoir of Vietnam and the Pentagon Papers*

"Faith, hope, and love have long been considered the essential virtues of the religious life. James Baraz has done us all a great service by elevating joy to its rightful place alongside the trinity of sacred emotions."
—PATRICIA E. DE JONG, senior minister, First Congregational Church of Berkeley

"This is an inspirational and practical resource that helps us identify where we are or are not experiencing joy in our lives. This original book addresses the primary obstacles or beliefs that hinder our access to joy, and includes timeless practices and ways in which we can expand, cultivate, express, and experience more joy in our lives and within our own nature. Well-written, informative, and a significant contribution to everyone's well-being."
—ANGELES ARRIEN, PH.D., cultural anthropologist, and author of *The Second Half of Life: Opening the Eight Gates of Wisdom*

"I have been deeply touched and inspired by James Baraz's accessible, practical wisdom. His genuine caring for people and enthusiasm for life generously pours forth and permeates everything that he teaches—now in the pages of this book."
—RABBI MARGIE JACOBS, Institute for Jewish Spirituality

"*Awakening Joy* is a wise treasure house of valuable information, anecdotes, potent quotes, and creative suggestions to step into one's power and live life to the max. This book is a rich, inspiring resource I'm excited to share with my yoga students."
—GABRIEL HALPERN, founder and director of
the Yoga Circle, Chicago

"To awaken joy in oneself and others is one of life's great skills, a skill taught by sages across the centuries, and now distilled in this book."
—ROGER WALSH, M.D., PH.D., University of California Medical
School, author of *Essential Spirituality: The Seven Central Practices
to Awaken Heart and Mind*

"Grounded in brain science and positive psychology, and illuminated by the practical wisdom of Buddhism, this book shows you many effective ways to have more happiness, love, and inner peace. Honest, powerful, and profound, each page comes alive with James's warm and friendly voice, sharing his own hard lessons and the stories of others, and guiding you toward an unshakeable joy of your own. A gem."
—RICK HANSON, PH.D., founder, Wellspring Institute for
Neuroscience and Contemplative Wisdom, and author of
Buddha's Brain: The Practical Neuroscience of Happiness, Love, and Wisdom

AWAKENING JOY

AWAKENING
JOY

10 STEPS TO HAPPINESS

James Baraz

and Shoshana Alexander

PARALLAX
PRESS

Berkeley, California

Parallax Press
P.O. Box 7355
Berkeley, California 94707
www.parallax.org

Parallax Press is the publishing division of Unified Buddhist Church, Inc.

Cover and text design by Gopa & Ted2, Inc.
Cover image © iStockphoto
James Baraz photo by Fred Goldsmith
Shoshana Alexander photo by Judith Pavlik

Published by arrangement with Ballantine Books, an imprint of The Random
House Publishing Group, a division of Random House, Inc.

Library of Congress Cataloging-in-Publication Data
Baraz, James.
Awakening joy : 10 steps to happiness /
James Baraz and Shoshana Alexander.
p. cm.
Includes bibliographical references and index.
ISBN 978-1-937006-22-8 (alk. paper)
1. Happiness. 2. Self-actualization (Psychology)
3. Buddhism—Psychology. I. Alexander, Shoshana. II. Title.
BF575.H27B36 2013
158—c23
2012042578

2 3 4 5 / 16 15 14 13

To:
Arnold Baraz, who taught me how to love,

Neem Karoli Baba, who showed me that love and goodness
are all around if you look for them,

H.W.L. Poonja, who helped me reclaim my natural joy, and

Jane Baraz, my life partner, who teaches me to keep letting in
the love and sending it out, no matter what.
—JAMES BARAZ

To my son, Elias, and the late Buddy-gi, my fountains of joy;
to an emerging world where love and compassion make the
Earth beautiful again; and to Life—can't live without it.
—SHOSHANA ALEXANDER

Contents

Note on the Paperback Edition

Our intention when we first wrote *Awakening Joy* was to make a positive difference in people's lives. Since publication, it's been gratifying to receive regular feedback from readers on how the material has genuinely supported them in greater well-being. Additionally rewarding has been the fact that many groups in the US and around the world—book clubs, meditation groups, those participating in the Awakening Joy course—have practiced the principles together with great benefit.

My personal favorite response so far was the gratitude booklet Shoshana and I received signed by thirty inmates from the Jessup Correctional Institution in Jessup, Maryland (one of several prison groups that have gone through the material together). For ten weeks Drew Leder, a Professor of Philosophy at Loyola University, led a group of inmates in practicing the principles in *Awakening Joy*. I first received an email from him in which he spoke about the "very moving graduation ceremony where each of the thirty men spoke about the most valuable lessons they had learned." A few days later a booklet with a beautiful drawing of a lighthouse and the words "Thank you" on the cover came, and I treasure it. One group member, Douglas Arey, explained, "The lighthouse, (drawn by Fortunato Mendes) symbolizes the light you shine on the otherwise dark obscure corners of the penal system. We are grateful for your great support." Another inmate, Brother John Woodland, signed, "Thank you for writing this book. It has helped provide me with tools and examples to face life's challenges. It was so instrumental that I shared it with my son and daughter. Grateful and thankful." Vincent Greco wrote, "Seeking joy after thirty-one years in prison can be a daunting endeavor, but your guiding insights have helped. Thanks so much."

Receiving that gratitude booklet confirmed a basic belief I hold about our potential for well-being: No matter what our circumstances, we can train our hearts and minds to access the goodness inside us and, in the process, allow it to shine through so that we become a field of positive energy and love that awakens it in others as well.

With the publication of *Awakening Joy* in paperback, it is my hope that the material will reach many new readers, awaken their noblest qualities and, in its own way, be a source of healing in the world. I hope you enjoy it!

May you be happy and share your love well!

James Baraz
Berkeley, CA
June 2012

FOREWORD
Jack Kornfield

Y OU HOLD IN YOUR HANDS a book that can change your life—filled with inspiration and practical wisdom on how to live with more joy and well-being. James Baraz, my longtime colleague and dear friend, has always delighted in sharing teachings that inspire the mind and open the heart. This book is James at his finest. It draws on his wonderfully successful Awakening Joy course, which has shepherded thousands of students, even die-hard "unbelievers" and cynics, into a more joyful and happier life.

Without understanding the importance of happiness, spiritual life can feel like a grim duty or be confused with an endless self-improvement project. James Baraz and Shoshana Alexander, who were my students in my early years of teaching, skillfully build on principles and practices from the Buddhist tradition to offer a pathway to true happiness.

As human beings, we all participate in the eternal dance of pleasure and pain, gain and loss, praise and blame, and birth and death that make up our lives, what Oscar Wilde called the "tainted glory" of worldly incarnation. In *Awakening Joy,* you will learn how to find and live with joy in the midst of all life's changes. To be joyful does not mean ignoring the great measure of suffering in the world, nor avoiding responsibility for alleviating as much suffering as we can. James and Shoshana show us how joy enables us to be a part of the solution to suffering, as it enables us to uplift all those we touch.

Joy is our birthright. All young children (if they are not traumatized) have it; it is innate to our consciousness. Joy is a reflection of our true nature—a pure, timeless, inviolable spirit found in each of us. In these pages, which include modern neuroscientific research as well as inspiration from exemplars like the Dalai Lama, you will discover how the transformative practices of *Awakening Joy* can lead each of us to live with dignity, compassion, and gracious freedom.

Read these words slowly. Savor them and practice the exercises in this book. Use them to open your heart and transform your life. Your days on Earth will be full of blessings.

May it be so.

Jack Kornfield
Spirit Rock Meditation Center
Woodacre, CA
May 9, 2009

PREFACE

Ram Dass

JOY GIVES LIFE COLOR, and it counteracts the negative around us in people and in society. I am finding that old age can be joyful. There's wisdom in it; it's unhurried. Even the absence of memory has its good points. By connecting to the joy in myself, I find the joy in everybody else. Our own joy becomes something we share, and that helps awaken it in others.

Real joy is deeper inside us than the happiness we get from external circumstances. Knowing that you're going for true happiness is a very joyful thing. My guru, Neem Karoli Baba, would become joyful just knowing that his devotees were all aiming for the purest place in their hearts. He said that if you love everyone, serve everyone, and remember God—that will naturally bring you joy.

Love and contentment bring me very close to joy. Contentment leads you deeper into the moment, and there you find joy because you see that everything—the grass and the trees and the clouds—is a manifestation of the Divine. Everything becomes radiant. If you're a good lover of life, you will be tapping into joy.

I've known James Baraz for a long time, and he is skilled at presenting teachings on happiness in an accessible way. *Awakening Joy* is fun to read. The stories are marvelous and the information is to the point. It's a very friendly book, appealing to all readers. And if you happen to be a practitioner of Buddhism, you will find that it's a deliciously Buddhist book—with the accent on *delicious.* This book shows that the celebration and love of life can go together with deep wisdom. This is a beautiful, beautiful book. Enjoy it.

Ram Dass
Maui, HI
July 15, 2009

Introduction

B<small>Y HIS OWN ADMISSION</small>, Warren was a pessimist. "You're looking at someone who tends to see the downside of things," he warned me when he started coming to my classes. He had some reasons for feeling this way. Life had thrown him a few curveballs, among them an accident in his youth that had left him with chronic pain. Despite being pretty well committed to "the downside," when he heard that I was creating a course called Awakening Joy, and would be teaching it in Berkeley where he lived, he was intrigued. He actually told me he wondered if changing his way of seeing things could make him happier. I wondered that myself, especially as the class got under way. Although I could see that the strategies and techniques were helping the other participants find more joy in their lives, after each session Warren would express his skepticism. I just figured, "Well, you can't win 'em all."

Then one evening he arrived at class with a noticeably different expression on his face. I was curious to hear what had happened. We started the class with each person reporting how the practices I gave as homework had been going since our previous meeting. To my surprise and delight, when Warren's turn came he told us that something quite unexpected seemed to be happening to him. "As I was driving into the city," he started, "there was a whole lot of really slow traffic. I tend to get frustrated when I'm caught in that, and I started, as I often do, thinking about everything that's wrong in our society. I was really getting on a roll."

We all nodded our heads, easily identifying with the scene. Warren continued, slowly speaking the words, as if amazed that they were coming out of his mouth. "Suddenly I stopped and said to myself, 'Now wait a minute. Is there any joy here?' I saw that I could just switch the channels. I looked out and I saw the water in the San Francisco Bay. I looked up and it was a clear day. I opened my sunroof and I said to myself, 'You know, it's not so bad.' I realized there is a switch that I'm starting to find that I didn't know was there before."

He looked at us and smiled as if to say, "Go figure." At that moment I knew that the tools in the Awakening Joy course had undeniable potential to unlock joy.

Joy and happiness are more than just good ideas. They can be the baseline on which we live our lives. The purpose of this book is to show how to access that switch inside and live life with greater joy. It's based on the program I've been teaching since the first course in my living room in 2003. Within a couple of years, it became an online course with people enrolled from around the world. Repeatedly I've seen that by cultivating certain behaviors and attitudes, participants can indeed bring greater well-being into their lives.

> *My life has taken a positive turn I'd have never believed possible. I truly believe my new focus is what made it possible to let go of a collapsed marriage, foreclosure on a home, and a bankruptcy. I now wake up and go to sleep with a conscious feeling of happiness.*
>
> —A COURSE PARTICIPANT

THE MANY FLAVORS OF JOY

Awakening Joy is based on a key principle: Our joy and happiness is up to us. Our suffering or well-being is not solely determined by what's happening in our present circumstances but to a large degree by our *relationship* to what is happening. As happiness experts Rick Foster and Greg Hicks say in their book *How We Choose to Be Happy*, happiness is a choice, and over time we can learn how to make it a habit.

This book will not create joy for you. Joy is already there inside you. It is inherent in every one of us, an innate capacity, like the ability to learn a language or to love. As innocent babies we came into this world with a natural joy, and we can discover it again.

The feeling of well-being I'm calling joy comes in many different flavors. And it can look very different from person to person, from a quiet sense of contentment to bubbly enthusiasm. For some people it's an energetic radiance; for others it's a quiet feeling of connection. Joy can arise as a belly laugh, or as a serenely contented smile that accepts life just as it is. We experience a profound joy when we let ourselves be touched by beauty and nature. We can feel an energetic lightness when we let ourselves be silly and playful. Acting with generosity or compassion uplifts our heart, as does the feeling that comes from living with integrity. We delight in seeing others happy, and we can be moved when we behold goodness and truth. We each have our own unique ways of experiencing and expressing joy based on our individual temperaments. Your happiness may not look like someone else's, but you can find the expression that is uniquely yours. One of your discoveries as you follow this program will be the many flavors of joy you can find in yourself.

"WHAT IF I'M NOT A JOYFUL PERSON?"

Is there a limit to how happy any one of us can be? Yes . . . and no. The idea of a "happiness set point" became popular for a while among psychologists and the general public. Early studies suggested that no matter what events or experiences happen to us—good or bad—we return to our typical level of happiness. However, recent research has painted a more complex picture, showing that in general, people have a changing happiness level that can rise and fall over time, and that we have the opportunity to improve our own level of well-being.

For example, Dr. Richard Davidson's research at the University of Wisconsin has been demonstrating the brain's ability to change and develop, even in adults. In her book *Train Your Mind, Change Your Brain*, Sharon Begley writes extensively about the results of Davidson's experiments. She concludes: "The basic finding that cognitive activity can alter activity in one of the brain's emotion regions supports the hope that mental training can shift the happiness set point." Davidson's intention is to demonstrate how such training can transform "the emotional mind." Whether you consider yourself a joyful person or not, you have a brain that is capable of changing.

Some people are uncomfortable with the word "joy." Perhaps the thought of "being happy" makes your eyes roll as if you're being asked to wear a permanent smiley face. Maybe it brings to mind syrupy TV ads of couples skipping through meadows of daisies. Don't worry. Truly happy people are not happy all the time. This is what Rick Foster and Greg Hicks found in their research, identifying and interviewing over three hundred individuals who live genuinely happy lives. Being sad and angry and feeling the whole range of human emotions is part of being alive. I'm not talking about adopting a Pollyanna attitude or living in denial. What I'm calling joy is a general feeling of aliveness and well-being that is characterized by meeting the ups and downs of life with authenticity and perspective.

This course has been superb! The fog of depression in which I began the year has almost entirely lifted. I am unspeakably grateful.

—A COURSE PARTICIPANT

If "joy" and "happiness" bring up resistance, see if there's another word that resonates better with you—well-being, contentment, delight, ease, aliveness—and substitute it as you participate in this program. You might use a variety of words to describe these uplifting states as I will do throughout this book.

FINDING JOY IN DIFFICULT TIMES

The thought of finding joy may seem out of touch with reality, especially during times of great challenge in your own life and in the lives of others.

What Is Joy?

Take a few moments to reflect on what the word "joy" evokes in you. What images come to mind? How is joy most naturally expressed through you? Notice any resistance you may have to the word and, if you need to, find the words that most closely express a state of well-being you value. Begin to pay attention to this state whenever you experience it in your life.

Every day we read stories in the news that make our hearts ache—from global climate change, to ideological wars, to mass foreclosures and company layoffs. Or we see in our neighborhoods and among our friends the fear that comes with economic uncertainty or health problems. Perhaps closer to home, we feel that fear ourselves. Awakening joy might seem like a frivolous endeavor.

I know the course has had a positive impact on me—but it is amazing to see how it can benefit others in my life. This stuff is absolutely contagious.

—A COURSE PARTICIPANT

For those of us who tend to carry the world on our shoulders, being joyful in a world of suffering can feel self-centered or like sticking our heads in the sand. Someone with this perspective stood up to speak at the opening session of an Awakening Joy course, his voice both thoughtful and troubled. "I'm having a big reaction here," he confessed. "All this talk of well-being and joy seems so disconnected from what's going on in the world. It's like we're all sitting around, safe and comfortable, singing, 'Someone's crying, Lord, Kumbaya.'" There were lots of nodding heads in the group.

Together we ended up dubbing this roadblock the "Kumbaya Factor," and it is one of the most convincing reasons to stop looking for joy before we start. While this critical issue will be considered more fully in Step Four, something was said in the discussion with this young man that made sense to him. Focusing only on the terrible things in the world, and overlooking the beauty and goodness, can lead us to pull back from life and fall into despair. Staying in touch with the well of joy enables us to be part of the solution, rather than part of the problem. It can motivate and support us in making a positive difference in our lives and in the world, not only through actions we might choose but also through the uplifting effect we can have on those we're in contact with.

In 2004, historian Howard Zinn published an inspiring article in *The Nation* magazine, entitled "The Optimism of Uncertainty." In it he wrote:

An optimist isn't necessarily a blithe, slightly sappy whistler in the dark of our time. To be hopeful in bad times is not just foolishly romantic. It is based on the fact that human history is a history not only of cruelty, but also of compassion, sacrifice, courage, kindness. What we choose to emphasize in this complex history will determine our lives. If we see only the worst, it destroys our capacity to do something. If we remember those times and places—and there are so many—where people have behaved magnificently, this gives us energy to act, and at least the possibility of sending this spinning top of a world in a different direction.

In Taoism it's said that life is made up of ten thousand joys and ten thousand sorrows. If we focus only on the sorrows, we're not seeing the full picture. When we open up to the joys—the beauty and goodness around us—we can view our suffering with a wider perspective. This course is not about denying the hard stuff. In fact, dealing with sorrow wisely when it comes is one of the essential practice themes of the Awakening Joy course.

The ten thousand joys and ten thousand sorrows are part of the full tapestry of life. Life is often hard; to awaken our joy does not mean to deny that. Those who discover the secret of well-being are capable and centered, able to be authentically engaged with whatever circumstances life presents. Although they feel the full range of emotions, they also know that anger, sadness, and fear are temporary visitors.

Trying hard to be joyful or happy will just be frustrating and work against you. When you're feeling sad or worried or angry or having other difficult feelings, don't pretend they're not there. Allow your experience to be just as it is while opening to the possibility of joy.

As we awaken to all that is good in ourselves and in others around us, we are reminded of how much we love life and care about this planet. Cultivating our goodness, aliveness, and joy not only feels good, it also helps us express our love more and awaken it in others. Our own joy becomes a gift to everyone we meet.

WHAT RELIGION IS A JOYFUL HEART?

Because I've been a teacher of Buddhist meditation for more than thirty years, many of the basic principles and time-tested practices in the Awakening Joy program come from that body of teachings. The Dalai Lama, a Tibetan Buddhist, says in *The Art of Happiness,* "The purpose of life is to be happy." The Buddha himself was known as The Happy One. He encouraged each person to discover where true happiness is found, saying if we aim for the highest happiness—a mind free of all negativity and confusion—every other kind of happiness will follow.

However, this is not a Buddhist course on happiness. There is no "Buddhist" happiness or Christian, Jewish, Muslim, or Hindu happiness. Our natural state of well-being is not exclusive to any particular spiritual tradition. Ministers, rabbis, and people from every faith—as well as those who follow no religion—have found this course beneficial. In fact, many people, including myself, consider Buddhism to be more a philosophy than a religion, a way to live a harmonious life. Because of its emphasis on discovering the truth for oneself rather than living by a set of doctrines, its basic principles can be put into practice by anyone.

CAN A BUDDHIST HAVE A GOOD TIME?

I was first drawn to the teachings and practices of Buddhism when I saw they could help with the insecurity and anxiety that had been my longtime companions. It was a great relief to hear what is known as the First Noble Truth: There is suffering in life. Finally someone was telling it like it is, rather than saying I should cheer up, count my blessings, and go shopping.

But it made me wonder if there was any room for enjoyment. I couldn't help noticing that dancing and singing didn't seem to be an integral part of the practice. I could see that the Buddha was smiling in most depictions of him, yet as I sat silently in meditation practice, sometimes in pain, there didn't seem to be the potential for a lot of what I was used to defining as "fun." In fact, we were being taught that seeking pleasure could lead us into the trap of unhealthy attachment—a kind of addiction to pleasure that causes us to suffer.

Soon after my introduction to these teachings, I hit a real snag about what this was supposed to mean for my life. In 1974, I was at Naropa Institute in Boulder, Colorado, taking a class from Joseph Goldstein on Essential Buddhism, and we were learning how to meditate. Trying my best to focus on my breath and be in the present moment, suddenly I remembered that I had put on my New York Knicks T-shirt that morning. I was not only a passionate fan, but a season ticket holder as well. Some of the most ecstatic moments in my life had occurred in Madison Square Garden as I wildly cheered for my beloved team. My mind wandered off, reliving those peak highs until, with a bit of a start, I woke up to the fact that I was supposed to be seeking a stillness and calm that would bring me peace. Unnerved, I wondered, *What effect would full-on commitment to meditation have on my enthusiasm?* The dissonance between exhilarating passion for the game and the calm of meditation was so unsettling that at the end of the class I mustered up the courage to speak with Joseph for the first time.

I approached him and, with some embarrassment, explained my quandary. After becoming proficient at meditation, would I end up at a game in Madison Square Garden, head turning serenely as I followed my team from one side of the court to the other, equanimously acknowledging, *Nice shot, Frazier. Very good move, Havlicek.* "If that's where this is heading," I confessed, "I'm not sure it's for me."

Joseph smiled. "Don't worry," he assured me. "I think you'll still be able to enjoy the games just as much. If anything changes, it will probably be that you'll be able to get over a loss sooner with less devastation." He couldn't have given me a more satisfying answer. And he was right. Learning to live with a mind at ease doesn't mean giving up our enthusiasm for life.

Some of us were taught in our religious upbringing that rejecting the world would make us holy—the "vale of tears/hairshirt" approach to religion. This same attitude can be found in Buddhism, with students mistakenly believing that if they enjoy and appreciate life, they risk getting caught up in imprisoning attachment. But closing yourself off to the life that's here before you is simply another form of aversion, a belief that says, "It's dangerous to enjoy positive experiences." Buddhist monk Ajahn Sumedho has a different perspective. He was born in the United States and, after serving in the Navy and the Peace Corps, became a monk in Thailand. Sumedho has been able to interpret the ancient teachings in a way that is applicable to our contemporary lives. In his book *The Way It Is*, he writes:

> Sometimes in Buddhism one gets the impression that you shouldn't enjoy beauty. If you see a beautiful flower, for instance, you should contemplate its decay. . . . This has a certain value on one level, but it's not a fixed position to take. . . . Once you have insight, then you find you enjoy and delight in the beauty, and the goodness of things. Truth, beauty, and goodness delight us; in them we find joy.

It's important to remember that a major goal of Buddhist teachings is to find happiness in the here and now, and that includes appreciating all the beautiful gifts of life that are right in front of us.

THE AWAKENING JOY COURSE

In recent times, the subject of happiness has become increasingly popular. Many wonderful books have been written pointing people in that direction. *Awakening Joy* is joining that effort by offering a slightly different approach. This course introduces practices that have been used through centuries as methods of training the mind to learn new ways of thinking. What makes the Awakening Joy course so effective is that it presents these ancient teachings in an accessible form and combines them with strategies to change habits and behaviors that are informed by contemporary psychology and science.

This book is based on the ten-month Awakening Joy course, building on the same themes offered there and in the same sequence of steps. While using this book can allow you to move through these steps at your own pace, it is the process of cultivating new habits over time that will bring about a sustained quality of well-being. You might read the book straight through and then go back and focus on the exercises and topics that are particularly relevant to you. Or you may want to go through it chapter by chapter, spending as much time as you need on each step.

I refer to each chapter here as a "step," but the journey of Awakening Joy is not a linear process. All of the practices interact with each other—a kind of hologram to open you to more joy. And it's based on a systematic program that has been tested over several years by a large population and proven to be effective.

Throughout the book you will see quotes from those who have benefited from this course. Some of them are from participants who responded to online surveys, some from personal communications or from interviews done specifically for this book. Many of the moving stories in these chapters are drawn from the experiences of students attending the silent mindfulness meditation retreats I lead. Many of the personal stories I tell about my own life, as well as those from Shoshana, are drawn from experiences we've had on retreats ourselves. Silent retreats are a kind of crucible that reveal the workings of the mind in a unique and illuminating way. However, these stories are not intended to suggest that training your mind or learning how to be happy can happen only on retreats. These insights about human experience can be realized in many different ways, as you will also see in these pages.

I have been quite amazed by how powerful it is to pay attention to things that make me happy instead of overlooking them. As you say, when the mind is inclined this way, my brain seems to change gears and look at everything more positively.

—A COURSE PARTICIPANT

People can participate in the Awakening Joy course either over the Internet, through video and audio recordings, or in live classes. All include presentations from various happiness experts, neuroscientists, and spiritual teachers. Words of wisdom from those who spoke at the course held in Berkeley in 2008 are included throughout this book.

There are many sophisticated theories about happiness and the mind. I combine three particular Buddhist teachings to form the cornerstone of the Awakening Joy course. The effectiveness of applying these principles to developing happiness has been corroborated by neuroscience research, some of which will be referred to in the book. The three principles at the heart of the program are:

- **Inclining the Mind toward Joy.** As the Buddha clearly stated, "Whatever the practitioner frequently thinks and ponders upon, that will become the inclination of the mind." But our minds can be trained. A central aim of the course is to incline the mind toward states that give rise to joy.

- **Developing and Increasing Wholesome States.** When we are kind or generous, at ease or calm, we experience genuine happiness and well-being. These are called wholesome states in Buddhist teachings. Once we understand what healthy activities help support these wholesome states, we can intentionally invite and cultivate them.

- **Focusing on the Gladness that Arises with Wholesome States.** While engaged in a healthy activity, we experience an actual positive uplift of energy. The teachings speak of the value of strengthening this "gladness connected with the wholesome" and the delight that "gladdens the heart." Increasing that gladness is what I've come to mean by awakening joy.

In creating the course I reasoned that if over several months participants "frequently think and ponder upon" as well as deliberately focus on these wholesome states and the "gladness" that accompanies them, that would become "the inclination of their minds." Over time your mind and heart have become accustomed to certain habits that may be limiting your full potential for happiness. With practice you can change your default setting so you can consistently access your natural joy.

SUPPORT PRACTICES

Besides the principles and practices presented in each step of this Awakening Joy program, there are a set of activities I encourage you to bring into your life to support your journey. Use these suggestions in any way that works for you, without making them a burden or one more thing you *have* to do. Don't worry about what you haven't done. Feel good whenever you do *any* of them:

- **Move your body.** Walk, exercise, dance, or do yoga regularly. Develop a healthy relationship with your body. Stretch it. Walk it. Exercise it. Move it around vigorously if you can. This will clear the cobwebs, get you out of your head, help you live longer, and make you feel more alive. Your body tries to serve you as best it can. Be nice to it. All with the intention of awakening more joy.

- **Regularly engage in some kind of creative expression,** like singing, writing, drawing, playing an instrument, or dancing. I especially suggest singing, since it opens up the throat and tunes you to a vibration of well-being, and many participants have found it to be a key to increased happiness. Even if you feel silly singing, try it anyway! Studies have shown that exposing ourselves to music helps boost our immune system. You could also experiment with listening to music that uplifts your spirit. I've put together my own compilation of music that brings me joy, and every time I play it (and sing along), it works. Any form of creative expression, however, will help lift your state of mind and keep the joy juices flowing.

- **Create a Nourishment List.** One of the supports to greater well-being is recognizing ways you can nourish your spirit and then regularly fitting them into your routine. Creating a Nourishment List will help you make that come about. Take time to write down everything that brings you joy. It can be a simple thing like eating a peach, or something exotic like windsurfing, or anything in between (walking the dog, having tea with a friend, etc.). Which ones could you actually see doing to bring more joy into your life?

- **Do something nourishing** for yourself three or four times a week, daily if possible, no judgments if less. Your ability to access joy is greatly enhanced by nourishing your spirit. This does not necessarily mean maximizing pleasure. You can eat three helpings of ice cream and, although there might be lots of quick pleasure, your spirit will probably not be nourished.

In fact, you'll get indigestion! Nourishing your spirit is usually connected with engaging in healthy activities and experiences. Sink into a hot bath. Go for a walk in nature. Meet a friend for lunch. Do any of the support practices mentioned here. You might do these as a reward or just because you deserve it. Instead of leaving joy up to chance, recognize what evokes it and then prioritize that in your schedule. Let yourself have fun and play.

- **Meditate or take some time by yourself regularly,** every day if possible. Even if you don't meditate, try sitting with a cup of tea for five to ten minutes as you look out the window. See what it's like to be quiet without doing anything else. Getting in touch with your internal life helps access the goodness and joy that is there. Course participants find that doing this has a major impact on their well-being. Neuroscience confirms that meditation actually creates positive changes in brain structure that support greater happiness.

- **Keep a Joy Journal** to keep track of your experiences as you do the practices suggested throughout the book. At the end of each day, you might write down what brought you joy, well-being, and happiness that day. It doesn't have to be volumes. No judgments if you can't think of anything. But remember that even the smallest things count, such as nuzzling with your dog, hearing a favorite song, or talking to a friend. Writing them down allows you to reflect back on those moments and bring them to life.

- **Find a Joy Buddy or Joy Group.** Having a buddy, especially someone who is also reading the book or taking the course, to check in with regularly can be a tremendous support for this process. This is like having an exercise buddy—someone to keep you on track. Stay in touch with your buddy by email, phone, or face-to-face. You'll want to agree on how to do this in a way that serves both of you (time, frequency, mode of communication). Even a five-minute check-in will help keep you both inspired. The purpose is to support each other in discovering the effects of the practices and to share insights. It's also okay if you choose not to have a buddy.

The online Awakening Joy course helps set participants up with a buddy. All over the world, groups (including e-groups) have formed for people to work on the materials together, which is a very supportive way to do it.

Building Up a Storehouse of Positive Experiences

"To help us survive, the brain has evolved to register negative experiences more readily than positive ones. A single bad event with a dog stands out more vividly than a thousand good ones. In other words, the brain is like Velcro for negative experiences and like Teflon for positive ones. The amygdala, a little almond-shaped bunch of neurons in the center of the brain, plays a big role in storing emotional memories, and it's primed to look for bad news.

"Because we're set up in this way, we can go through life doing the things that confirm our worst fears. We look for what's negative in a situation, just in case it's a survival threat. Because our brain is set up to be wary, we have to help ourselves toward happiness by inclining our attention to positive experiences by consciously intending to do so. Through conscious attention you can gradually build up a storehouse of positive experiences to neutralize the negative ones. The most powerful method I know is to deliberately look for positive experiences and take them in by being present with them. This helps the brain register the positive experiences long enough for those neurons that are firing together positively to start wiring together."

—RICK HANSON, PH.D., AUTHOR OF *Buddha's Brain:*
The Practical Neuroscience of Happiness, Love, and Wisdom
AT AWAKENING JOY COURSE, BERKELEY, 2008

USER-FRIENDLY EXPERIENCE

I want to make clear at the outset that there should be no guilt as you do this program. Guilt is counterproductive to cultivating joy! No failing, no pressure. Take this as a nourishing experience. Whatever you do as part of this experiment, please feel good about it. You may decide that simply reading this book is all you want to do. One course participant told me that reading the program materials was the only thing she did but that it reminded her that there's another way to be in the world, and she felt a significantly positive impact.

What I've noticed is how often I actually feel well-being already! I've always thought of myself as moody and anxious, but as I've been paying more attention, I'm realizing that I actually feel joy way more than I thought I did. This isn't going to be as hard as I thought.

—A COURSE PARTICIPANT

Thousands of people from all over the world have gone through this program and experienced its benefits. It gives me great pleasure to share it with you through this book. My sincere hope is that it will help you change habits that don't serve you and strengthen those that lead to more well-being and aliveness. Beyond the personal benefits, I believe finding more joy in your life will also have rippling effects that can touch everyone you know and make a real difference in the world. And it begins with making the choice to be happy.

AWAKENING JOY

Step 1

INCLINING THE MIND TOWARD JOY

With our thoughts we make the world.
—THE BUDDHA

ONE EVENING after hearing me give a talk on real happiness, a student approached me. "I have something to show you," he said, opening a slick magazine to a two-page advertisement. There, in shimmering glory, was a beautiful woman draped in gold jewelry, looking satisfied and happy. Across the pages in bold lettering were the words: "The Gold Shivers." I felt both amused and appalled as I read the pitch:

> *From the First Small Shiver*
> *when a Shimmering Necklace of Gold Beads Catches a Woman's Eye.*
> *To the Great Shivers of Delight*
> *when the Coveted Object Actually Becomes Hers . . .*
> *Among Life's Pleasures, Count this Deeply Held Euphoria as Unique.*
> *The Only Way to Get the Gold Shivers is by Getting the Gold.*

Because we're bombarded with thousands of marketing messages like this every day, it's easy to think that gratifying our desires is the way to find happiness. We might even know, as one bumper sticker says, "The best things in life are not things," but we can still believe that something else out there will make us happy. *When I find my soul mate, or when I write the great American novel, or when I retire . . .*

There's no denying the hit of pleasure we feel when we fulfill a desire for a particular experience or object or goal. But how long does the satisfaction last once we receive the "coveted object"? Perhaps until we notice there's something else we want. When we equate true happiness with getting something (or someone), we can end up like hamsters in an exercise wheel—running but never arriving.

If genuine happiness is not based on objects or experience, where can it be found? And how? Like following a road map, once you know where you're going, it's easier to figure out how to get there.

TAKING THE FIRST STEP

The journey of awakening joy begins with setting a clear intention. Although we all want to be happy, most of us don't place an explicit wish for that at the center of our lives. We think if we are successful, rich, or liked by others, happiness will come. We tend to hope that achieving certain goals in the future will make us happy. But these are roundabout ways to get to happiness, and they don't necessarily work. What *does* get you there is starting where you are and discovering what you are looking for in the midst of your current life.

You might think that the circumstances of your life will have to change a lot before you can find happiness in the midst of them. While it's true that our well-being is affected by how we live, we also know that even in the best of circumstances we can be unhappy. And sometimes in very challenging situations, we can feel surprisingly at ease. While this book will encourage you to bring experiences and circumstances into your life that contribute to your well-being, the key factor is deciding to change your

I tend to ask myself what I have to be joyful about. I'm still out of work, I'm overweight, and the relationship and life I was hoping for didn't happen. But slowly, with just this one question and being present in the moment, I've begun to realize, my answer is: EVERYTHING! I'm alive, I'm facing my difficulties, I'm actually living my life and not hiding from my pain. I realize I'm just happy to be here. I can feel my breath, the sun on my face, the movement in my limbs as I go walking, the pleasure of smiling, laughing, and singing. It's not delusion or hiding or shutting down in denial: It's being present and taking things one moment at a time!

—A COURSE PARTICIPANT

mind. As my colleague Sylvia Boorstein puts it, "Happiness is an inside job." When we consciously *intend* to be happy, actually saying that intention aloud or to ourselves, we set in motion a radical transformation. Profound changes begin to take place inside us, in our body and our mind. The momentum of positive change grows as we learn to choose actions and situations that align us with our intention.

THE GOLD OF TRUE HAPPINESS

I was a gloomy existentialist in college until one day it struck me that I actually wanted to be happy. I believed the only way to achieve that was to get and to do what I wanted. My personal strategy to ensure happiness was trying to string together enough moments of pleasure and gratification that the underlying unease couldn't get through. Getting the latest album of cool music felt good—for a little while. Having fun at a wild party was exhilarating—at the time. But no matter how many happy moments I had, I still didn't feel any closer to being a "happy person." I felt like I was on a roller coaster, and the ride down seemed to last a lot longer than the occasional trip up. There had to be another way.

Go Ahead, Say It: "I Want To Be Happy."

What happens when you let yourself say, simply and clearly, that you want to be happy, that you want joy to become part of your daily experience? Do you feel like you need to look over your shoulder to see if anyone is watching as you dare to consider such a thing? Maybe you wonder if it could really be possible. Or perhaps you feel a sense of relief at finally letting yourself say it. Whatever your response, this is how you take your first step toward awakening joy.

That was what led me in 1974 to Naropa Institute, a kind of spiritual summer camp, in Boulder, Colorado. I'd read some books on Eastern philosophy that made me question a lot of my assumptions, and I wanted to check things out for myself. When I walked into meditation class that first day, I was excited about the promise of an exotic new teaching. There in the front of the room a man was sitting cross-legged—but he didn't at all fit my image of the great spiritual guru I was expecting to see. In fact, he didn't seem very different from me. He was Jewish and sounded like he was from New York, and I wondered if this guy could really tell me something new. But after spending the first ten minutes of the lecture judging the package, I decided to start listening to what he was saying.

Within moments it was clear that Joseph Goldstein understood something about genuine freedom and happiness and how to get there. I saw for the first time the possibility of not being a slave to my neurotic thoughts and fears. By the end of the class, I knew I had found a sure road to happiness, and I was determined to follow it.

Joseph talked a lot about one of the basic teachings of the Buddha—the recognition that everything we experience in life is impermanent. No matter how good things are, they will change. *Well, that's for sure,* I thought. *That's the story of my life.* We don't get what we want and feel frustrated. We get what we don't want and feel upset. Or we get what we want and then find out it doesn't quite satisfy us in the way we thought it would. We find that the pleasure of the gold shivers lasts for a few moments, then fades away. As those famous "philosophers," the Rolling Stones, so profoundly put it: "I can't get no satisfaction."

Because everything changes, no circumstance, experience, or object can give us lasting happiness. Our bodies change, our minds change, the seasons change. Yet we try to hold on to pleasure, youth, summertime, happiness. As Joseph puts it, trying to hold on to anything in an ever-changing reality is like holding tight to a rope you're sliding down. All you get is rope burn. And the more you hold on, the more you suffer.

What is the way out of this predicament? Awakening joy isn't about fulfilling goals or changing particular circumstances. It's about training the mind and heart to live in a way that allows us to be truly happy with our life as it is right now. Not that we stop aspiring to grow and change in positive ways, or that we remain in harmful situations, but we begin to find the joy inside us right where we are. As you work with the practices offered here, you will discover that happiness is not a place you arrive at but rather the result of training your mind to ride with ease and flexibility the roller coaster of life.

DECIDING TO BE HAPPY

Vickie was hoping for a miracle. For five years she had been living with chronic pain, unrelieved by anything doctors and healers had been able to offer. By the time we spoke, her disappointment had spiraled down into severe bouts of depression. "Often I break down and cry just from trying to get through the day," she told me. Vickie had come to talk about whether or not she should enroll in an Awakening Joy course. "But I just can't believe it's possible for me to be happy," she said.

Recently her situation had gotten even harder. Friends who had been trying to help for years had begun to drift away, afraid of being pulled into the black hole of Vickie's despair. "And my boyfriend has real doubts about our future," she said through tears. "I know he loves me and feels a lot of compassion for me, but he says he wonders if I haven't given up on life."

"You're going through so much, Vickie," I said softly. "But I've seen other people going through really hard times make major changes when they decide to. I think you can do it."

Despite her doubts, Vickie decided to enroll in the course. The very first meeting of the group proved to be a critical turning point for her. As usual I opened the course by asking participants to get in touch with their intention to bring more happiness into their lives. The evening was spent exploring this uplifting prospect, and by the time the class ended, the room was filled with enthusiasm and promise. Some participants lingered to talk with friends, and others came up to ask questions or make comments. I noticed Vickie sitting quietly at the side of the room, and when the others had left, I went over to see if she was okay.

"I just don't see how this will work for me, given my physical condition," she began. "I can't even conceive of what it would be like to be joyful."

"I understand how you can feel that way," I said, taking a seat next to her. "And don't try to be any different from how you are at this moment. But I think the most important ingredient in changing your situation is letting yourself open to the *possibility* of finding joy in your life. That needs to happen before you can get clear on your intention."

I knew there had to be a way to help her realize she had the capacity to enjoy her life. I had seen so many people, including myself, turn their lives around once they had embraced that possibility.

"Vickie, are there ever any moments in your life when you're enjoying something?" I asked her.

She replied, a little hesitantly, "Yes . . . when I play with my three-year-old niece."

"Can you right now bring to mind an image of playing with your niece?"

Vickie settled into her chair and closed her eyes. Almost immediately a tiny smile appeared.

"Now just stay with that image and those feelings for a few moments," I suggested. I could see a subtle change pass over her face as she sat there in silence. When I asked her to describe what she was feeling, it took her a while to find the words.

"I feel a kind of tingling throughout my body . . . a lightness in my mind . . . my heart feels warm."

"Okay, good. Now let yourself breathe in that feeling, allowing it to deepen with each breath," I suggested, knowing that letting the experience fully register in her body and mind was a key to making the shift she wanted.

"Now project your mind forward in time and imagine that you've practiced accessing this feeling of well-being regularly during the next ten months of the course. Can you tell me what your life would look like then?"

I could see Vickie's body relax as she reflected.

Imagining a Change

Doing an activity repetitively changes the structure of the brain. However, even just imagining the same activity has an impact on neural structure. Researchers at Harvard Medical School demonstrated this with an interesting experiment. They asked one group of volunteers to play a five-finger exercise on the piano over the course of a week. A comparison group was asked to merely imagine moving their fingers to play the same exercise. Though actually doing the action had a greater impact on brain structure than simply imagining it, by the end of the week, the same region of the brain in both groups had been significantly affected.

By actively imagining feelings of happiness or recalling happy experiences, you can help to make those changes in your brain that can bring more joy into your life.

"I have less stress . . . I enjoy being with my friends again . . . I see myself taking more walks in nature, and letting myself have more fun."

"Great. If this feels worth going for," I said softly, "take your time to get in touch with your intention to make it happen. See if you can decide that you'll do your part to bring it about."

As she silently contemplated that suggestion, it looked to me as if Vickie's body actually grew lighter. When she finally opened her eyes, the smile she gave me was genuine and bright. "That was amazing," she offered. "Something in me said not only *can* I do this but I'm *going* to do this." That decision began a process within her that would eventually look like the miracle she had longed for. As the saying goes, "God helps those who help themselves," and Vickie's "miracle" was actually set in motion when she was willing to open to the possibility of joy.

FINDING THE "MAGIC" WORDS
FOR YOUR INTENTION

As Vickie found, setting the intention to awaken joy works best once you've recalled your capacity to be happy. Trusting that knowledge, you can make the heartfelt decision to do your part to make that happen. This is the heart of setting your intention to be happy—your determination to do what you can to fulfill your vision.

Finding a phrase that encapsulates your intention is a useful way to remind yourself of your direction. You might say something like, "I intend to allow more joy into my life," or "I want to experience more happiness each day," or "May I live with a greater sense of well-being." The exact way you phrase your intention doesn't matter, and the wording may change over time. What's most important is to begin.

Joan wrote from Canada about the struggle she got into when she tried to find the perfect way to state her intention. She had joined the Awakening Joy course in order to find more joy in her relationships with her husband and two children. "I keep falling into knee-jerk reactions such as irritation and negativity with them," she wrote. Because the change she was looking for felt so important, Joan wanted the phrase she used to state her intention to be exactly right.

After several frustrating days of trying out various possibilities, she decided to just sit quietly and see what came. The words that arose were "I'm going to give joy a shot." Not at all the profound phrase she was looking for! "I felt almost repulsed by the words and dismissed them," she wrote. But the phrase kept coming back. At some point Joan realized, "I can just be silly with the intention and stop worrying about the 'right' words. Instead I can try to stay connected with the raw energy behind these 'silly' words and go for it!"

A GAME OF REMINDERS

The more you do something, the easier it gets. The more often you remind yourself that you are actually intending to bring more feelings of

Inviting Happiness into Your Life

Think of a time when you felt real joy. Maybe skiing down a fresh powder slope; watching your dog bound across a field; being with a close friend; receiving an award for a job well done. As you imagine this experience vividly and in detail, paying attention to colors, sounds, smells, notice what you are feeling in your body. Where does the joy register? Maybe a slight swelling in your chest or tingling throughout your body. You may find that you are smiling. What is your *state of mind* as you experience this memory? Maybe a sense of being uplifted or feeling open and alive.

Now let those feelings of well-being register deeply. Breathe them in, feeling them pervade your body and mind. How would your life change if this kind of joy were increasingly part of each day?

joy and well-being into your life, the more you will be open to them when they arise. And when you remain aware of your intention to grow in happiness, you're more likely to make choices to support it.

Shirah came to an Awakening Joy course highly motivated to get herself out of a rut. At the end of the second week, she reported to the group that she had discovered a successful strategy. On her computer at work, she set a timer to chime every twenty minutes. Each time she heard that little musical signal, she reminded herself of her intention. "The first week I would say, 'May I be open to more joy and well-being in each moment.'"

As she continually worked with that statement, she began to recognize that fulfilling her intention depended upon making choices in what she was doing or thinking. By the second week, each time the chime sounded,

Meaning What You Say

Are you ready to bring more joy into your life? If you are, take whatever time you need right now to make the heartfelt decision to do so. Allow a phrase or a statement to arise that can remind you of your intention. Whenever you say that phrase, rather than just repeating empty words, let it remind you of your capacity for joy. Be willing to be open and receive the feelings of well-being you are inviting.

Shirah had begun asking herself, "What would make me happy right now?" Would it make her happy to complete the task she was working on? To take a needed stretch break? To offer encouragement to a coworker? "I really like the question," she added, "because it engages me in an exploration and makes it more difficult to go on automatic. And it works."

One person's magic trick doesn't necessarily work for another, however. You may feel that having a chime go off when you are trying to concentrate would drive you crazy. Be creative and find what works for you. A playful spirit can help deepen your commitment to well-being.

My friend Ina developed a unique way to remind herself of her intention. A New Yorker with a sarcastic bent, she found the word "joy" to be just too sugary for her. Each time she thought about "joy," instead of opening up, she found her body and mind recoiling in aversion. A sure way *not* to fulfill her intention! Ina devised an ingenious alternative:

> I love the color green. It lifts my spirits. So I decided that instead of "awakening joy," I'd start telling myself, "I'm awakening green." That was something I could relate to. I could never have guessed the effect that little device would have. I started noticing green all around me, and each time I did, it made me happier. Now I look for the green, and it seems to

trigger that response automatically. Who would have guessed this cynic would become so joyful!

One online participant made up a set of cards using inspiring quotes from the course materials and sent them to the website for others to download. Other participants' suggestions have included:

- I put little signs that say "BREATHE" on my refrigerator and on my bathroom mirror. Every time I see them and take a conscious breath, I remind myself to incline my mind toward more joy.
- I posted cards all around my kitchen: Sing! Meditate! Laugh!
- My two young boys and I start out each morning saying to each other: "Let's make this a happy day." One day when we were *not* having a happy morning, my son reminded me we'd forgotten to say our happiness chant. We said it together, took a deep breath, and started the day again. Things worked out much better the second time around.
- Before I fall asleep at night, I bring my awareness to my whole body, feeling the sheets surrounding me and the comfort of the bed. I say to myself silently and inwardly the following words: "I open my heart to the universe to accept love and peace." This often brings a wonderful feeling of well-being and contentment into my heart. I let this feeling permeate my entire being as I fall asleep.

As you remain aware of your intention, lots of surprising transformations can come about. Katy wrote from Ireland to say that keeping her intention in mind made her aware of how much she was afraid of going into new situations. Whether at work or at parties or traveling, she had always been asking herself, "What will happen to me in this situation?" She realized that what she'd really meant was "What can go wrong here?" As Katy continued to remind herself of her intention to bring more happiness into her life, she found a new question instead: "What is the *best* thing that could happen in this situation?" And of course, as her expectations changed, new situations were no longer so frightening.

WHAT GETS IN THE WAY?

You've set your intention, come up with a phrase and some ways of reminding yourself, and suddenly you find yourself doubting the whole process. It's not unusual during the first few sessions of the Awakening Joy course to hear protests and resistance from some people. I've noticed, in fact, that the course seems to be a magnet for skeptics who want to be happier. Michael came up to me after the second class and told me that he just didn't think this "awakening joy business" was for him. He had been practicing seeing the glass half empty his whole life. "That's just the way I am," he told me, the resignation in his voice betraying a certain frustration.

As we continued talking, Michael relaxed and joked about being such a cynic: "I think I'm going to be one tough nut for you to crack." As we laughed together, I suddenly asked, "With that big smile all over your face, what are you feeling right now?"

"Light . . . playful," he confessed.

"There it is," I said. "Let yourself feel that fully."

After a pause, Michael admitted that he felt pretty good, although he was a little surprised to think that those feelings had anything to do with happiness. I assigned him the task to have his radar out for moments of well-being and to slow down and feel them fully. He somewhat reluctantly agreed to "give it a try." Over the next few months, Michael began to see that those moments arose more often than he might have expected. After the last session of the course, he sent me a note:

> Being happy had always seemed like luck or some sort of accident, and when I wasn't happy, I felt like I was a victim of life's circumstances. But I realize now that I have a lot more to do with experiencing joy than I thought. I can choose to be happy—and I can choose to be unhappy, even miserable.

"THE COMMITTEE"

Like Michael, many of us go through our days on the lookout for what can go wrong. We carry around a lot of voices in our heads that tell us all of the bad things that have happened, or could happen, to us in our life. One colleague refers to these voices as "The Committee." Each voice in that group is trying to get us to follow its own particular direction, with the result of not only confusing us but limiting what we believe is possible. You might want to be happy, but subtle thoughts may be lurking not far from the surface: *Who am I fooling? I know I'll only be disappointed again. How can I bring more joy into my life when . . .* You can probably fill in any number of reasons. Even if we believe we can create more happiness for ourselves, negative voices can undermine our intention.

Max wrote from Australia to say that he'd begun doing the practices with great enthusiasm and was actually seeing progress. But soon he encountered a major obstacle:

> When I notice myself feeling happy or joyful in the midst of some activity, almost simultaneously there arise memories and feelings of failure and worthlessness, which send the message "You don't deserve happiness/success in awakening joy." It takes real effort to disregard these nagging negative thoughts, which form an almost constant, day-long backdrop to my ongoing efforts to awaken joy. I need to get on my own side totally in this endeavor! But how? Why do these voices want me to fail? And how can I silence them?

Max isn't to blame for those voices that "want him to fail." They are probably not so different from thoughts he had when he was a little boy and doubted he could hit a baseball or make friends in a new school. When we're learning new and healthier ways of being, all our old self-sabotaging patterns of thought can become more evident. The contrast between how we want to be and the way we have been is painfully obvious, and the voices of doubt and fear are often loud and clear. This is not a bad thing. Becoming more aware of them is actually very good,

I have found having the intention of being joyful can have an amazing effect on my mood. When I'd wake in the morning on weekends, I used to think of depressing things until I didn't want to get up. The more I lay in bed the more down I would get. Now, as long as I remember to do it, I can completely switch off those feelings which sapped my energy. I can just say to myself 'Get up now, the sun is shining and it's going to be a good day full of new things.' And I end up full of energy.

—A COURSE PARTICIPANT

because then we can see what gets in the way and understand the conditioning that we're dealing with. When we don't recognize these negative voices, we're under their spell with little idea of how powerful and persuasive they are.

Sometimes course participants get waylaid by believing that awakening joy means they must have only positive thoughts. I'd like to make it clear that you don't have to get rid of all negative thoughts. In fact, that's nearly impossible, and trying to do so has the opposite effect. Right now, try to get the thought of a pink elephant out of your mind. Now try harder! Is it gone? Our attention gives life to thoughts, and the more we try to push them away, the more persistent they become.

Other chapters in this book will offer ways to work with negative or unwelcome thoughts, whether they are in the form of undermining voices, critical perspectives, or pink elephants that won't leave the room. For now the key is to stay in touch with your intention and be patient and compassionate with whatever gets in the way.

THE COMFORT OF THE FAMILIAR

Although you may want to be happier and more at ease in life, changing habits you've grown used to usually requires moving out of your comfort zone. Many years ago during a workshop I was participating in, I witnessed a conversation between a teacher and a student that made clear to me how caught up we can get in resistance to change. At the end of one of the movement sessions, a number of us had gathered around the teacher with our questions. One of the students had been experiencing some pain in her hip joints during the session, and it was distracting her from quieting her mind. What might the teacher recommend? After making sure she didn't have a medical problem, he suggested an exercise to gently stretch her tight muscles. She responded with a sigh saying she feared the stretch might put some pressure on her knee, which sometimes acted up. Could he suggest something else?

The teacher then recommended a different exercise, which avoided flexing the knee. "Oh no, I couldn't do that," she shook her head, explaining there was a chance her back would then flare up. Was there another alternative? He patiently gave her a third option, which she once again deftly parried, saying it might cause another problem. After a few intense moments of silence, the teacher said, in a kind and compassionate tone, "I think your intention to stay the same is greater than your intention to change. When you're ready to change you will."

You may think that bringing more joy into your life is a good idea, but until you're willing to stretch yourself and alter the patterns that have maintained the status quo, change won't happen. It's all too easy to fall back on the safety of the familiar and avoid putting yourself in potentially uncharted territory. In doing so, you stay stuck in a prison of predictability. It may feel comfortable, but is that what you want to settle for? Stretching beyond your comfort zone will lead to the happiness you're looking for.

Hearing a New Voice

What are some of those inner voices that try to keep you from being happy? Each time you notice them come up, rather than believing them or giving them energy through reacting, just let them pass. Restate your intention, recalling if possible the positive feelings that accompany joyful experiences. As you incline your mind toward well-being and happiness, those negative voices inside will begin to diminish.

Stretching Beyond the Familiar

When you join a gym and begin working out, those first few days of exercise can leave your muscles really sore. But if you keep going, using those muscles over and over, you arrive at a new level of fitness. Be willing to go through the natural discomfort that comes from letting go of the familiar as you move to a new level of well-being. Be patient. Don't put pressure on yourself. Keep reminding yourself of your intention, knowing that little by little you're bringing about greater well-being in your life. There will be ups and downs, but each time you try the new way, notice how good it feels.

DOING YOUR PART

Once you consciously set out on your pathway with a clear intention to be happy, it might look like something magical or mysterious is happening as you actually find more well-being in your life. It's like when you learn a new word, you suddenly notice it everywhere. Neuroscience tells us that setting an intention "primes" our nervous system to be on the lookout for whatever will support what we intend to create for ourselves. In his book *The Mindful Brain,* Daniel Siegel talks about the effect paying "attention to intention" has on our brain and thus our experience of our surroundings. He writes: "Intentions create an integrated state of priming, a gearing up of our neural system to be in the mode of that specific intention: we can be readying to receive, to sense, to focus, to behave in a certain manner." This suggests that when we pay attention to the intention to bring more happiness into our lives, we are more likely to notice the actions, opportunities, people, and things that can bring that about for us. It's sort of like recognizing which piece of a jigsaw puzzle will fit the picture.

Life is always presenting us with unexpected circumstances—obstacles as well as opportunities. Remaining aware of your intention helps you to more readily recognize, from the multitude of options life offers, those that support your vision.

Setting your intention for joy doesn't mean that you're going to *make* joy happen, but rather that you will *allow* it to happen. When you plant seeds in your garden, you can't will the vegetables to grow. You can only do your part by tending and caring for them, seeing what they need in order to develop as fully as possible. Likewise, you support your intention by keeping it in your consciousness and doing your part to help it manifest.

BUILDING ON SMALL SUCCESSES

Establishing your intention is not the same as setting a goal with a fixed timeline, such as, "I'm going to be happier in two months." Although goal-setting can be a very skillful motivator in certain circumstances, it can be counterproductive in this program. If you're trying to "get joyful" on a schedule, or in a particular way, you're likely to end up assessing whether you are succeeding or failing. *Am I there yet? What do I need to do now to meet my goal?* This creates a tightness in the mind rather than the spaciousness that allows your natural joy to arise. To open to more well-being, let go of timetables and scorecards and just do your part by staying connected to your intention, and see how things unfold.

When asked by a reporter how it felt to fail so many times before successfully inventing the lightbulb, Thomas Edison replied, "My good man, I did not fail. I invented the lightbulb. And it was a 2,000 step process." We might say something similar about awakening the joy inside us. It's a process that not only requires commitment but patience as well. The conditioned patterns of a lifetime don't shift overnight. It would be

Rather than wishing friends would ask me to visit, go to the movies, or have a meal together, I approached three different acquaintances and asked if they would like to go out to a movie. I know it's so simple, but I've been afraid of 'no.' I'm now sharing enjoyable outings, like walks, movies, meals, and coffee chats, and I have three new friends.

—A COURSE PARTICIPANT

wonderful if we could just declare, "From here on out, I'm going to be happier," but unfortunately it doesn't work that way. The path may not always be as simple and smooth as we would like, but if we're facing in the right direction, in time we'll find what we're looking for.

During the 1980s, the San Francisco 49ers, my local team, were the best team in all of football. (Well, everything changes . . .) They didn't try to go for the long touchdown every play, or even much of the time. The secret to their success was chipping away five to ten yards at a time, getting into a rhythm and building on their success as they slowly marched down the field. I learned a lot from watching them. Keep building on your small successes and feel good about what you've done.

When you're on the lookout for it, you will find joy right where you are, even in those places where you might least expect it. Edith, who was taking the course online in Germany, had a revelation when she stopped looking for something special and simply opened up to the feeling of well-being. She wrote:

> I had been looking for some kind of "spiritual joy," some other-world joy (that I'd failed to find), and totally overlooked how much "ordinary joy" was already present in my life. As a matter of fact, I sometimes find myself in very ordinary situations—noticing the beauty and radiance of one of my children, for example—and experiencing a kind of ecstatic joy. Isn't it amazing how believing that there is some kind of "worthier joy" elsewhere can keep one from seeing and experiencing all the joy that is already there?

Most of the things that bring us joy are not elaborate or costly. Charlie, another course participant, reported that after checking in with his Joy Buddy one night, he got inspired to write to several friends he had been out of touch with for a long time. That simple act brought him immeasurable joy. Florence had been worried about the prospect of taking care of her four-month-old granddaughter for a couple of weeks, but she remembered her intention "to live this life fully, with joy and gratitude always." Afterwards, she wrote:

I didn't miss a moment of this wonderful experience with my granddaughter and was completely joyful, mindful, very alive and conscious, even with a sometimes not-totally-happy baby. I feel my own peace, love, gratitude, and joy were a wonderful influence on her as well. I did lots of singing to her and much walking to help her be happy, soothed, peaceful. I learned so much, am continuing to learn so much—about myself and about fully enjoying this short, beautiful experience called life.

Michelle found that setting the intention to be joyful before doing activities such as washing dishes, folding laundry, and walking the dog made these routine activities so much more pleasant. "These days," she writes, "I sing and dance while cleaning and end up getting much more done than I used to."

As you allow joy to be part of your daily life, you will find that, little by little, it builds on itself until it becomes a natural way to live.

Despite the chronic pain she had told me about after her first Awakening Joy session, Vickie did continue with the course. Accepting that it was possible to be happy helped her let go of some conclusions she had made about her own life and about life in general. Over the following months as the course continued, rather than focusing her attention day after day on how hard things were, Vickie increasingly paid attention to what she loved in life and to her vision of well-being. And life began to

Focus on Success

When you check in with your Joy Buddy, don't dwell on what you haven't done. Focus on what you *have* done. Share how that feels, and inspire each other with your successes, even if they seem small.

unfold in a way that supported major changes for her. At the end of the course, she sent me a note:

> The changes I've experienced in myself over these months have been amazing. Setting the intention to be more alive and to experience joy has been incredibly powerful. I find that I am less afraid of my constant physical pain. My friends are noticing also that I am having fewer episodes of extreme despair. And my boyfriend recently proposed marriage. I was very surprised, and he explained that he had seen so much progress in the stability of my moods and my ability to live life that he no longer doubted my commitment to "getting better." I'm so very grateful.

LIKE A TENDER SAPLING

When we get clear on our intention to change, we set in motion a process that ripples out, like a pebble dropped in still water, affecting everyone

Frame It with Joy

What routine chores or other activities do you usually feel resistance to doing? Bills? Cleaning the house? Laundry? Commuting to work? Before you begin, set an intention to let that activity bring more happiness into your life. You might try: *Paying bills contributes to my well-being*, and then see if something new can happen. Or your intention might be: *I enjoy traveling in my car*, and then notice if any ideas arise that help make that happen. You might begin listening to recorded novels or singing along with favorite music during your commute. Let yourself be surprised by the possibilities.

and everything around us. A shift occurs in how we are perceived, not only through our own eyes but through the eyes of those who know us. As the positive results of the practices begin to make a difference in your life, some friends will be cheering you on. "It's wonderful to see you so happy!" Others may be threatened. "Don't you think that going out for a drink after work is a lot more fun than a yoga class?" Or, "You're not like you used to be, and I'm not sure I like this new you." In the early stages of this program, your own belief in fulfilling your intention may be fragile, so it's important to minimize the influence of those who do not want to change the status quo.

The Buddha likened the needs of someone in the process of change to those of a newly planted sapling. In order to establish itself, a young tree first needs proper placement, with enough sun to be nourished yet enough shade to keep it from being overexposed. It needs the right amount of watering. And it needs a fence around it to protect it from hungry animals eyeing the luscious green shoots. In short, it needs tender loving care so

Nourish Your Intention

Your intention to awaken joy is at first vulnerable and needs to be protected from negative outside influences. Spend time with those who support you in bringing more joy and well-being into your life. Nourish your intention through choosing activities that keep reinforcing it. Stay in touch with your Joy Buddy. Spend time with good friends, good books, and nature. As best you can, do the supportive practices suggested for this program. No guilt for what you don't do. Feel good about *any* practices that you do. And avoid the negativity of those who doubt your efforts. Instead of getting into debates with anyone about the value of what you're doing, simply try to maintain boundaries that respect and support your needs.

that the roots can take hold and it can develop into a healthy, vital tree that can offer shade and protection.

Once the seed of your intention takes root and grows, it will bloom and provide refuge and support for everyone you meet, including those who may have initially questioned your attempts to be happy.

WIDENING YOUR INTENTION

Whatever motivates you to grow in happiness becomes the wind in the sails of your intention. It might seem pretty obvious *why* you would want to be happy, but if you take a close look at your motives, you might find a few other reasons. Maybe you believe that if you have more joy, you'll make more money, or you'll get the right guy or gal. Those are not necessarily bad reasons for intending to be happy, but you might also consider opening up to other options. The more inspiring your motivation, the more energy you can bring to fulfilling your intention.

In 1994, I was invited to a conference for Western Buddhist teachers to be held in Dharamsala, India, with the Dalai Lama. When I mentioned to a friend that my flight called for a stop in Frankfurt, Germany, she immediately said, "Oh, you should visit Mother Meera. That's where she lives." I'd heard about this holy woman before and said I'd consider it. My friend looked directly at me and, as if channeling instructions from on high, she repeated, "You should meet her. She's known to grant one's deepest wish." That was hard to resist, and I set about arranging a visit to the Mother's Center.

There was a buzz that evening as I waited in line with a crowd of about 150 others. We all were shepherded into a softly lit room with an empty chair in the front for the master. After about thirty minutes of silence, there was a rustle of excitement as a beautiful young Indian woman entered. The purity and serenity Mother Meera radiated was palpable. For a while I watched as, one by one, people would bow at her feet in respect, look into her eyes for a few moments, and leave with a blissful smile. Then I turned to the question that had been at the back of my mind for days. If this holy person could actually fulfill my deepest desire, what would I ask for? Over the next hour as I waited my turn, I dropped deeper and deeper into my heart, moving past layers of desire, dismissing the luxurious vacations, new cars, and houses that crossed my mind. What really mattered to me?

By the time my turn came, I knew clearly what I would wish for. I knew what my deepest intentions were for my life—to live with a pure heart and embody my highest ideals as I serve others. I kneeled before her, silently repeating the simple phrases I had arrived at, each one feeling both authentic and humbling. At one point I looked up into Mother Meera's eyes, and it was like gazing into a vast ocean of eternity. As I continued to fervently repeat my intentions, I felt as if they were being seared into my heart.

I don't know what powers Mother Meera might possess, but I do know that getting clear on my deepest intentions that evening set in motion a process that has increasingly aligned the elements of my life to fulfill them. Getting clear on our highest intention establishes our most authentic connection to our heart and is a powerful part of awakening the joy within us.

SINCERE MOTIVATION

The intention in our minds at the moment of any action determines whether we are planting seeds of future happiness or future suffering. If

Following Your Heart's Desire

What do you hold as the purpose of your life? What are your ideals? If a holy person or a magic genie could grant you your heart's deepest desire, what would it be? Take a few moments to contemplate those questions. Can you align your intention to be happy with those deeper desires? The more encompassing your vision of happiness, the greater the potential for joy.

What Is "Wholesome"?

In Buddhist practice the actions and attitudes associated with well-being are called "wholesome," because they help us feel healthy and whole, and they contribute to the well-being of everyone and everything around us.

we want the seeds we plant to produce huge beautiful blossoms, our intention for greater well-being must be motivated by a big beautiful desire. So don't hold back. Let your intention be about fulfilling your highest potential, or letting your actions come from love, or bringing more happiness into the world.

I came to understand the power of that kind of motivation through something the Dalai Lama said at that 1994 meeting in Dharamsala. He sat before us, beaming ease and joy and compassion, yet he had in his life faced a number of life-threatening situations, and he had listened to thousands of fellow Tibetans pour out the stories of abuse and torture they had undergone when their homeland was invaded. One participant asked him how he had managed not to be overwhelmed when faced with so much tragedy and suffering. He answered: "My sincere motivation is my protection." Later when I asked him how it is possible to remain calm and balanced in threatening situations, he gave the same answer: "My sincere motivation is my protection."

I'd heard him use that phrase before, but the meaning of it sank in this time. Aligning our intention with the goodness of our heart keeps us from getting swept up in fear, confusion, or negativity. When our intention to be happy is based on our highest values, we can rely upon it to lead us in the right direction. Even when we are caught up in the challenges of life, we know we can choose to be kind or to act with compassion. This in itself opens us up to well-being and contentment.

A verse in the *Dhammapada*, a collection of sayings of the Buddha, sums up this promise:

> Speak or act with an impure mind
> And trouble will follow you
> As the wheel follows the ox that draws the cart.
>
> . . .
>
> Speak or act with a pure mind
> And happiness will follow you
> As your shadow, unshakable.

There are many levels of pleasure and happiness, but the joy I am talking about here is what the Buddha called "the gladness connected with the wholesome." This gladness arises naturally from the goodness that is within every one of us. We know the warm and uplifting feeling we have when we are kind or generous. Contrast this with the unpleasant feeling that accompanies something hurtful or insensitive—telling a lie, putting someone down, putting ourselves down. There is a direct connection between true happiness and thinking and acting with a clear mind and kind heart. If you want to be truly happy, causing harm to others won't get you there. The more you are motivated by kindness and the desire to act from the goodness of your heart, the greater the possibility of awakening joy.

Noticing when you're acting with mixed motivations can help you sort out which ones you want to cultivate. For instance, you may feel motivated

Last night I had a restless sleep. My husband woke me at 5:00 a.m. with a cup of coffee; how lovely of him to do so. Instead of staying in bed, I got up with the intention of enjoying my day, tired or not. He was listening to a radio show and the song 'Soul Man' came on. I was suddenly hit with the inclination to move to the song. As I began dancing, I was struck with the thought, 'Don't do this, it's silly.' Remembering my intention for the day and my intention for taking the course, I just let go and started dancing. It felt great. After a few minutes I looked up and saw my husband, who was across the room, dancing too. I realized then that my joy was rubbing off on him. I now intend to dance more often.

—A COURSE PARTICIPANT

to do a kind act for a friend because you know it will make both of you feel good. However, you may also have a slight hope that perhaps that friend will do you a favor back. If you become aware of that kind of mixed motive, instead of dwelling on the less noble intention, turn your

Empowering Your Intention to Awaken Joy

You may want to write the answers to these questions in your Awakening Joy journal, and refer to them from time to time in order to remember what you are envisioning for yourself.

- What do you want to experience as a result of doing this program? Find a phrase that best expresses this—perhaps something like: "May I be open to experiencing more joy (happiness, well-being) in my life." This is your intention.
- Imagine what your life might look like six months from now if you stay connected with this intention. A year from now? Two years?
- Get in touch with a heartfelt decision to do your part, to the greatest extent possible, to bring about the joyful life you want to live.
- Repeat your intention to yourself as you start each day, and then throughout your day remind yourself of your intention to develop more joy. You might also repeat your intention whenever you begin a new activity at work or at home.
- Spend a few moments at the beginning or end of your meditation or quiet time focusing on your intention and imagining how you feel and what your life looks like as you fulfill it.
- If you have a Joy Buddy, discuss your intention with him or her. That way you can support each other in realizing your visions.

attention to that more wholesome impulse. We might have ninety percent pure motivation to help and ten percent ego-based hope for acknowledgment. If we focus on the ten percent, we might get down on ourselves for being phony and end up dismissing the value of the ninety percent. The real magic is that even if we initially have only ten percent selfless motivation, the more we stay connected to that, the more it grows.

To live with joy and well-being is possible for all of us, and it is a gift we can pass on to others. Setting our intention launches us on the journey.

Step 2

MINDFULNESS:
BEING PRESENT FOR YOUR LIFE

---

*There is a most wonderful way to help living beings overcome grief
and sorrow, end pain and anxiety, and realize the highest happiness.
That way is the establishment of mindfulness.*
—THE BUDDHA

IT WAS A WARM April afternoon in Yucca Valley where I was leading a meditation retreat. During a break from teaching, I was in the staff room with my son Adam, then two years old. On the table was a huge bowl of luscious ripe strawberries, which happened to be his favorite food. I lifted Adam to a chair so he could take one. He started stuffing one strawberry after another into his mouth, the red juice streaming down his shirt. As I watched him, the naive notion occurred to me that I could teach him the value of enjoying the moment. I would show him, as I do with adults through "eating meditation," how to slow down enough to fully taste the strawberry in his mouth before taking another. I moved the bowl out of his reach and coaxed him to finish what he already had. Adam would have none of it. He began howling. His mouth filled with juicy red fruit, he lunged for the bowl, imploring at the top of his lungs, "Strawberry!"

That image has stuck with me over the years as a symbol of our human predicament: We often don't enjoy the experience at hand because we're so caught up with reaching out for the next one. The way Jane, my wife, once put it: "Sometimes I think there's something more out there that will make me happier when really the best thing to do is to settle back and enjoy the moment I'm in." The secret to awakening joy is being present with whatever part of life we're tasting right now. The key to this secret is the practice of mindfulness, and it is the underpinning of all the other practices in this Awakening Joy program.

With mindfulness we live in the present moment. This is not, however, where most of us spend a lot of time. We topple forward into the future and worry about the next day or month or year. We think about what happened yesterday or last week or five years ago. We plan a vacation for months, then when we're finally lounging on the beach, our mind drifts off to the problems we left at home. The habit of being a little (or a lot) ahead of ourselves, living in the past, or lost in fantasy, exacts an enormous price: We miss out on our life.

Of course, there's a place for conscious planning or holding an inspiring vision of the future. And we can learn valuable lessons from our past or recall with fondness moments that connect us with joy. But if you spend most of your time in the past or future, you're lost in your thoughts instead of experiencing the actual moments of your life. As meditation teacher and psychologist Jack Kornfield likes to point out, the signs in Las Vegas casinos have it right: "You must be present to win."

The power of mindfulness to affect our well-being is widely recognized and is increasingly integrated into healthcare systems. Mindfulness-Based Stress Reduction, a program developed by Dr. Jon Kabat-Zinn at the University of Massachusetts in the late 1970s, is used throughout the United States to help people with chronic pain, fear, panic, anxiety, and other health problems. The value of mindfulness meditation in bringing about positive changes in the mind and body has been verified by numerous research studies. In one such study, Kabat-Zinn paired up with Dr. Richard Davidson, head of the Laboratory for Affective Neuroscience at the University of Wisconsin, which is known for the groundbreaking research on the brain wave patterns of Tibetan lamas in deep meditation.

Davidson and Kabat-Zinn studied the effects of mindfulness training on a group of employees in a high-pressured biotech industry. During a period of two months, participants learned mindfulness meditation in one class a week, and they attended a one-day retreat. They were also asked to practice mindfulness meditation at home for forty-five minutes each day. At the end of the study, not only did they report that their "negative emotions went down and their positive emotions went up," but in comparison to the control group—those who did not practice mindfulness—the meditators also showed increased immune function.

Training your mind to enhance your well-being can happen in a number of ways. In this program I emphasize mindfulness, because I have seen and experienced its undeniable efficacy over the course of many years. If you're not drawn to meditation, you don't have to jump right into that in order to learn mindfulness. As you will see in this chapter, there are ways in which you can gradually bring mindfulness into your daily life. However, as with learning anything, the more you focus on developing a new capacity, the more you will get out of it.

Mindfulness has many benefits, but for our purposes the most important is that it can help you live a happier life. You can't *make* joy or well-being happen, but you can help create the conditions in which those states more naturally arise. This starts with allowing yourself to be right where you are. Mindfulness is a tool that helps you learn to do that.

WHAT IS MINDFULNESS?

Mindfulness is commonly described as "nonjudgmental awareness" and refers to a specific practice of consciously paying attention to what is happening in the mind and body in the moment without judging it, without getting tangled up in a commentary about the experience, without wishing it were different. The ability to pay mindful attention depends upon awareness or consciousness. As long as we're alive, awareness is happening. It's an automatic process, but as mindfulness reveals, we can also direct it. This is the essence of the practice of training your mind.

Stopping for a moment to just listen is a simple way to experience what awareness is. Right now, take a few deep breaths, relax your body, and focus on listening. You may hear sounds nearby, other sounds far away. You might even notice the sound of silence. Notice too that you are not trying to hear. Hearing happens naturally because *awareness* is functioning.

As you listen, tune into the experience of *knowing* that hearing is happening. This knowing is the faculty of your mind that is engaged when you are being mindful.

Here's an example of how this works in the midst of daily life. As I sit here in my backyard, I can feel the soft breeze on my arms. I hear my wife Jane through the open door putting things away in our kitchen. I also hear a bird cawing and traffic in the distance. With mindfulness I know that right now I am hearing. Looking at the dance of leaves in the sunlight, the patches of blue sky peeking through, the Buddha statue at the base of the tree, and the books piled on the table next to me, I mindfully know that seeing is happening. I am also aware of the continually changing itches, throbbings, and vibrations inside my body. With mindfulness, I am aware of being a creature with five senses constantly interacting with my environment.

Likewise, I can also notice what is going on in my mind, which Buddhism considers to be a sixth sense. I am aware of my current mental state, knowing that I'm both relaxed and interested as I wonder what words will come next from my pen on to the paper. I notice the succession of thoughts coming and going—my mind commenting on how much I love soft breezes; the thought that says, along with a tinge of guilt, *You should be helping Jane wash the dishes!* But instead of diving into the guilt, I notice the uncomfortable feelings it creates in my body and the way my thoughts suddenly begin to weave a story about what I'm doing wrong, what I should be doing, how I always do this, and on and on. Fortunately, being mindful, I recognize this familiar pattern, label it as "guilt," and notice when those thoughts are replaced by the next experience that catches my attention.

Mindfulness focuses on the *process* of our experience—the fact that we're seeing, hearing, sensing, feeling an emotion, or thinking a thought. This keeps us from getting lost in the "stories," or the content of our thoughts, or our reactions to what we're experiencing.

Most of the time, we carry on a running commentary about our experience: *This is the way it should be.* Or, *If I were in charge of the universe, I would certainly do a much better job than this!* When we add that kind of report card to what's happening, we continually set up a test for life to pass or fail.

In a sixth-century text, "Verses on the Faith Mind," Sengtsan, the Third Zen Patriarch of China wrote: "To set up what you like against what you dislike is the disease of the mind." This disease disconnects us from the truth of our experience.

Sergeant Friday's signature line from the old TV series *Dragnet* would be a good slogan for mindfulness: "The facts, Ma'am. Just the facts." This is not a cold, disconnected assessment but rather a simple, clear acknowledgment: "Oh, this is what is happening." Mindfulness calls it like it is, without embellishing our experience—not making it more dramatic or intense, nor pretending it's easier than it is. If we're sad, we're sad. If we're peaceful, we're peaceful. When we are clear about our actual experience, we can be completely authentic. This authenticity is a basic component of a joyful life.

Although mindfulness is nonjudgmental awareness, this doesn't mean that we abandon the faculty of discrimination. In fact, when we are aware of what we're actually thinking and feeling, we can clearly discern the

Just As It Is

Pause for a moment and notice right now how you're feeling, physically and mentally. You may be seated comfortably somewhere as you read this or on a crowded subway train in New York. Wherever you are, check to see if your body feels tired or energetic. Notice the sounds coming and going. Rather than just looking around you, become aware of the fact that you're seeing. Notice any tension in your shoulders, neck, hands. Observe the thoughts going through your mind: *I love sitting here reading.* Or, *I can't wait to get off this train and get home.* Your experience might be pleasant or unpleasant, but allow it to be just as it is without wishing anything were different. You might notice how restful it is to simply be aware of what is happening in you, instead of getting caught up in making an assessment of it.

difference between those thoughts and actions that are harmful and those that are beneficial. When we're blind to our thoughts and impulses, they run our lives. Becoming aware of our habits and the automatic ways we react when we're confused or upset is the first step to freeing ourselves from their power. Mindfulness helps us untangle the tangle, as some Buddhist scriptures put it, and then we can act with greater clarity.

BRINGING THE WORLD ALIVE

In *The Little Prince,* the simple but profound book by Antoine de Saint-Exupery, the Prince is puzzled by the way grown-ups get so caught up in what they consider such grand "matters of consequence." Often we are those grown-ups, so busy with important things that we have no time for what the mathematician in the story calls "loafing or balderdash." But what in our lives are the *real* matters of consequence? Our child presents us with a drawing for our birthday, our partner prepares a delicious meal, we wake up in the morning to find the first snowfall of the season has transformed the world. Too often we can barely pause to notice, because we've got to get to our next appointment, check our email, finish a project. Such "matters of consequence" can distract us from recognizing the blessings that life is offering us over and over each day.

I was dealing with a really hard situation at work and came home feeling bone-tired and despondent. I went out to dinner with my partner and had this epiphany as I looked across the table at him. I realized that my life is incredibly full and that I'm so thankful for having a loving partner and for our life together. A switch went off in my mind, my problems at work were reframed, and I was flooded with gratitude for the gifts I have in my life.

—A COURSE PARTICIPANT

There's magic all around us if we just take the time to notice. With mindful presence we activate the natural curiosity we all came into the world with as innocent children. Look closely at the mystery of a spider web. Or stop to think for a moment how amazing it is that you can read the word "blue" and see a color in your mind, or hear the word "pizza" and taste a slice. When we are mindful, even the most ordinary experiences become wondrous. In his book *Peace Is Every Step*, the great Vietnamese meditation master and poet Thich Nhat Hanh writes:

> To my mind, the idea that doing the dishes is unpleasant can occur only when you are not doing them. Once you are standing in front of the sink with your sleeves rolled up and your hands in warm water, it really is quite pleasant. I enjoy taking my time with each dish, being fully aware of the dish, the water, and each movement of my hands. I know that if I hurry in order to eat dessert sooner, the time will be unpleasant and not worth living. That would be a pity, for each minute, each second of life is a miracle. The dishes themselves and the fact that I am here washing them are miracles!

We don't always have time to move at such a pace or to be so attentive, but when we can bring a wholehearted presence to what is right before us, life becomes more fulfilling. For the Little Prince, paying attention to a single flower gave him great pleasure. The wise Fox tells him, "It's the time you spent on your rose that makes your rose important." While taking the Awakening Joy course, Art shared this insight about being mindful:

> I once considered my life to be relatively bland and uneventful. It was even hard for me to remember what had happened during the day, since it was almost by definition "unimportant." But I now think this is more a matter of perception than fact. Seeing the wonder in what is, rather than looking for something wonderful and disregarding the rest, has been a big discovery.

When you slow down and pay careful attention to what is happening inside you and around you, a new world opens up. Everything comes alive. In fact, you *may* notice that surges of joy arise in you spontaneously, even when nothing special is happening, and even in the midst of difficult times. When my coauthor Shoshana was going through a particularly trying period in her life, her only relief was remaining in the present moment. Thinking about the future brought up too much anxiety. "To my surprise, I'd be walking down the street, for instance, and suddenly I'd be feeling inexplicably joyful, even though the circumstances I was in looked so dire. I began to recognize that little instances of joy arise on their own from time to time, simply as part of life."

With mindfulness we can appreciate that every moment of life, whatever our experience, is precious. When we live in this way, a certain kind of vitality comes into our lives.

KALEIDOSCOPE OF CHANGES

As we live more mindfully, something we saw in Step One becomes increasingly clear: The present moment is constantly changing. This might seem obvious, but most people do not live as if this is the case. Mindfulness directly reveals this truth of impermanence. All the tinglings, pulsations, tightenings in your body—even the discomforts—come and go. Look at your mind and you'll see how quickly your thoughts and feelings change.

When we see this truth of change for ourselves, our relationship to experience dramatically shifts. We learn to enjoy pleasant experiences without holding on to them when they pass (which they will), and we are able to remain present with unpleasant experiences without fearing they will always be this way (which they won't).

When times are hard, instead of thinking *I'm never going to get out of this mess*, remembering that things will change allows you to be with your experience without fighting or pushing it away. Without this struggle, you can respond wisely to the situation rather than reacting from confusion. One of the participants in the Awakening Joy course wrote:

I am noticing, with a much keener sense, how often my state of mind changes in any given hour, no less any given day. It brings me hope to realize that everything is always changing. I embrace CHANGE! Whoa, that's pretty amazing.

—A COURSE PARTICIPANT

> Combining mindfulness with the intention to be happy, I have found the surprising result of being more present with unwelcome experiences. With mindfulness I can say to myself, "This

is an unpleasant experience I am having, and I am unhappy," and yet I can feel it completely and let it move through me with the confidence that I can be happy again soon, that happiness is nearby, not so hard to find. So this negative experience need not overwhelm me or cause panic and aversion. This has been a great relief.

The same truth of impermanence holds when life is good to us. If we forget that everything changes, we may start thinking, *Wow! I finally have gotten my life together! I've worked really hard to get to this point and now I have arrived.* Then when things change, we wonder, *What happened? How did I blow it?* Knowing that change is an inherent part of life allows us to fully appreciate the good times when they come, without thinking that life has been unfair to us when they go.

Mindfulness develops our capacity to see the ups and downs of life not as an obstacle course but as an adventure. Being mindful of the ongoing

The Emotion Trap

In his book *Emotional Awareness*, coauthored with the Dalai Lama, psychologist Paul Ekman talks about how we can be blinded by emotions like desire or anger once they are triggered. "Once the emotional behavior is set off, a refractory period begins in which . . . we cannot perceive anything in the external world that is inconsistent with the emotion we are feeling. We cannot access the knowledge that would disconfirm the emotion." When we're caught up in anger, for instance, we tend to interpret anything that is said or done as more fuel for the fire. We can be lost in these emotions for hours. The good news, Ekman says, is that mindfulness seems to reduce the length of the refractory period to help you more wisely assess the situation.

kaleidoscope of changes gives you the opportunity to transform your life. Your mind and body become your laboratory for understanding how to awaken joy and well-being.

THE PAUSE THAT MAKES THE DIFFERENCE

We are creatures of habit. Like rats in a maze, given a particular stimulus we will predictably react the way we have practiced over time. For example, you're walking down the street on a hot day and pass someone eating an ice-cream cone. For many of us, that sets up the desire for a pleasant experience that starts us looking for the next store to get something cold and sweet to eat, even if it's not on our diet. As the thought of the ice-cream cone makes you salivate, a surge of desire says, "Go for it. It'll feel good." When you don't pay attention, the voice of desire easily wins out. But when you pause long enough to listen, and notice what is happening inside, instead of reacting in ways that don't serve you, you might choose a different response.

The practice of mindfulness interrupts the habits that put your mind on automatic. For instance, when you get to the ice-cream shop and see that there is a special on the double-cream vanilla, you might think, "Well, 320 calories won't matter, just this once." But when you pause for a moment of mindfulness, your image in the mirror that morning might pop into your mind, and suddenly you remember the promise you made to yourself to get in shape. Now you can either choose the double-cream vanilla, decide to get a nondairy sherbet, or let go of the impulse altogether. You're no longer the rat driven by habit.

Likewise, a negative stimulus can set us off in a very unpleasant direction. A coworker says something critical to you. When you hear the words and feel the anger begin to rise, pausing to be mindful allows you to notice what is happening inside. Your face may feel hot, your throat tight, your heartbeat rapid. You might be thinking, *How dare she say that to me? After all I've done!*

Instead of launching into defense and attack, if you pay attention to the sensations in your body and to your state of mind, you might make a wiser choice. Perhaps in that pause you recall how venting your anger in the past only made things worse. So you decide to say, "Could we talk about this later, please? I need some time to think." This doesn't mean that you roll over and let yourself be mistreated, but at least you can choose to respond in ways that don't leave you later regretting what you say or do. With mindfulness you begin to develop the freedom to make choices that lead to greater happiness and well-being instead of suffering and regret.

"YOU BREATHE OUT AND IN"

Kate has been teaching mindfulness to children at inner-city elementary schools as part of a program called Mindful Schools in Oakland, California. Many of the students are from poor families who live in neighborhoods plagued by violence. In a survey of a fourth-grade class, 40 percent of the children knew someone who had been shot, and 70 percent knew somebody who had gone to jail. The challenges these students experience daily became clear when Kate asked her first-grade group to practice being mindful of sounds at home. Some of them came back reporting gunshots, people screaming, the police at the neighbor's door. "They're experiencing mini-traumas all the time," Kate says. "But these kids have so much potential. They're very smart, and I can see that the right tools bring out all the love and wisdom that's right inside of them."

Kate uses mindfulness exercises to help the children become aware of their thoughts and feelings. "They're like sponges," she says. "When they start to realize how their minds work—that instead of being present, they're sometimes in the past, sometimes in the future—it gets really exciting. I've had kids run up to me saying things like, 'Miss Kate! Miss Kate! I've just had a future thought!' They're building a new muscle in the brain to pay attention to themselves."

Kate's young students have also been using mindfulness in their interactions with others. "Many of these kids understandably are dealing with anger," Kate reports, "and often they believe that showing they're strong, or even hurting people, will feel good or help them survive. By learning mindfulness, they can see the difference between *feeling* an emotion and *acting* on it. We talk about how mindfulness can squeeze in between the two and create a space. I tell them, 'When you feel the sensations of the emotion in your body, it's a cue to create that space.'" Kate and her students talk about ways to do that, whether it's breathing, walking away, or telling someone to stop and give them a minute. "As we've practiced together, they've become willing to stop when they're angry, take a breath, and say, 'Okay, maybe there's another way.'"

In fact, one child shared how he used mindfulness during his summer break to make a better choice. He told one of the mindfulness teachers that he'd gotten really angry at his brother and decided to go get a weapon. On his way, he remembered what he had learned during that previous year at school, and he actually decided to stop and pay attention to his breath and his emotions. He never did pick up the weapon. Without his ability to let go of that impulse, things might have turned out very differently.

Just as the tool of mindfulness is helping these children get perspective on fear and destructive anger, it can do the same for us when we are trapped in negative

Last week two much-loved family members did something that made me unhappy. Instead of my typical pattern of getting more and more upset, going over and over in my mind how and why I'd been wronged, I was able to ask myself: Do I really want to feel bad? Do I really want to prolong and deepen my suffering? Will it help me or the others involved for me to assign blame and feel self-righteous? Or do I want to create a more positive path—one that accepts that something didn't go the way I wanted—and choose to let go and move on. *I diffused my anger, went on with my day, and then later talked with them, without blame or anger, about my hurt feelings over what really was an unintentional action on their part. This saved all of us from what could have escalated into a lot of anger and chaos.*

—A COURSE PARTICIPANT

thoughts. Whether you're holding on to the belief that the world is dangerous, as many of these inner-city kids have learned, or the expectation that life should always be pleasant and something's wrong if it isn't, using the tools of mindfulness will "create the space" that frees your mind. Like the child who let go of his desire to harm his brother, letting go of blind reactions by being mindful of them lets you make choices you won't later regret.

RELEASED FROM THE PRISON OF THE MIND

One of my favorite examples of the power of mindfulness to influence positive choices was told to me by my friend Mary Reinard, who teaches mindfulness meditation in maximum-security prisons. One of her students, Matt, seemed an unlikely candidate for meditation. Matt was big and buff and had a temper to match. Before being imprisoned for a violent crime, he had been a Green Beret in the U.S. military, trained to react quickly and forcefully. One day in class Matt suddenly asked, "Can you teach me to control myself?"

During that session Mary talked about mindfulness as a way to harness the power of the mind. Rather than being at the mercy of every whim, she explained, the more conscious we are, the more choice we have. She ended the class with a challenge: "Before acting, pay attention to your thoughts and the feelings in your body, and choose the way that will serve you best." A few weeks later Matt arrived at the class excited to report his success.

"You won't believe what happened this week," he began. One day at lunch someone at Matt's table had started "razzing" him. Inmates are assigned seats in the huge cafeteria, and sitting elsewhere can get them in trouble. Stuck at his table, Matt tried to ignore the man but found himself feeling more and more annoyed. Then he remembered what Mary had talked about in class.

"I noticed what the anger was doing to my body. It was tight all over. It was really uncomfortable. I was thinking that if I punched this guy out, there'd be some release. At least it would shut him up. But then I thought, 'Hey, the challenge was to choose a different way.'" Even though Matt knew he could get in trouble, he picked up his plate and moved to another table. "I decided to just suck it up and move," he told the class. "And get this, as soon as I sat down at another table, I saw all the tension in my body just disappear, like magic! Lunch tasted great!"

The positive result of Matt's action didn't end there. "The best part of the story is that this guy came up to me after the meal and apologized! No one ever apologizes in prison, and here was this guy saying he was sorry. You know, I think we both left feeling satisfied. Imagine that."

If Matt had reacted in his usual way, this scene would likely have ended in a fistfight, maybe a brawl in the cafeteria. He, and perhaps others, could have been put into solitary, people might have been hurt. But being mindful of what was going on inside him—the tension in his body and the angry thoughts in his mind—enabled Matt to make a different, more positive choice.

When I'm fully present, everything becomes more interesting. I feel complete and whole. Nothing needs to be added or taken away to make it a better moment. When I'm fully here, it feels so good I wonder why I'd want to be anywhere else.

—A COURSE PARTICIPANT

Matt wasn't an evil or bad person. As a Green Beret he had received highly effective training to react to aggression with aggression. By learning mindfulness, he was able to start changing a pattern that was not appropriate to his circumstances. If Matt can do it, I believe we all can.

BEING PRESENT FOR YOUR LIFE

Because we're so used to not being present, being mindful takes practice. You can begin right in the midst of your daily life. Setting aside even five minutes a day to do nothing but sit still and notice what is happening inside, you can begin to teach your mind to be more focused and present. Or you might choose something you do each day, such as relaxing with a hot cup of tea or coffee. But rather than reading the newspaper at the same time, or talking on the phone, just be there with your experience. Notice the taste, the warmth of the cup in your hands, the liquid moving down your throat as you swallow.

Also notice when your thoughts move out of the moment. You may be smelling the fragrance of the coffee one instant and five minutes later realize you drank the entire cup without noticing. Instead of being present with your actual experience, you were caught up in thoughts about what you were going to do later in the day, or you were going over last night's conversation with your partner. Don't be discouraged. You're just learning how the mind works. Keep a sense of humor, and gently turn your awareness back to the moment. The very act of inclining the mind to be present is potent and will soon begin to bear fruit.

I like to make a game of being mindful during my daily activities. That makes the practice less "work" and more fun. Here are a few of the ways I remind myself. Experiment with what works for you.

- When the phone rings, take a few mindful breaths before answering.
- When you're waiting in line—at a store, at the movies, in traffic—especially if you are feeling agitated or frustrated, notice those feelings. Then turn your attention to what you're experiencing in your body. Notice how you are standing or sitting. Take a slow deep breath and feel that you are alive in this moment.
- Take a mindful walk around your neighborhood. Feel your feet on the ground with each step. Just walk and know that you are walking. When your mind wanders, bring it back to your steps.
- I know this one is radical: Instead of multitasking, try *unitasking*. That is, try doing one thing at a time. It's much easier to be present for your experience when you do.

The more often you practice paying attention, the easier it gets to steady your mind and remain present. You will notice that being present in itself awakens a feeling of well-being.

THE PRACTICE OF MINDFULNESS MEDITATION

As you will readily discover, the mind is hard to rope into the moment. For this reason, a very effective way to train yourself in mindfulness is by practicing it in a structured period of formal meditation, as in a class or on a retreat. In these environments, free of the usual distractions that keep you from noticing your inner experience, you sit in silence for periods of time long enough to let you see how the mind works. Mindfulness meditation is traditionally called "insight" meditation or *vipassana*, which means "to see things clearly." In contrast to other forms of meditation, in which you might focus on an object or a mantra or an inner image to bring about a certain state of mind, mindfulness is about simply being present for your experience, whatever it is. Mindfulness meditation practice does typically begin with focusing on the breath, but then the attention is turned to whatever else is happening in the body and mind.

Whether doing formal meditation practice or just taking a few minutes to quiet the mind, most people find that soon after they begin to pay attention to their breath or to some sensation in their body, without even knowing it, they're gone, lost in their thoughts. This is not bad. It's just the way it is. The eye sees. The ear hears. The mind thinks. Thoughts are not the enemy, and the mind can be trained.

How we respond when we realize the mind has been wandering is critical to the process of developing mindfulness. If you get lost in a thought, patiently bring your attention back to the moment, remembering that you're sitting and breathing. It's important to do this with kindness, because reacting with frustration or annoyance only strengthens those qualities. You're in the process of training your mind, and just like training a puppy, it's patient repetition rather than punishment that works best. Rather than feeling aggravated because you've been lost, you can

The Mindful Moment

"Several times a day I take sixty seconds or less to be mindful. Often it's before a meal. I reflect on the actual physical nature of the food I'm eating. Where did this chicken come from? Where did this corn come from? I think about the people driving the trucks, and the gasoline that propelled those trucks. The sunlight, the DNA in domesticated corn. I feel all that going into my body, which gives me a sense of being part of that whole process in a very direct way. That's a moment of mindfulness."

—RICK HANSON, PH.D., AUTHOR OF *Buddha's Brain: The Practical Neuroscience of Happiness, Love, and Wisdom*
AT AWAKENING JOY COURSE, BERKELEY, 2008

appreciate that you've woken up from the dream. Each time you return your attention with patience and kindness to the moment, you strengthen those qualities as well as your ability to remain present. Over time you will find negative patterns naturally unwinding and wholesome attitudes increasing.

HOW DOES MINDFULNESS WORK?

How can mindfulness help free us of negative habits? A method that uses observing the mind in order to change our actions may seem pretty

How Do You Do It?

Sit in a posture that allows you to be comfortable and relatively still but not so relaxed that you fall asleep. You want to be both alert and at ease. Now, begin with paying attention to your breath. How do you know you're breathing? Where in your body do you feel it most clearly? You might notice the breath coming into your nostrils and passing out again. You might instead feel the rising and falling of your abdomen. Or you might simply be aware of your whole body sitting and breathing. Each time your mind wanders, gently return to the breath. Paying attention to breathing helps focus and calm your mind so that it can more easily stay present in the moment.

In addition to the breath, you can be mindful of other experiences inside you as they call your attention—various sensations in your body, your moods, your thoughts as they come and go. One moment you might notice a breath, the next you're aware of an itching in your back or arm, then a sound, then a thought, then the breath again. The key to being mindful is remaining aware of any of these experiences as they arise, without getting lost in the story or thoughts connected with any of them.

mysterious. However, the Buddha tracked the process with a precision that some psychologists and neuroscientists are beginning to recognize the validity of today. Changing negative habits depends upon paying mindful attention to what is happening inside us when they arise. As I've been emphasizing in this chapter, the key to success is in *not reacting* to what is going on in our thoughts, our feelings, and in our body.

The mind and body are interconnected, each affecting the other. We take in information through our five senses, and that's where the process begins. The first thing that happens in any situation in which we might react is that one of our senses is stimulated. For instance, we hear someone say something to us. If we were hearing only the sound, with no evaluation of it, we would have no reaction. But that's not the way we're set up as humans.

When we hear that sound, our brain immediately evaluates it, primarily based on our past experiences. If the sound is soft and warm, it is equated with loving experiences we've had, and it's called a "good" sound. If it's harsh and explosive, it's most likely connected with painful experiences in the past (unless you're a heavy metal fan), and it's evaluated as a "bad" sound.

Simultaneously, whether we are aware of it or not, the sound registers in our body. If it's a pleasant sound, we may feel little ripples of delight; our muscles may relax. If the sound is unpleasant, we may feel prickles of fear, and suddenly we're tense.

Finally, depending upon whether the sound is pleasant or unpleasant, we react. We like it or we dislike it. We want more of it, or we want none of it.

In releasing old habits, the trick is not to get caught up in that last part—the reaction. There is no way to interrupt the first three steps in this process. They all happen automatically. You can't *not* hear a sound if your ears are open, though if your attention is engaged elsewhere, you might not register it consciously. This happens all the time and can lead to typical misunderstandings. "I called you to dinner three times!" "But I was reading and didn't hear you."

The point in this process where you have a choice to create more happiness is in the reaction of wanting or aversion. This process can also

Changing Your Mind

As neuroscience expert and psychologist Dr. Rick Hanson says, the mind and the brain are a unified system. As the brain changes, the mind changes. As the mind changes, the brain changes. This means you can use your conscious mind to make lasting changes in your brain to bring about more well-being and happiness in your life.

Each time you repeat a particular thought or action, you strengthen the connection between a set of brain cells, or neurons. The phrase neuroscientists use to describe this phenomenon is: "Neurons that fire together wire together." This means that the more often you repeat a thought or action, the stronger the related neural pathways become, and the more easily that thought or action can recur. That's bad news if you're caught up in some negative habits. But the good news is that you can interrupt old patterns and put new ones in their place. Over time, the brain actually changes structure by strengthening the new, more frequently used circuits, and the unused ones fall away.

take place entirely in your mind, that "sixth sense." You might remember something someone said to you, and all those same inner responses can take place. Whether you are interacting with someone, or you are alone and recalling something that happened to you, if you simply remain present and aware of the experience in your mind and body, you are no longer feeding the habit through reaction, and it begins to diminish. As neuroscience would explain it, the synaptic connections that are not strengthened through repetition begin to weaken.

This effect of mindfulness is known as freeing or purifying the mind. As negative patterns are released, they are no longer obscuring the beneficial mind states. Therefore, your natural joy and goodness can express themselves.

CHOOSING THOUGHTS THAT LEAD TO JOY

The Buddha was a preeminent mind researcher 2,500 years ago. Before his enlightenment, he wandered the countryside of northern India for six years, trying many methods in order to understand the nature of life and where true happiness can be found. As he investigated his mind in meditation, he noticed two different categories of thoughts: those that led to suffering and those that led to happiness. The first group included thoughts connected with blind desire, ill will, and cruelty which led, as he put it, "to my own affliction and the affliction of others." The other set of thoughts—those of contentment, kindness, and compassion—had just the opposite effect. Not only were they harmless to himself and others, but they actually led to happiness.

We have little control over what thoughts arise in any particular moment. If we did, we would probably have only thoughts of love and goodwill toward all of humanity. But a few others seem to slip through. We have profound thoughts, bizarre thoughts, and ugly thoughts. Seeing some of what goes on in our mind—the fears, the pettiness, the judgments—can be humbling. I once heard a Tibetan Buddhist teacher playfully refer to looking at what's going on in our minds as "one insult after another." Or, as a common saying goes, "Self-knowledge is usually bad news."

But actually it's very good news. While what arises in our mind is somewhat random and out of our control, we do have control over which thoughts we choose to dwell on. By training ourselves to pay attention to what is happening in our mind and body in any situation, we make it more likely that we will empower those thoughts that support our well-being.

At one Awakening Joy class, meditation teacher Sylvia Boorstein told a story about how becoming aware of what she was thinking helped reframe an experience. One evening when she was staying in New York City, she had arranged to meet a friend for a theater performance and decided to take a bus to get there. As the bus crept along through the heavy traffic, Sylvia started worrying: *I'm going to be late. I'll miss the curtain. My friend will worry about what happened to me. I shouldn't have taken the bus. The subway would have been so much faster.* Figuring she could walk faster than the bus was going, Sylvia got off, "and of course as I'm walking, the bus passes me by . . . and now I'm thinking, *I should have taken a cab.*"

Sylvia has been meditating for years, but she has also, by her own admission, been fretting for years, so it was an easy reaction to fall into. Continuing her story, she describes running down Broadway—in high heels with a cold wind whipping around her. And then:

> All of a sudden I have the thought: *What am I doing? I'm grumbling.* That's a moment of mindfulness. Up until then, I was caught up in a habit-driven narrative, an editorial comment about what was happening. The moment at which the mind says, *Sylvia, you're grumbling,* the lens switches, and suddenly the truth of that moment is: *I'm a seventy-one-year-old woman running down Broadway in the middle of winter in high heels. That is far out! That is an extremely fortunate thing to be able to do.* It changed everything. I felt proud, and I actually hoped a lot of people saw me.

When we are mindful, we can let go of thoughts that undermine our well-being and thereby frame our experience in a way that invites more ease. As Sylvia puts it, "A moment of mindfulness is always a moment of freedom. We can have the courage to make choices that result in a positive difference for ourselves and others."

After recounting to his followers his experience of seeing the two kinds of thoughts and their outcomes, the Buddha shared with them the secret of training the mind in states of well-being: "Whatever a practitioner frequently thinks and ponders upon, that will become the inclination of his mind." We strengthen habits of thought through repetition. If you often think unkind, negative, or

When we're in the car, my husband and I often quibble about which route is the fastest. The other night I was about to yell at him when he was driving, but I stopped myself and took some deep breaths. I said to myself, I don't have to act on these thoughts. I don't have to say what I'm thinking right now. Then I started noticing the way my breath felt going through my body. I ended up feeling more relaxed and didn't care which street we drove on or how much traffic there was.

—A COURSE PARTICIPANT

depressing thoughts, you'll tend to continue thinking in that way. If you choose thoughts that uplift, nourish, and bring kindness to yourself and others, your mind will increasingly lean in that direction.

Mindfulness teaches us to incline our mind toward joy by helping us wisely choose our thoughts and actions. And the more we do this, the more readily it happens. Research psychologist Sonja Lyubomirsky says in her book *The How of Happiness* that "an unhappy person spends more than twice as much time thinking about unpleasant events in their lives, while happy people tend to seek and rely upon information that brightens their personal outlook."

FINDING REFUGE IN THE PRESENT

It started out as an almost imperceptible phenomenon. I was preparing for a talk I was going to give at a retreat in Southern California, and as I looked over my notes, I had the sense that a shade was ever so slightly being drawn over my upper right field of vision. I dismissed it as just my imagination. Although I'd had no vision in my left eye since childhood, my right eye had been serving me well enough. The next day, however, that mysterious little pull-down screen happened again, and I thought I should probably check it out. Little did I know what lay in store.

The doctor at the clinic was friendly, and I felt at ease as she dilated my eyes and began the exam. But a few minutes later I felt her demeanor change. She turned the lights back on, and I could see in her face this was not good news. "I'm afraid you have a giant retinal tear," she said with concern. "Since this is your one good eye, it's particularly serious. You could end up completely blind. Either we perform an operation immediately and you stay here for the next five or six weeks to fully heal, or you get on the next plane back to the Bay Area and hope for the best."

I was stunned. When I could finally think, I told her I'd rather be at home with family and friends for the procedure. She warned me against any sudden movements or lifting, told me to be very careful, and wished me luck. During the forty-five-minute drive back to the retreat center, I would experience firsthand the benefits of mindfulness practice.

I made my way to the parking lot. I don't know if it was the time of

Three Levels of Mindfulness

"I see mindfulness as distinctly connected to joy on three levels: the physical, the personal or psychological, and the universal.

One: Mindfulness is thrilling on the physical level. Something happens neurologically in the body when the attention is brought in from all the ways it gets scattered. To feel your hands touching each other, or to simply put your foot down and know that you're putting your foot down, is tremendously pleasurable. Being present in that very action sends a thrill of rapture through the body. When the mind is focused on one thing, it's not caught up in the inner narrative of fear or yearning.

Two: Each of us has our own idiosyncratic set of memories, views, and opinions based on our personal experience. These play over and over like a tape loop. Mindfulness illuminates the habits of our mind and sets us free from being held captive by them. These moments of clarity can happen at any time simply by inclining the mind toward being present. Over time the mind becomes used to being clearer, and we learn how to live wisely.

Three: Mindfulness illuminates truths that are universal. Things pass. Everything—you and I and everyone and everything—has a life span. This moment is all there is, and to the degree we can remember that, we can actually experience the joy of living, even in situations that are quite difficult.

We often imagine or plan that when this or that happens, we'll have a good time. But who knows if this or that will ever happen? A million things can happen on the way there. There's only now. So mindfulness is about being in this moment. It's the only one in which joy is available."

—SYLVIA BOORSTEIN, AUTHOR OF *Happiness Is an Inside Job*
AT AWAKENING JOY COURSE, BERKELEY, 2008

day, but as I turned on the car ignition, everything suddenly seemed darker both outside and inside. Hands gripping the steering wheel a bit more tightly than usual, I took the familiar route through the stark landscape of the desert hills. Although I wasn't driving fast, my mind was racing. *I could be blind next week. What will my life be like? Will I be totally dependent on Jane?* Then something curious happened. It was like a voice reminding me from a distance, "You don't know about next week. Just be here now."

My attention turned to my hands on the wheel, and I realized I could relax my white-knuckle grip. I began noticing my breath move in and out of my nostrils. My mind calmed down . . . for about a minute or so before the next swirl of disturbing thoughts arose. *Adam is just eleven years old. What will his teenage years be like if I can't be there for him the way I want to?* Once again the words inside gently and firmly reminded me, "You don't know what the future will be like. Just come back to this moment."

This process of my mind spinning out with fearful images, followed by a return to the breath and a calming down, took place at least another twenty-five times as I made my way back to the retreat center. What was so illuminating was not that my mind was filled with worry, but that it didn't kick into outright panic. My years of meditation practice proved to be my greatest ally. I was experiencing the power of mindfulness. Each time the nightmare fantasies were starting to take over, they were interrupted by a return to the present moment and a recentering on my breath. Remaining mindful carried me safely back home and even helped me get through the operation a few days later with a level of calm and acceptance.

This refuge from our fears—the present moment—is always available to us. And with practice we learn to more easily return to it, even in the

I struggle with being the best mom I can be to my two kids. Being at home all day with my four-year-old daughter and seventeen-month-old son can try my patience. Recently I yelled at my daughter. Before learning mindfulness, I would have told myself I was a bad mother, that I was stupid, useless, and so on. But instead I just said to myself, 'I yelled at Sasha' and moved on. That actually let me be a better mom, because I wasn't being so hard on myself. This freed up more time to have fun with her and be happy.

—A COURSE PARTICIPANT

midst of confusion. As we do this over and over, we begin to understand how the mind works and what choices incline it toward well-being and joy. In time our experience shows us that mindfulness can indeed, as the Buddha said, help us "overcome grief and sorrow, end pain and anxiety, and realize the highest happiness."

HOW CAN I TELL IF I'M HAPPY?

Knowing whether or not we're happy might seem like a no-brainer. You might feel on top of the world, but if it's because you're jacked up on a double-cappuccino and your heart is racing, are you really happy? A colleague who works in a high-powered industry told me she had been wondering about this very thing. "I can think I am 'happy' about something happening at work, but when I notice that I'm speedy and breathless and my stomach is tight, I'm not so sure." If we don't know how to recognize when we're actually happy, we can end up choosing states of mind and body that lead us in an entirely different direction. As you might know from experience, that caffeine high can suddenly subside yet keep you wired for hours. So how can you recognize the kind of happiness that is connected to genuine well-being?

In the early 1970s, a remarkable little book came out—*The Lazy Man's Guide to Enlightenment* by Thaddeus Golas. One of the many points that rang true for me was Golas's idea of "expansion and contraction" in describing various states of mind. He said: "We experience expansion as awareness, comprehension, understanding." In contrast, "contraction is felt as fear, pain, unconsciousness, ignorance, hatred." Recalling this distinction helped me define something basic to happiness. Genuine happiness goes along with a feeling of openness and ease in the mind and body. Even when your focus is acute, as in mountain climbing or playing a musical instrument, the mind is not rigid.

Being mindful of your internal state is a great aid in helping you discover what will bring you more happiness. By noticing if your body is feeling contracted or open, you will realize whether or not you are in the midst of an experience you want to strengthen and repeat or one you want to let go of. Likewise, you can check if the mind is tense or at ease

Noticing Contraction and Expansion

When you find yourself in a contracted state, what do you notice in your body and mind? Course participants responded:

- ▸ Like it's hard to breathe.
- ▸ I want to go away and curl up somewhere.
- ▸ Like I hate everything.
- ▸ A little sick to my stomach.

When you're feeling expansive, what do you notice in your body and mind?

- ▸ Every one of my cells feels like it's smiling.
- ▸ I feel unafraid and open.
- ▸ I feel connected to the people around me.
- ▸ I feel warm and happy and also like crying, which surprises me.

to know if you're moving toward or away from joy. As you do so, you'll begin to discover that certain ways of thinking and acting lead to a deep satisfaction and well-being.

At first it might be a bit tricky to discern the distinction between the two states. Contracted states can disguise themselves as uplifting. The adrenaline rush that comes with anger can make us feel powerful and in charge. The excitement that comes with desire may feel like bliss. But how does your body actually feel when you are angry or filled with desire? What state of mind are you in? That rush of anger can make you feel great, but watch out if someone dares to disagree with you! And that driving desire to get what we want, from window shopping to lust, can feel exciting and invigorating, but rarely peaceful and open-hearted. When we burn with anger or desire, our body is tight, our mind is in turmoil, and joy is nowhere in sight.

States of well-being are the opposite of stress and agitation. How does your body feel when you're giving a gift to someone you love, delighting in the antics of a cute toddler, or reveling in the satisfaction of a job well-done? When my wife Jane walks through the door of my office and gives me a hug, I notice that my heart instantly feels warm. The smile on my face tells the rest of my body to relax. My breath gets slow and easy. My mind, too, feels spacious and at ease. This is the quality of expansion that accompanies happiness.

This difference between expansion and contraction is directly linked to the Buddha's distinction between wholesome and unwholesome thoughts and actions. When we're kind and compassionate, we feel open and happy; when we're angry or fearful, we feel contracted and dissatisfied. The trick here is not to resist whatever you're experiencing. It's all part of being human. Instead of tightening up in reaction, be mindful of what is happening, noticing without judgment how and what you're feeling. Then choose thoughts and actions that expand your heart and your understanding.

As you will see throughout this program, the wholesome states presented in the following chapters are invariably connected with what is beneficial to yourself and others. This not only brings us genuine happiness but also develops, as the Buddha said, "a mind that is without hostility or ill will"—in other words, a mind at peace.

AMPLIFYING YOUR JOY

Mindfulness did help me get through that critical eye operation, and over the course of the following year it would offer another and unexpected gift. While my eye had been saved, the operation had left me with a complication—the world looked like a Jacques Cousteau underwater documentary filmed on a cloudy day. I carried around a magnifying glass to read with; my notes for teaching were written in big letters with brightly colored felt pens; students' faces were a blur. By the end of that challenging year, my joy in life was subtly dimming along with my vision. When the options were presented to me—going slowly but surely blind or undergoing another high-risk surgery—I took my chances.

Once again I found myself facing the unknown and, moment by moment, trying to remain present to avoid sliding into fear. And then came that unforgettable experience after the operation when the bandages were removed. I could actually see! Not only notice what was around me but *see*, clearly and sharply. I remember the words to Johnny Nash's song ringing in my mind: "I can see clearly now the rain is gone. . . ." Every chorus of that song lifted me to a higher level of gratitude. "It's gonna be a bright, bright sunshiny day. . . ."

Far from subsiding, the gratitude I felt at my good fortune became a continuous backdrop to everything else in my life. I could see Jane smile. I could see the sparkle in Adam's eye when he did something that made me proud. I could read books and newspapers, I could see the joy of understanding on the faces of students, I could watch a sunset, I could travel alone. Whatever pain and travail that arose was short-lived whenever I'd remember *I can see.*

I was waiting in my car, with barely enough time for lunch, as a group of elderly individuals, whose car occupied the only available parking space, slowly maneuvered a walker into their trunk. I began to realize that I didn't need to define this situation as being about me and my desire for a parking space but could instead see the situation as an opportunity to recognize our human connection. By the time I called out the window to ask if they wanted any assistance, my offer was not primarily about getting into the parking space faster but mostly about seeing whether I could help make their lives easier at that moment. They didn't need help, and as I continued waiting, I allowed myself to notice some beautiful, red, sunlit leaves on a plant right outside my car window. I realize how much choice I have in defining the moment.

—A COURSE PARTICIPANT

I had trained for years to examine my experience carefully, not only for my own spiritual growth but also to share my findings with students. Clearly the topic now up for investigation was this tremendous feeling of gratitude. I became fascinated with the question, "What is gratitude?" Bringing all my attention to the experience in my body and mind, I became an explorer of the landscape of the grateful heart. I became intimate with the expansive feeling in my chest, with the lightness that seemed to course through every cell.

As I paid close attention to the feeling of gratitude, I began to notice

Building Your Happiness Muscle

You can actually strengthen the happiness circuits in your brain. Whenever you are experiencing a moment of joy or contentment—walking, listening to music, watching a sunset, being kind, feeling grateful—DON'T MISS IT! Pause to notice the feelings in your body and the state of your mind. Do you feel warmth in your chest? Tingling through your body? Does your mind feel light, open? Now consciously intensify that feeling. Some psychologists call this "memorizing" the feeling. Either way, you are causing the same neural circuits to fire repeatedly, thereby strengthening them. Dr. Rick Hanson, author of *Buddha's Brain,* calls this "taking in the good" and suggests first intensifying the experience in your body, then letting it calm down, and then intensifying it again. He says, "As with any positive state of mind, see if you can develop a strong 'sense memory' of the experience so you can re-activate it deliberately when you want to."

that being mindful of this state actually seemed to increase it. I had always taught the principle that when we pay attention to wholesome states, they increase. Now it wasn't just theory. In a very real way, I was experiencing in my body and mind a profound truth—simply paying mindful attention to the experience of gratitude was intensifying the feeling of gratitude in the moment. And besides that, it was also giving rise to a sustained sense of happiness.

Mindfulness has a unique power. It weakens all mind states that lead to suffering, such as anger, greed, and fear, while awakening and strengthening within us all the mind states that lead to happiness such as kindness, love, and clarity. As you bring the practice of mindfulness into your life, take note of how your life changes. Besides enhancing your positive states of mind, when you pause to notice what you usually overlook, a new world opens to you. Instead of worrying about the future, regretting the past, or being lost in fantasies of what you long for or fear, when you are mindful, you're brought into the immediacy of *now*. Whatever your experience is, you can hold it as a sacred moment of life worthy of your attention.

Step 3

GRATEFUL HEART, JOYFUL HEART

*Be grateful for your life, every detail of it, and your face
will come to shine like a sun, and everyone who sees it
will be made glad and peaceful. Persist in gratitude, and
you will slowly become one with the Sun of Love, and
Love will shine through you its all-healing joy.*

—ANDREW HARVEY
Light Upon Light: Inspirations from Rumi

A STUDENT ONCE complained to Nisargadatta, a great twentieth-century spiritual teacher from India, that daily life seemed so tedious to him. "You've done the most amazing thing," the sage replied. "You've made life boring!" In this culture of thirty-second sound bites and blockbuster action movies, we can easily get into the habit of looking for a never-ending diet of peak experiences. When only highly stimulating events and fantastically wonderful things are worthy of our appreciation, we easily end up disappointed and feeling that life is mostly dull and uninteresting. In the midst of abundance, we find life lacking.

The founder of Gestalt psychology, Fritz Perls, used to say, "Boredom is simply lack of attention." As we've seen with mindfulness, when we pay attention, anything can be interesting. My friend Joe Kupfer discovered this in college, and it set his life in a new direction. Joe and I attended the same rigorous high school in New York City, and we came out with an almost identical grade point average—decent but not stellar. Neither of us had been that interested in going for top academic honors. Four years later we both graduated from Queens College, and while I had continued my casual scholastic attitude, Joe had achieved magna cum laude and went on to become a professor of philosophy. What was his secret? (Unfortunately for me, I didn't ask him until my senior year!)

When he started college, Joe told me, he'd made the decision to excel. I remember him saying he figured that the more interested he was in the course material, the easier it would be for him to learn the subject. So he devised a game: At the start of each semester, no matter how boring a class might appear to be, he would ask himself, "Why has the professor devoted his whole life to specializing in this subject? Why does he find it so interesting?" In searching for the answer, he invariably found something valuable and even fascinating in the material. Joe had interrupted a pattern of not appreciating what was before him and supplanted it with an eager openness that enabled him to shine.

I'm allowing myself more time to appreciate what I see, be it the clouds in the sky, a fallen leaf, the trees changing, or my friends and loved ones. As I do this, I find myself loving life more and feeling the joy that's inside me.

—A COURSE PARTICIPANT

I've been thrilled to watch my daughter flourish and feel free when I allow myself to relax and feel the love and openness that gratitude rewards me with. It's almost like watching myself in a mirror.

—A COURSE PARTICIPANT

As Joe discovered, you don't have to wait for appreciation and gratitude to spontaneously arise. You can consciously cultivate this powerful ally to a joyful heart. Each day of your life, you have many opportunities to develop a grateful heart by paying attention to the blessings, big and small, that are all around you. Even if things are uncomfortable, or not as you might wish, it is still possible to find something you can be grateful for.

You can miss those blessings when your mind is contracted with stress or filled with negativity. There's no room for them to enter. But the moment you pause and let yourself notice something to be grateful for, even in the midst of a challenge, it is virtually impossible to continue being lost in worry about the future, or regret about the past. Negative states like anger, bitterness, and resentment dissolve in the presence of gratitude.

One Tibetan lama says gratitude is like a satellite dish. When we feel grateful, our receptors are wide open to receive the abundance available to us. The very act of appreciating someone or something instantly calls forth joy. You can try it right now for yourself. Think of someone or something you feel grateful for, and notice what happens. It is impossible to feel genuinely grateful and not have a little rise of joy.

What does gratitude feel like, in your body and mind? Course participants offered these reflections:

- I breathe more deeply.
- I feel a glow in my chest, a tingling in my fingers, and a half-smile appears on my face.
- It feels like a blanket of goodness descending upon me.
- It brings me energy and peace at the same time.
- It makes me feel loved by God.
- I like myself and my muscles relax.
- I feel like my body is resting on the perfect pillow created to hold all of me.

As you notice all you have to be grateful for, pay close attention to the many different ways the experience of gratitude manifests inside you. Developing gratitude is for some people a turning point in their practice of awakening joy. It becomes immediately apparent how available joy really is. With practice, the grateful heart increasingly sees the goodness and wonder around us. As you explore this new step, notice the effect cultivating gratitude has on your life and the lives of those around you.

THE GLASS HALF EMPTY

What gets in the way of feeling gratitude? Most participants in the Awakening Joy course name the culprit as the frenetic pace of their lives. They write comments like these:

- Rushing through the moment, I often get fatigued and then tend to take things for granted.

- In my usual goal- and achievement-oriented attitude toward life, every moment has to be spent productively.
- I have the belief that I must complete a list of "to dos" before stopping to enjoy anything.

Many of us probably can relate to those statements. We can get so focused on what we're doing (or on the next thing we have to do) that we overlook how much we have to be grateful for. There just doesn't seem to be enough time to smell the roses. While there's a place and time for not being distracted from our goals, we can become so habituated to a fast pace that even when we don't have to get somewhere or get something done, we just keep going.

Feeling Gratitude

Take a few minutes to think of some of the people and things you feel gratitude for in your life. You might begin with being grateful that you can read these words. As each person or quality or thing comes up in your imagination, say silently to yourself, "I am grateful to . . . or for. . . ." Pause with each to feel the experience of gratitude that arises in your body and mind.

Before you finish with this exercise, stop and take in the fullness of the feeling of gratitude itself. Breathe it in deeply, and let it pervade your body and mind.

When Laurinda broke some bones in her foot, she was forced to slow way down. As she hobbled around the house with a supportive brace, she began to notice that even though she couldn't move quickly, inside herself the rushing pace she was used to was still driving her. It was as if she would miss something if she wasn't fast enough. As Laurinda made the effort to pull back and literally take it just one step at a time, she began to see how much she really had been missing. She wrote:

Every night I brush my hair, but suddenly I saw that I had been going at it like it was a chore. Instead of a wonderful pleasure that I could relax and appreciate, it was just something to get done. Rather than quickly counting off the one hundred brushstrokes, I started feeling each one and noticing how good it felt to lift my arm and draw the brush through my hair. I found I could actually slow down inside and give myself this simple joy. I felt so grateful, not just to change this small habit, but to begin to release the tension that has been a lifetime habit.

GRATITUDE SQUELCHERS

Gratitude grounds us in the present. When we're lost in galling regret about something in the past or overwhelming concerns about the future, we can forget what we have to be grateful for right now. Before I met my wife, I spent many a painful moment feeling sorry for myself and fantasizing about how good it would be when I found the love of my life. Caught up in longing, I overlooked the fact that I had many wonderful friends, but they didn't really count, because I was so focused on what I didn't have. When we get lost in fantasies of "My life could (or should) be better," we're missing the only life we actually have. Having a positive vision of the future is healthy, but in order to get there, it helps to appreciate and build on what's good in our life right now.

One thought away from "It could be better" is "*I* could be better"—a sure gratitude squelcher. When we think we're not good enough, we can spend our energy trying to prove the opposite to ourselves and to the world. We can get caught up in a kind of perfectionism that keeps us from appreciating ourselves as we are.

We can also be retroactive perfectionists, living in regret that things could have or should have been better. While we certainly can learn from past mistakes, playing over and over in our minds what might have been is guaranteed to keep us unaware of anything we can be grateful for, then or now. For example, you might go out for dinner and a movie with a new friend, and although you both obviously had a good time, you end up later replaying in your mind the one sentence that didn't come out the way you meant it to. *I'm such a dummy,* you berate yourself. *I guess that's the end of that friendship.* The next thing you know, that friend tells you how great it was to spend time together. And there you've been, lost in regret rather than remembering the joys of that evening. What a waste. The same kind of thing can happen with months or even years of our lives when we focus on what went wrong rather than on what went right.

Another equally useless version of regret is wishing things were like they used to be in "the good ol' days." When we look at people or events through a rearview mirror, they often seem better than they really were. An argument with your partner might leave you feeling nostalgic for the single life, forgetting how excruciating the dating scene was. When we're attentive and grateful for our lives right now, we can make sure that our present moments, soon to be our "good ol' days," are fully lived and appreciated.

RIGHT UNDER OUR NOSES

In one of my favorite stories about Mulla Nasruddin, an eccentric wise fool from the Sufi tradition, Mulla and his donkey have been frequently crossing the border between Persia and Turkey. As time goes on, the customs officials on both sides of the border notice that Nasruddin seems to be getting increasingly richer. His clothes are finer and he is wearing elegant perfumes. The officers are sure he is smuggling contraband. They thoroughly search him, his donkey, and the donkey's straw, but each time they can find nothing. For several months the situation continues in this way. Nasruddin looks richer and richer, yet despite careful inspections of both him and his donkey, nothing is found.

Many months later, one of the customs officials sees Nasruddin shopping in the bazaar. He approaches him and says, "Mulla, I have retired from my post as a customs official. I now have a generous pension and want nothing from you except one thing. We all know you were smuggling something across the border but could never find anything on you or the donkey. I swear I won't tell a soul if you share your secret with me. What was it you were smuggling?"

Nasruddin looks at him with a mischievous grin and replies, "Donkeys."

Often the precious riches we are looking for are right under our noses but we miss them. We can find valuable gifts in the most unexpected places if we get in the habit of being grateful for whatever is before us. Sometimes they are even hidden right inside the challenges we face.

My friend Abby developed cancer of the throat. During an eight-month ordeal of chemotherapy, radiation, and receiving nourishment through a feeding tube, she chose to focus not on the pain and discomfort but on how fortunate she was to have access to good medical care and the fact that the doctors caught the tumor in time. Her recovery was extraordinary and, of course, she was a true inspiration to everyone who knew her.

About three months later, however, Abby received the startling news that there were signs of malignant cells in her lung. The specialists gave her two choices—the less invasive procedure would remove some tissue in the lung, but there was some chance that this would not completely remove the problem. The more dramatic choice, while the surer solution, would entail removing the entire upper lobe of the lung. On the advice of her doctor, Abby chose the second option.

"When the surgery was over, my doctor informed me that they hadn't found cancer in the lung after all. It had been a false read," she told me. I think most people in the same situation would have understandably been very upset. But Abby was determined to incline her mind toward appreciation rather than regret or anger. Even though she might have seen little to be grateful for in this situation, she chose to look at this as another opportunity to be open to what life was giving her. "My prayer going into the operation was that I would come out of it with no cancer in the lung. And in the end, that's what I got!" she says. "My prayer was answered." Rather than being brought down by bitterness, Abby's ordeal deepened her capacity for gratitude, and she was invigorated by the joy she felt from focusing on what there was to appreciate.

Abby's ability to respond to her ordeal with gratitude was grounded in years of spiritual practice. She knew that anger and frustration, though justified, wouldn't change what had happened and would only lead to more emotional upset. While it usually takes time and practice to develop this kind of wisdom, it begins with realizing you have a choice. The shift toward responding with gratitude in the midst of difficult circumstances can be a gradual process or it can happen in an instant. As you keep in mind the fact that what you really want is happiness and peace, you learn to act in ways that are more likely to bring that about.

Author Carolyn Hobbs suggests that we try saying yes to whatever we're experiencing. This means we're not fighting our circumstances. Any situation, even the most disappointing, may have a hidden gift we can be grateful for. Sometimes we see that better in retrospect, but by then we may have spent many unhappy moments bound up in anger or depression. When we remain open to whatever is happening to us, we are far more likely to find the valuable gifts hidden in our challenging times.

"GRACE DISGUISED AS OBSTACLES"

For decades Ram Dass, a much-loved spiritual teacher and author of *Be Here Now*, mesmerized audiences with his fascinating lectures. Then in 1997 his life radically changed when he suffered a major stroke. He went from being able to cast a magic spell with words to struggling through long silences just to construct a simple sentence. In his book *Still Here*, Ram Dass describes how painful this process initially was as he tried to hold on to his old identity, remembering how things used to be.

One of his first public events after the stroke was held at Spirit Rock Meditation Center in California, on a day dedicated to celebrating him. The talk he gave was short and halting. Although everyone was moved by his presence, when I saw him afterward, he expressed sadness that he would never be able to do what he had done before.

Besides losing his eloquence, Ram Dass could no longer do most of the activities that had given him great joy. Of course he had to go through a period of grieving. But eventually he was able to say yes to this new version of himself and transform his frustration into a profound gratitude. He writes in *Still Here*:

> I used to say, "I'm a golfer and a sports car driver." . . . But now I'm someone telling that story. I can't golf or drive anymore. If I cling to that identity, I suffer. . . . The stroke was like a samurai sword, cutting apart the two halves of my life. It was a

demarcation between two stages. Before I had the stroke, I was full of fears about aging. . . . The stroke took me through one of my deep fears, and I'm here to report that "the only thing we have to fear is fear itself" . . . The stroke cleaned out some of the pockets of fear. It's happened, and here I am.

The result of this change, Ram Dass says, is that he has grown closer to God than ever before. "What more could I ask?" he writes, acknowledging the gift deeply hidden in his suffering.

Over time Ram Dass has not only adjusted to his new identity, he has become even more of an inspiration than before. He invites his adoring audiences to use the pauses in his speech to enter into a meditative silence. In allowing his stroke to be a teaching, he now conveys, in an even more profound way, the wisdom he's been communicating for decades.

I was extremely frustrated when I tore the meniscus in my knee. However, not being able to work out every day, one of my favorite things to do, ended up giving me more time for meditation, gardening, listening to music, and spending time with my family. I've found new paths to joy.

—A COURSE PARTICIPANT

Gratitude in our darkest times is more than a matter of remembering our blessings so we can hold the hard stuff in a bigger perspective. With understanding, we see that often it is the suffering itself that deepens us, maturing our perspective on life, making us more compassionate and wiser than we would have been without it. How many times have we been inspired by those who embody a wisdom that could only come from dealing with adversity? And how many valuable lessons have we ourselves learned because life has given us unwanted challenges? With a grateful heart, we're not only willing to face our difficulties, we can realize while we're going through them that they are part of our ripening into wisdom and nobility.

GLASS HALF FULL

Lisa came to a retreat at Spirit Rock eager to get away from all the distractions of her busy life. Instead, what was revealed in the silence was the continual complaining taking place in her mind. When she came in for her interview, the fifteen-minute check-in with the teacher scheduled during silent retreats, the look on her face was a combination of frustration and humor. With a sigh she began, "I can't believe the way I talk to myself all day. No wonder everything seems so heavy. I'm constantly whining! And I'm so tired of it."

"What kinds of things is that internal voice saying?" I asked.

"It's always the same refrain," Lisa answered. "No matter what I'm about to do, my mind grumbles, 'Oh now I *have to* do this. Now I *have to* do that.' When I'm in the meditation hall and the bell rings at the end of the sitting, the thought comes, 'Oh, now I *have to* do walking meditation.' Then when the bell ends that period, my mind says, 'Oh now I *have to* do sitting meditation.' Even when the bell for lunch sounds, my response is 'Oh now I *have to* go to lunch.' And I know that's what I always do in my daily life as well. I wish I could stop it," she went on. "But I don't know how to break the habit. Now I see why I often feel that life is a drag. I make it a drag!"

Lisa had actually pinpointed the problem herself. "What if you just change one word in there?" I asked. She looked at me quizzically. I continued, "I wonder what it would be like if, whenever you hear yourself complaining about what you *have to* do, you try saying instead, 'Now I *get to* do this' and 'Now I *get to* do that.' That way each activity would feel less like a chore and more like a change of scenery for you to appreciate." She agreed to give it a try.

A few days later Lisa came in for her next interview, beaming. "What a difference that one little word makes!" she began. "I haven't minded the bell ringing these last few days at all. I've even been looking forward to my work meditation folding the laundry. I'm taking each activity as a new adventure, and so I notice all kinds of things I used to miss. I don't want to jinx myself by saying it, but I'm actually having fun!"

I'd been delighted to learn that Lisa had

After a week of overwhelming generosity bestowed upon me, instead of enjoying it, I started to feel fear and caution about becoming too joyous, as this might mean I'd let my guard slip and get sideswiped when I least expected it. This revealed my tendency to limit joy or feel like I somehow have to "pay back" for the joy I receive. I wonder how often I have limited joy in my life. Funny, as I don't seem to put limits on the pain.

—A COURSE PARTICIPANT

From "Have to" to "Get To"

Choose a particular task or situation in your life that feels like a burden. Try changing "have to" to "get to" and see if you get a different perspective. "Now I get to take out the garbage" just might make you feel grateful to the people who come and take it away. The more you notice what there is to be grateful for, the sooner your half-empty glass begins to look at least half-full.

discovered on the retreat a new way to relate to her life, but even more impressive was that she sustained it. Several months later in Berkeley, I ran into her by chance. She said that keeping up her "Now I *get to*" practice was having a profound effect. "I'm so much lighter now," Lisa smiled. "Changing that one little word has changed my life."

The habit of seeing what's wrong in our lives is like reading only the depressing articles in the newspaper. Taking in a steady diet of bad news, we can forget about the cartoons or the inspiring feature stories. Gratitude helps us shift the perspective so we can see what is filling our cup rather than what might be missing.

FRAME IT WITH GRATITUDE

One year I was in Los Angeles visiting my then eighty-nine-year-old mother. I brought with me a copy of *Greater Good*, a magazine published by a couple of brilliant minds at the University of California at Berkeley. Their focus is on reporting the breaking research on altruism and well-being. The topic of the particular issue I had with me was the beneficial effects of gratitude. As we sat at the dining room table eating the special eggplant dish my mother always makes for me, I told her about some of the findings. She said she was impressed by the reports, but admitted she had a lifetime habit of looking at the glass half empty. "I

The Benefits of Gratitude

- ▸ Martin Seligman, the father of Positive Psychology, asked people who considered themselves severely depressed to write down three good things that happened to them each day for fifteen days. At the end of the experiment, 94 percent of these subjects had a decrease in depression and 92 percent actually said their happiness had increased.
- ▸ Leading gratitude researchers, UC Davis psychologists Robert Emmons and Michael McCullough, divided volunteers for a study on the benefits of gratitude into three groups. Once a week for ten weeks the "Gratitude Group" wrote down five things they were grateful for. The "Hassle Group" wrote down five things that displeased them. And the "Neutral Group" listed five things that affected them but without emphasizing the positive or negative aspects of their experience. The results? On a scale used to calculate well-being, the Gratitude Group registered 25 percent happier than either the Hassle or the Neutral Group. They also felt better about life, were more optimistic, had fewer health complaints and symptoms of illness, did more physical exercise than the Neutral Group and *significantly* more exercise than the Hassle Group.

know I'm very fortunate and have so many things to be thankful for, but little things just set me off." She said she wished she could change the habit but had doubts whether that was possible. "I'm just more used to seeing what's going wrong," she concluded.

After dinner my mom and I broke out the Scrabble set, as we often do. (She's a terrific player and derives great joy from trouncing her poor son!) Our conversation continued as the lines of tiles filled the board.

"You know, Mom, the key to gratitude is really in the way we frame a situation," I began. "For instance, suppose all of a sudden your television isn't getting good reception."

"That's a scenario I can relate to," she agreed, with a knowing smile.

"One way to describe your experience would be to say, 'This is so annoying I could scream!' Or you could say, 'This is so annoying . . . *and* my life is really very blessed.'" She agreed that could make a big difference.

"But I don't think I can remember to do that," she sighed.

So together we made up a gratitude game to remind her. Each time she complained about something, I would simply say "*and . . .*" to which she would respond "*and* my life is very blessed." I was elated to see that she was willing to try it out. Over the next few days, as the complaints rolled off her tongue, we had many chances to play our little game. We'd both chuckle each time she dutifully gave her agreed-upon reply. Although it had started out as just a fun game, after a while the exercise began to have some real impact. Her mood grew brighter as our week became filled with gratitude and a genuine good time.

After I got home I called my mother a lot during the first few days to support her in keeping her gratitude practice alive. Miraculously she kept at it, and the new habit took hold. My sister, who had been out of town, called me when she got back. "What did you do to Mom?!" she asked.

To my delight and amazement, my mother has continued doing the practice, and the change has been revolutionary. Seven months after my visit, she sent a card for my birthday. As is our family tradition, it contained a poem she wrote for the occasion. This one I especially cherish. Even though she started losing her sight during those months, the effects of her gratitude practice are evident in this poignant excerpt. And it goes to show you that you *can* teach an elder human new tricks!

> *Ninety is just fine with me, I no longer rant and rave*
> *About where the world is heading and my exclusive job to save.*
> *I wallow in contentment and know that I am blessed*
> *Awakening to the joy of living at its best.*
> *I'm happier than I've ever been and truly mean each word.*
> *The thoughts that caused the worries now all seem so absurd.*
> *Though my eyesight has been dimmed I see clearer than before,*
> *The glass is not half empty, it's overflowing to be sure.*

The choice is ours. We can go through life focusing on the burdens or letting our challenges serve as reminders of the blessings that also surround us. Maybe the story of my ninety-year-old mother can inspire you to remember in the midst of life's hassles that your life too is really very blessed.

STRENGTHENING YOUR GRATITUDE MUSCLE

If appreciation and gratitude feel so good and lead directly to joy, why aren't we going around all of the time counting our blessings? Because, as with other wholesome states, it takes practice to get in the gratitude habit. But even putting a little time into it can have a significant impact on your level of well-being.

For a number of years, Jane, my wife, has been doing a daily gratitude practice. It started with her taking five minutes each night to exchange emails with a friend, reporting on what they were grateful for that day. The results have been dramatic, but in the beginning she remembers that it took focused effort.

"When we first started the gratitude practice, it was a stretch for me," she recalls. Raised in a family where it was considered smart to be cynical, she had become an expert in scanning the horizon for problems instead of for what was going well. "I would sometimes struggle to think of something to write if it hadn't been a particularly positive day. If I'd been hassling with my teenager, working on taxes, or getting stuck in traffic, it was sometimes pretty hard to feel grateful." But Jane stayed with her commitment, and as she kept her radar out, she began to notice things she had taken for granted:

During my first bike ride of the season, I encountered a very steep hill and watched my mind fret and body tighten. In that moment I also realized how grateful and lucky I am to have a healthy body and to be alive on this beautiful spring night. I smiled at my fretting mind and took one pedal at a time. I slowed down, turned the gears down (literally and figuratively), and got present. I did not focus on the top of the hill. I focused on the foot on the pedal, the movement of the body, and the beauty, freedom, and immediacy of the practice of gratitude.

—A COURSE PARTICIPANT

I began to see how much I have to be grateful for. I have clean drinking water and food on my table. I've had the opportunity to get an education, I have a loving family, and I like my job as an ESL teacher. I also learned that I could choose what to focus on. When my car needed repair, I could get grumpy, or I could feel grateful that the mechanic caught the problem before the car broke down on the freeway, grateful that I could afford to have it repaired, and grateful that I have a car at all.

. . . and my life is really very blessed.

Each time you find yourself worrying or complaining, try adding on that little phrase. Even if it seems false at first, let yourself play with it and see what happens. You might find it helpful to enroll an ally to keep you on track—your partner, child, or Joy Buddy. Remember you're in a learning process, and be patient with yourself. Every time you succeed in shifting your outlook to a more relaxed sense of gratitude, tune in to how good you feel, and pause to anchor that in your body and mind.

It used to seem wrong to feel any joy when I was filled with sorrow. But I realize now that I need joy for myself and for those around me especially during a time of sorrow.

—A COURSE PARTICIPANT

Knowing she would be reporting each night on what she was grateful for gave Jane the extra impetus to notice people, things, and events that she appreciated. Before long, her gratitude emails flowed with an abundance of appreciations. As we cultivate the habit of being grateful, the mind naturally comes to rest on the goodness in our lives. As Jane found, if you have the intention to awaken gratitude, over time it will gradually become the natural rhythm of your heart, strong enough to hold even suffering.

THE GRATITUDE PERSPECTIVE

Several years after starting the nightly emails, Jane's partner in the gratitude emails, Bonnie, was diagnosed with breast cancer. Bonnie would find that her years of gratitude practice were a major support as she went through the intense treatments. She wrote:

> The second round of chemo has been difficult, but I don't add to the difficulty. What I feel most is gratitude. I cry now just feeling this. I'm perhaps more aware than ever of the suffering in the world. Yet when I woke up the other day and looked at the full moon through the skylights—clouds surrounding it, then moving to cover it—aahhhhhh, life.

Gratitude for the small wonders continued to carry Bonnie through her healing. Her messages would say, "I can't walk hills, but this week I can walk . . . I'm very grateful for the beautiful spring days . . . Wishing you mindfulness of the preciousness of this life."

When we're faced with challenges, gratitude opens us to a larger perspective that helps us more effectively address them. When we're unhappy—depressed, angry, in pain—we contract. The simple practice of gratitude actually begins to relax the mind. Instead of seeing things from only one perspective, we become "open-minded." The causes of suffering don't go away, but the context in which they're happening gets bigger.

Mary is a social worker at an elementary school in a large urban center. Many of the students she works with live with their grandparents or in single-parent families; some come from large families in which the parents struggle to make ends meet. "The children who come to me are, for the most part, experiencing grief and loss," Mary told me. "There is much poverty, death, incarceration, divorce, domestic violence, and violence in general in their young lives." Doing the gratitude step in the Awakening Joy program, she began to remember times in her life when being actively grateful had made such a difference in how she felt. "I decided to try bringing some balance into their days by doing 'gratitude rounds'

Deepen Your Happiness Groove

▸ Spend five minutes at the end of each day writing down what you are grateful for. In addition to the more obvious blessings, be sure to include simple things, such as seeing a sunset or your child's smile. You can do this in your private journal or set up an email exchange with a friend or Joy Buddy.

▸ Each time you eat, pause to say some version of a "grace before meals," remembering the many elements that have made your meal possible.

▸ A course participant said she has started saying thank you to her family members when they do even routine things around the house. Try this and see what happens.

Whenever you feel that open and delightful experience of gratitude, deepen your "happiness groove" by pausing to consciously notice what's going on inside you. Just a few seconds is long enough to let the sensations in your body and the state of your mind register in your awareness. As you become familiar with the landscape of gratitude, you will more easily and naturally access it.

with the children. We'd sit in a big circle, and one by one they'd say what they were grateful for that day. They are such amazing teachers, and with little prodding they thought of, and were eager to share, their deep and heartfelt gratitude."

Seeing the positive effect on the children at school, Mary gave them the assignment to interview each of their family members about what he or she was grateful for. She encouraged them to come back with some specific examples from a sister, a grandparent, a mother or father. It turned out that their family members welcomed the chance to answer the question, and those reports brought another level of joy into the

Authentic Happiness

Psychologist Martin Seligman is an expert on what makes people happy. In his book *Authentic Happiness,* he reports that of all the exercises he has developed for his Positive Psychology classes, one is particularly effective—writing a gratitude letter. He suggests that you pick someone you feel great gratitude for and write a one-page letter appreciating all the ways that person has enriched your life. Then slowly read it to him or her, face-to-face, and listen attentively to the response. I offer this exercise in my meditation classes and Awakening Joy course, and have found that mailing the letter or reading it over the phone can also be very meaningful for both appreciator and appreciated. Even if the recipient of gratitude has passed away, I suggest that people write a letter anyway. Just the action of expressing your gratitude has a major impact on your own well-being.

group. Even though the basic circumstances in the families of these children didn't change, some light shone through. "Every time we do our gratitude rounds," Mary reports, "there is extra cheer as we say our rousing good-byes."

A note of caution: You can't force gratitude, and if you try, you'll just feel frustrated and want to close down. If you are in the midst of great challenges and you don't feel grateful, just notice that and let the feeling be as it is. Bring a kind awareness to the resistance you're feeling, and know that there is one thing you can be grateful for—that you don't *have to* be grateful!

SCATTERING GRATITUDE LIKE JOY

When I was in the sixth grade my teacher, Mrs. Oxman, taught us that the secret to adding a new word to your active vocabulary is to use it three times in conversation. "Then it becomes yours," she told us. Years later, a school teacher myself, I would try to have my students not only take in important information by reading or hearing, but also by discussing it, drawing it, and writing about it. The more senses that were involved, the deeper the material was absorbed.

Several years ago I had to decide what to give my dad for his sixty-fifth birthday. He has everything, wants nothing. So I wrote him a letter detailing why I'm grateful that he's my dad and that he is who he is. Then I went to a shop that makes handcrafted wooden boxes and found one that suited him and gave it to him as a 'Gratitude Box.' It turned out to be a great gift.

—A COURSE PARTICIPANT

In the same way, when we convert our thoughts, whether positive or negative, into words and actions, we increase their impact. For example, you might be thinking fond thoughts about a friend or your partner, but what happens when you actually tell that person you love them? Even in a relationship of many years, speaking the words "I love you" makes something come alive. Our loved one lights up, and we light up back. Like completing an electrical circuit, the life force moves through and between us. The same thing happens when you express your appreciation to others. Scattering gratitude spreads a joy that encompasses us as well as those to whom we are grateful.

Our lives are filled with people whose presence helps us to live and thrive. If you think about it, your list might include the mail carrier, those who grow your food and transport it to market, the civil servants who help sustain the systems that support our towns and cities, your teachers and clergy, your coworkers . . . the list is nearly endless. If you really want to develop a grateful heart, in addition to thinking about how grateful you are for these people, express your gratitude to them when the opportunity arises.

Besides opening your own heart, expressing appreciation to others makes them feel more comfortable around you. They're not on guard, fearing judgments. They can relax and feel your friendliness. Then they more easily appreciate you, which in turn allows you to feel more at ease. Expressing our appreciation and gratitude to others not only feels good, but it helps make the world a friendlier place.

BUT I CAN'T FEEL GRATEFUL TO *THEM*

When my son Adam was little, I often read books aloud to him at bed-time. One of our favorite series was Lloyd Alexander's *Chronicles of Prydain.* In the wonderful volume *The Black Cauldron,* a main character ends up on the side of evil. At the end of the final battle when the heroes are honoring all the dead who helped their cause, this fallen character is included in the tribute. Taran, the young protagonist, is filled with disbelief at the gesture. A wise mentor and companion explains to him that although this man had betrayed the group, he was also instrumental in many ways in their ultimate victory, and so it was fitting to honor the good he contributed.

After the assignment to express my appreciation, I decided at work to say thank you and really mean it. It made a huge difference for me. I felt more connected to everyone with whom I shared thanks.

—A COURSE PARTICIPANT

I vividly recall sitting in bed with Adam and, as I finished reading this to him, being moved to tears as I thought about all the people who had fallen off the pedestal I had put them on. Instead of appreciating them for how they had enriched my life at some point, a later disappointment had gotten in the way of fully opening my heart to them in a debt of gratitude. Tears flowed at

Practicing being thankful has made it possible to turn around my struggles with my teenage son, as I really am quite thankful he is in my life.

—A COURSE PARTICIPANT

the sorrow of having done that, as well as at the joy of allowing them back into my heart. This lesson has continued to help me remember that, in spite of difficulties, my heart can stay open to those who help me grow.

When we have a challenging relationship with someone, we can easily forget that we have reasons to feel grateful to them. My friend Rob came to this understanding during a meditation retreat. When he came in for his final interview, he had a big smile on his face.

"I just got in touch with something in the last twenty-four hours that I'd never really understood before," he began. He explained that he'd been blessed with a kind and supportive father with whom he shared a deep, loving relationship. His relationship with his mother, however, was not as easy for him. "She was often judgmental," he said, "and it felt like she was living from a place of fear and scarcity emotionally." In Rob's life story, Dad held center stage as the hero in the limelight and Mom was often in the wings. "But something shifted for me yesterday," he said and went on:

> As I looked back on my life, I got in touch with all the ways my mom was there for me. She was the one who taught me to throw a baseball. She loved literature and taught me about writing, which is now my vocation. As I thought about the positive ways she impacted my life, I understood that despite all our mother-son challenges, she really cared about me. In fact, in her own way, she really loved me. In the last few hours I've had a feeling of gratitude for my mom that I never allowed myself to feel before. It's wonderful! I feel so much more open now. I don't have to hold back fully loving her. She can share center stage with my dad. She belongs there too.

Often those closest to us can be the most difficult to appreciate. As with Rob, your relationship with your parents might be a place where opening up to gratitude can be transforming. Or you might experience that release by remembering what you appreciate about a coworker, your child, or your partner. When you think of those who have been a challenge, can you also see how they might have helped bring out qualities in you, such as patience, determination, caring, or wisdom? Or perhaps there are positive qualities in that person that you have overlooked. When you can look beyond the difficulties to what you appreciate, you open another door to joy.

IT WOULD HAVE BEEN ENOUGH . . .

When I was a child, each year in springtime our family would celebrate the Jewish holiday of Passover. At the traditional meal called a Seder, we ate special foods that reminded us of the hard times before God led the Jews out of bondage in Egypt into freedom. The parsley dipped in salt water recalled all the tears we shed in slavery. The horseradish or bitter

Open in Gratitude

A GUIDED MEDITATION BY PATRICIA ELLSBERG
AT AWAKENING JOY COURSE, BERKELEY, 2008

Open in gratitude . . .

. . . for the breath that nourishes every cell in your body and has sustained you from the moment you were born.

. . . for the miracle of your body that, despite whatever weaknesses or limitations, serves you and allows you to sense the wonders of the world.

. . . for your brain that coordinates all the functions of your body without your even being aware of it.

. . . for consciousness that allows you to perceive, feel, and be amazed.

. . . for the eyes that allow you to see the abounding beauty that surrounds you—colors and shapes, the face of a loved one.

. . . for the ears that enable you to hear birds singing, wind rustling in leaves, words people say to you, and the laughter of children.

. . . for the sense of smell that allows you to enjoy the fragrance of flowers, the scent of fresh air, your favorite food.

. . . for your mouth and tongue that enable you to taste the fruits of the earth, to enjoy a ripe peach or chocolate melting in your mouth.

. . . for the skin that protects you and yet allows you to touch and sense the world, feel warmth, coolness, softness, and the touch of a loved one.

. . . for your heart that beats faithfully your whole life, from even before you were born.

Open to a sense of wonder and gratitude for the amazing gift of being awake and alive in this precious human form. The fact that we exist or that anything exists at all is a wondrous mystery. We all live in the midst of a miracle.

The Buddha's Discourse on Blessings

It is a great blessing:

—To spend time in the company of wise people and to honor those who are worthy.

—To live in a place that is good for you, to do good deeds, and to keep yourself going in the right direction.

—To be well-educated, to develop your skills, to train yourself in discipline, and to use words carefully and beautifully.

—To take good care of your mother and father, to cherish your partner and children, and to engage in a livelihood that is harmless.

—To give generously to others, to live with integrity, to care for everyone you consider your family.

—To avoid doing harm, to refrain from intoxicants, and to develop wholesome states of mind.

—To be respectful, humble, content, and grateful, and to regularly bring spiritual teachings into your life.

—To be patient, open to learning, to be in touch with people on a spiritual path, and to discuss spiritual teachings.

—To live simply and in a holy way, to understand the deepest truth, and to realize the highest freedom and happiness.

—To have a mind that is steady, unswayed by the ups and downs of life, free of sorrow and shame, and at peace.

Those who act in these ways cannot be dragged down. Everywhere they go, they find well-being.

—ADAPTATION BY SHOSHANA ALEXANDER
OF THE BUDDHA'S *Mangalam Sutta*

herbs helped us remember the bitterness of those times. We also ate lots of matzo crackers to remind us that there hadn't been enough time to let bread rise before fleeing Pharaoh's army. Throughout the long service, we prayed, sang songs, and heard the story of the Exodus.

Then came the best part for me—not only could we finally dig into the sumptuous feast of "real food," but we got to sing the joyous song "Dayenu." This Hebrew word means "It would have been enough." Following each of the fifteen verses recounting the many gifts God had given—freedom from slavery, miracles in the desert, closeness to the Divine—we would all break into that rousing refrain: "Dayenu!" This one thing would have been enough, but then You did this. . . . Just singing that song of gratitude would fill me up with joy. It still does.

Sometimes I realize I can look at life with that spirit of *dayenu*. To be given life would have been sufficient. But not only that, to have a healthy body, a kind heart, a good mind . . . thank you, Life. To be able to enjoy the taste of ripe peaches, delight in listening to Beethoven and the Beatles, take in the sweet smell of gardenias and bay trees, feel someone's caring through their hug. Thank you. What's more, this body with all its senses and intelligence comes with a mind that can think creative thoughts, crack jokes, reflect on philosophical questions, and be aware of itself. And in this mind-body process called "James" is the capacity to care for another's pain, delight in their joy, express my love, and be touched by the world around me.

Yet can I take credit for any of these things? Can any of us take credit for the life we have? We don't own any of it. It has all been given. There is something about life that is miraculously generous. Instead of the gardenia, there could have been only the cactus! This benevolent abundance evokes tremendous gratitude in me.

THANKS TO LIFE

When I look back on my late teens and early twenties, I realize I did lots of crazy things. I was walking nonchalantly and unconsciously through a minefield of potential dangers. Yet, as many of us know, no matter how far we go in the wrong direction, our lives can turn around. Some inner call gets us facing in the direction of goodness, truth, and happiness. Think back to the turning points in your life that got you to where you are now. Could you have written that mysterious script? How can we not be grateful for the amazing grace that keeps us heading in the direction of wholeness? As part of your gratitude practice, you might consider writing a thank you letter to Life itself, not only for the endless blessings but also for giving you the lessons you needed in order to grow.

Once we start looking for blessings in our lives we see them everywhere. In her book *Attitudes of Gratitude,* M. J. Ryan writes:

> Gratitude is like a flashlight. It lights up what is already there. You don't necessarily have anything more or different, but suddenly you can actually see what is. And because you can see, you no longer take it for granted.

In a famous teaching, called the "Discourse on Blessings," the Buddha enumerates the many noble qualities and circumstances available to us in our daily lives. Among the qualities of the blessed person, he includes being grateful. To be grateful is in itself a blessing and an open door to joy. Each time you are grateful for something, stop to take in and fully experience that uplifting and joyful feeling. Gratitude can be an ongoing frame of reference from which to live your life. You might even, as Albert Einstein suggests, begin to see that everything around you is a miracle.

Step 4
FINDING JOY IN DIFFICULT TIMES

*In the middle of winter, I at last discovered that there was
in me an invincible summer.*
—ALBERT CAMUS, *The Myth of Sisyphus: And Other Essays*

WHEN THINGS ARE going well, it's easy to be joyful. "Isn't life wonderful!" you may say. "I'm so happy. Everything's on track." But as we all know, there's another side to life. How do we cultivate joy and well-being when we're in the midst of pain and suffering? Inclining your mind toward joy does not mean putting on a happy face, denying your feelings, or enduring pain with a stiff upper lip. But what does it mean when you're having a hard time?

The Buddha's teachings about life don't begin with: Be happy. Everything is cool. They start with the First Noble Truth: There is suffering in life. In *Pali*, the language of the Buddha, the word for suffering is *dukkha*, which also means stress, unsatisfactoriness, unreliability. Life is stressful, and it's often unsatisfactory and unreliable. We've all had some experience of that.

Circumstances beyond our control can turn our world upside down in an instant. Driving along, minding our own business, we get rear-ended. We go through our days taking our good health for granted, and suddenly, out of the blue, we get a diagnosis of illness. A dear friend dies. We lose a job, a house, a partner. Tragedies happen unexpectedly, as the newspapers remind us every day. As my teacher Joseph Goldstein puts it, "Anything can happen at any time."

Life was going well on all fronts for my friend Abhaya. She was teaching meditation, had completed a two-year training to get certified as a chaplain, and was working at a hospital with people facing life-threatening illnesses. Doing what she loved to do was greatly fulfilling. The last time I'd heard from her, she said she was very happy. Then one day I received an unexpected email from her, sent out to all her friends:

> I have had an interesting week and have some news to share. A physical therapy appointment led to an ER visit, which led to a CAT scan, which a few days later led to an MRI, which yesterday brought me to a neurosurgeon who showed me the results, which reveal a rather large tumor in my brain. No matter how I say it, it sounds so dramatic! The neurosurgeon believes he can remove most of the tumor, but not all of it. He will not know the full ramifications until he knows what kind of tumor it is, which he will not know until he is in there.

It's not a question of *if* the hard stuff comes but *when* it comes. Suffering and stress are part of the fabric of life. While some of us have easier lives than others, if each of us lives a normal life span, not one of us can escape old age, sickness, and death. These three facts of life shook Prince Siddhartha, the Buddha-to-be, out of his idyllic world at the age of twenty-nine and started him on the quest that was to transform him into the Enlightened One. Over the six years he spent as a wandering monk, he questioned how one could find true happiness in a world filled with so much suffering. His journey led him to the conclusion that the more we face the fact that suffering is a part of life, the greater the possibility of experiencing the happiness of a mind liberated from stress. In fact, when asked about the essence of his teaching, the Buddha's reply was simply, "I teach about suffering and the end of suffering."

Although everyone suffers, when things go badly we tend to think there must be some kind of mistake. My friend and teaching colleague, Rodney Smith, ran a hospice in Seattle for many years. He tells the story of a ninety-seven-year-old woman who, upon finding out that she had a terminal condition, began wailing, "Why me?!" My friend Abhaya, in contrast, was in her mid-forties when she found out about the brain tumor, and she responded by writing in the note that announced the news to her friends:

> My heart is very full today with all the love I am receiving. Know that I send this with love and gratefulness to all of you. Please be happy and feel some of the wonder of life.

What a difference in response between two people facing a similar challenge! Clearly one of them was happier, despite what she was experiencing. You have a choice as to how you deal with your suffering. You can try to avoid it and live in denial. You can resent it and grow bitter. You can simply endure it and resign yourself to your bad luck. Or you can discover that there's another way, one that opens you to wisdom and to life itself.

Abhaya's operation was successful and, despite the inevitable challenges she faced during a long recovery, she consciously chose to keep her heart open and remember there is more to life than just the difficulty she was going through. Recently she sent out an email message to the circle of friends who had in various ways supported her healing. She wrote:

> I continue to be very grateful to each of you. On many levels you have helped me sort out and deal with things I was facing. There has been fear and confusion, yes, but there has also been a larger perspective, based in humor, gratitude, and being held by the mystery and joy.

Our life circumstances change all the time. To a great degree, how much joy we have in our lives is determined not by what is happening but by how we respond to it. Sometimes we're in the flow, other times we're stuck in the mud. In eighth-century India, the scholar and philosopher Shantideva wrote:

If there is a remedy when trouble strikes,
What reason is there for despondency?
And if there is no help for it,
What use is there in being sad?

This simple and practical advice is as useful now as it was over a thousand years ago, and it's a good platform for a healthy relationship with the challenges in our lives. Pema Chodron, a school teacher in California who became a Tibetan Buddhist nun and renowned meditation teacher, gives a modern context to this advice. She calls it "Shantideva's advice for stress reduction." In *No Time to Lose* she writes: "If we're caught in a traffic jam, for example, what's the point in fuming? If there's a remedy, like an off-ramp, there's no need to be upset. But if there are cars as far as the eye can see and no way out, then obsessing makes us unhappier." In any situation, instead of looking for reasons for our suffering, or worrying about what will happen in the future, we can just take it a step at a time, like Abhaya, and respond openly to what life puts before us.

This fourth step in Awakening Joy shows that by being open to the suffering that comes into your life, rather than resisting it, you can learn to let the pain of life's inevitable challenges move through you rather than get stuck in you. You also create the conditions that allow you to be open to more joy. In this chapter, mindfulness is the primary tool I am suggesting, because the resistance that intensifies our suffering is in our mind. Mindfulness can ease what we're going through in hard times, and it releases us from mental states that cause suffering. Other tools are also offered to help you when the going gets rough. Mindfulness, however, gets to the root of suffering and frees us from its power. As we stop trying to protect ourselves from our painful experiences and mindfully open to them, all those positive qualities within us—understanding, compassion, kindness—can also come to life.

Two of the most inspiring people I am aware of who remain open in this way are the Dalai Lama and Archbishop Desmond Tutu. Both have seen enormous suffering in their lives, yet somehow they radiate an infectious joy. How is that possible? I believe it is because both know deeply that suffering is part of life and, because of their dedication to spiritual practice, they are not afraid to be with it. I've seen the Dalai Lama get very serious, even cry, upon hearing about a tragedy and then, as the subject changes, laugh a few minutes later. His complete openness to the sorrows of the world lets him also be touched by delight, goodness, and joy when these arise.

As you explore this step, it's important to keep in mind that you don't need to go out and look for suffering in order to practice what you're learning here. On one of my first silent meditation retreats, many people around me appeared to be going through profound emotional release. Tears and tissues were everywhere. I, however, was basically following my breath and having almost no difficult feelings. I wondered if I was somehow missing out on something. I went to see my teacher, Joseph Goldstein: "It seems like everyone else is going through stuff and having some kind of deep transformation. Should I be doing something different?"

"Don't go looking for trouble," Joseph smiled. "It will find you soon enough."

He was right. In subsequent retreats I would go through many a box of tissues myself and would realize that both ends of the spectrum have their gifts.

If you happen to be in a phase of your life that is easy and relatively unchallenged, you can just continue to incline your mind toward well-being and remain present for uplifting states as they come. When the difficult times inevitably come along, the tools in this chapter will prepare you to face your circumstances without being overwhelmed by fear or trapped in resistance. The willingness to be with any situation, no matter how challenging, trains the heart to stay open—an essential ingredient for a joyful life.

BABY STEPS

When things are going well in your life, doing the Awakening Joy practices may be fun and easy. But it's when you're facing challenges that you need them most. I'm not suggesting that you pretend you're not hurting. But finding moments of well-being during a hard time will begin to make a big difference.

Paula had a high-paying professional job, was living in her own home, which she loved, and had achieved "all the things I thought I wanted to do that were going to change the world." A year later she was unemployed and living in a low-income complex where many of the residents were sick and elderly. Enrolled online in the Awakening Joy course, she wrote to say that while she was actually discovering some "great moments of joy," the daily challenges could still drag her down:

> Many of your stories have such happy resolutions, so I wanted to give you an honest reflection from the middle of the process, not just the euphoric result of a singular success, important as that may be. Being in the trenches daily is quite a roller coaster ride. For a few days there is the grace of happiness, and then suddenly someone says something that activates the voice of doubt in my head, and I'm back in a bad place again.

Instead of giving up in despair, Paula was learning how to keep going. "It's all about putting in the baby steps," she says. "That's really the key—repeating your intention, sitting through the hard stuff consciously when it happens, staying inside the good stuff for longer periods and really appreciating it, practicing lovingkindness for yourself, not becoming discouraged or impatient, and then getting up tomorrow and starting all over again."

Despite the challenging circumstances Paula was living through, she says she actually feels as if her "heart is fuller than it's been in some time, and I feel more mature and wiser." Putting in those baby steps, day after day, eventually pays off by awakening in us a deep trust in life and the ability to flow with it.

LETTING IT ALL IN

When our dog Pal died last year, I was filled with sadness. He was a big, gentle labradoodle, and we loved him very much. Everyone who met him fell in love with his endearing sweetness. Pal had been my teacher of

Keeping Perspective

When you're going through a hard time, the suffering might feel relentless. But often there are moments when the sun peeks through the clouds. Keep in mind that everything is impermanent, including negative mind states, and notice any moments of well-being that arise—a smile when you see children playing, pleasure at tasting a favorite food, the warmth of sharing a hug with a friend, or the satisfaction in reading a good book. Don't miss these moments. You might also try gratitude practice to remind yourself of any blessings in your life. Whenever positive feelings arise in your body and mind, pause to notice and take them in.

patience and unconditional love for twelve years. Though I'd been saying good-bye in my mind for the previous few months as he'd grown weaker and weaker, it still hurt. I missed him terribly. I missed burying my head in his belly and smothering him with kisses.

For a while after he passed, I had little energy for anything other than taking care of basic needs. I gave myself space to grieve and the time to absorb and digest everything I was feeling. Even when I wanted to distract myself from my feelings, I knew there were more tears that needed to come out. I found myself listening to a certain melancholy piece of music over and over. The cello tugged at my heart while the guitar gently encouraged me to remember the beauty of my sweet dog. Even though Pal was gone, I would speak aloud to him in the same voice I'd used all those years, and the special love we shared would arise, along with the tears. I knew that denying all those feelings would not do justice to Pal and the rich bond we had shared.

One of the most painful sources of suffering is losing someone or something dear to us, a situation that is inevitable. We won't find happiness by trying to get around this unavoidable fact. There is a traditional

Buddhist practice that, ironically, is intended to make us happy by directly focusing on the inevitability of change and loss. The Buddha advised his followers to contemplate these truths every day:

1. This body will grow old; I am not beyond aging.
2. This body will become sick; I am not beyond sickness.
3. This body will die; I am not beyond death.
4. Everything near and dear to me will become separated from me.

While regular reflection on these might look pretty depressing, one of its benefits is to get us used to the truth of how things really are. Instead of running away from life, you're setting yourself up to be here for the whole show, in all of its sorrow and glory.

I decided one year to share this practice with the weekly meditation group I lead in Berkeley. Each week we were to keep one of these reflections in our consciousness as much as possible and investigate the impact of that on our daily lives. At first, staying aware of such a bald statement of truth felt quite heavy to me. There was no running away, no distraction. I saw the ephemeral nature of everything that I valued. All my relationships would end. Jane would be gone. I would be separated from my family and network of friends. My good health and abilities were just a set of temporary circumstances. I saw myself in a nursing home with people who might not even know me. And perhaps I wouldn't know or even recognize them!

Continuing with the practice, however, was like putting on a new shoe that takes a while to break in. After the initial discomfort, these truths became familiar, and with them came not only the acceptance that "this is the way it is" but an awareness of the preciousness of each person and each thing in my life. I felt strangely liberated as I relaxed into the facts and let go of hoping that I could avoid the inevitable. As the Roman philosopher Seneca said, "You cease to be afraid when you cease to hope, because hope is accompanied by fear." Understanding that death and the ravages of time are unstoppable lessened my fear of their approach.

Because my mind was not filled with resistance when Pal was dying, there was room to focus on appreciating all his wonderful qualities. I remember lying down next to his body, mainlining unconditional love. Love, sadness, acceptance, and appreciation were all in my heart and I could allow them to be there. No sorting, figuring out, wishing for a miracle. Just allowing all the feelings to be felt, to play themselves out, and move through me. In a peculiar way it felt good. My openness helped me connect to life instead of railing against it.

JOY IN THE MIDST OF GRIEVING

The more willing we are to be present for the hard parts of life, the freer we are to be open to all of it. When Alice's grandparents died, she said, "We barely spoke about it. We didn't even have a ceremony." So a few years later when her father died suddenly and unexpectedly at the age of sixty-six, she decided to respond to the pain in a new way. "Every day I set the intention to experience my grief and let it flow—rather, rip—through me without fear." Something she heard Sylvia Boorstein say in her talk in the Awakening Joy course stuck with her: "The essential wisdom is to know what is happening when it is happening and not to be in contest with it."

That's what Alice knew she wanted to be able to do. But when the time came to pick up the ashes of her beloved father from the crematorium, Alice found herself in tears of anguish and regret.

> I realized I was trying to push away what was happening. I was literally saying, "No!!" As I gently allowed the truth to sink in again, I could see that the "no" was an attempt to protect my heart, to control the experience. How could I protect my heart? It was already broken. How could I control anything? We die. I don't want to sugarcoat it. This hurts. The pain is powerful and often scary. But I am glad I'm here for it.

By being present with the truth of her pain, Alice was also able to flow with the full spectrum of feelings and experiences that were arising for her. She continues:

There have been many wonderful, joyful moments as well: connecting with my brothers and sister in a warm and open way, being washed over with powerful memories of my dad, feeling profound surges of love that erase all other difficulties, feeling connected to everyone else on earth who is grieving right now. Because I was able to talk about my feelings, everyone else in my family was free to do the same. In the end, we had the most beautiful, meaningful ceremony. I know the seed was planted by letting myself open to the pain.

When we fear that feeling our grief will be overwhelming, we may try to numb ourselves with alcohol or drugs, or lose ourselves in work or compulsive behavior. Or we get stuck, frozen in a state of sorrow or fear. As Alice found, remaining open and present with her feelings, without getting lost in them, allowed her to also be open to the joyful moments.

MEETING PHYSICAL PAIN WITH MINDFULNESS

We all experience physical pain; there's no way around it. However, when our bodies are going through their aches and pains, we might remember that useful distinction encapsulated in the popular quote attributed to M. Kathleen Casey: "Pain is inevitable, suffering is optional." This is not to minimize the plight of anyone in severe and relentless pain, but as a

Having Known Them . . .

Recall an experience of losing a loved one. Allow yourself to feel the sorrow with tender awareness. Feel the love you have for this person (or pet) and the way he or she enriched your life. Open to the gratitude you feel for having known him or her, and focus on sending that beloved being your thoughts of love and appreciation.

general guide it has value. We automatically contract from pain—it's a built-in response, warning us of something to avoid if we want to survive. But in the midst of pain we can't avoid, learning to respond with mindfulness can lessen our suffering. It is also a good training for remaining open and present with any kind of suffering in life.

Certainly you should reach out in various ways for relief and healing, but notice what happens when you try to just remain mindful of pain. (I say "try" because this is not always so easy, although practice helps.) Like all experience, pain arises and passes away. If you pause and pay attention to your stubbed toe, noticing the throbbing, the shooting pain, the heat, you may find that the sensations are not as solid as they first appear to be. There are moments of greater and lesser intensity. Eventually the pain in the toe subsides. Except in extreme situations, continuous pain is usually not our experience moment after moment.

When my ninety-five-year-old father was ill and dying, my grief was overwhelming. I felt exhausted, found it difficult to be with people and to keep my commitments. With mindfulness practice I came to see that the grief 'had me.' It had taken over my entire life. I saw that I could allow the grief and be fully with it whenever it came up, but that there were the other moments of the day when it wasn't there. This allowed me to 'have' the grief as well as be present in the moment with whatever else was there. I have since felt lighter, had more energy, and am once again engaged in my life.

—A COURSE PARTICIPANT

The suffering, in contrast to the pain, comes in when your mind gets involved. As Stephen Levine, a spiritual teacher who has worked extensively with the process of death and dying, puts it, "The resistance to pain may be more painful than the pain itself." We can intensify our suffering by our reaction. If you stub your toe, the pain might be excruciating. Or a migraine headache might feel like an overwhelming wall of pain. Of course you want the pain to end, but getting caught up in stories of what terrible things might lie ahead only adds another layer to your suffering. *What I'm going through now is bad, but what if it gets worse? Maybe I broke something? What if this pain never stops?* Or we get caught in an emotional cul-de-sac: *Every time things are going well, something like this happens.* Long after the physical pain is gone, we can still be stuck in mental and emotional pain.

In a similar vein, the Dalai Lama offers a prescription: "To diminish the

I suffer from terrible chronic pain. Every joint in my body is an issue and my spine is breaking down. I've recently lost my job after thirty-four years, pretty much as a result of my illness. Yet I have so much to be joyful about. I have a wonderful and caring family and a beautiful home. I can read and type a little, but the most important thing for me is that I can be happy. I am not worried about tomorrow. It is amazing what a difference that makes. I am never going to be the hiking/camping grandma I always thought I would be, but I am still the grandma.

—A COURSE PARTICIPANT

suffering of pain," says the Dalai Lama, "we need to make a crucial distinction between the pain of the pain and the pain we create by our thoughts about the pain. Fear, anger, guilt, loneliness, and hopelessness are all mental and emotional responses that can intensify pain." Especially with chronic pain, it's important to distinguish between the physical malady and the sense of helplessness that understandably can accompany it.

When physical pain is severe and constant, as for those suffering from cancer or other terminal diseases, to let down resistance and remain present with the sensations is nearly impossible. Yet mindfulness might still help to remind you that who you are is more than just the physical pain. In *Being Zen,* writer and Zen teacher Ezra Bayda says:

> We often think that being healed means the illness and pain will go away. But healing does not necessarily mean that the physical body will mend. . . . Healing is not just about physical symptoms. Many people heal and still remain physically sick or even die. Many who become physically well never really heal. Healing involves clearing the pathway to the open heart—the heart that knows only connectedness. . . . To heal, to become whole, means we no longer identify with ourselves as just this body, as just our suffering. We identify with a vaster sense of being.

THE SECOND DART

Much of the suffering addressed in this chapter is the mental and emotional suffering that pulls us down and can be at least as painful as physical suffering, often more. When we are depressed, lonely, sad, angry, we often add to those states by talking to our selves in ways that intensify the state: *What's wrong with me? I shouldn't be feeling this way.* Or we dig ourselves deeper into the emotion by feeding it with a story: *She did such and such to me. Of course I'm angry, and furthermore . . .* Or we try to deny the feeling: *Buck up. It's not that bad.* And the pain goes underground, only to express itself in other, sometimes even more painful ways.

To show how we multiply our suffering, the Buddha used a vivid analogy. If a person is struck with a dart, he feels intense pain. If he were to be struck immediately after with a second dart, the pain would be so much worse. That's what we're doing when we add negative thoughts to an already painful state. So how do you keep from launching that second dart?

As with physical pain, we take the experience one mindful moment at a time. Instead of compounding your suffering, with mindfulness you can learn to meet it with balance, clarity, and kindness. Chogyam Trungpa, the brilliant and iconoclastic Tibetan Buddhist master, used to say that every situation, no matter how challenging, is "workable." If you meet your difficult thoughts and feelings with nonjudgmental awareness—not getting lost in them, remembering that everything changes—you will find that you don't feel so overwhelmed. And in the process you also begin to deepen your understanding and open your heart.

I have been having a somewhat minor yet painful illness, and I'm finding I am able to feel my underlying joy and aliveness in addition to the pain. It doesn't mean that I don't feel the pain, but it helps me to know that the pain is not all consuming. I am not the pain. It is a part of me, just as joy and love are.

—A COURSE PARTICIPANT

CAUGHT IN THE SPIN CYCLE

Fiona came to her first mindfulness meditation retreat knowing very little about what to expect. A young woman in her twenties with a high-powered job in New York City, she thought that meditating on a silent retreat would be the perfect counterpoint, a way to find relaxation, peace, and stillness within. She didn't realize that the road to inner peace usually entails facing all the demons and fears that obscure it. In the silence and simplicity of a retreat, there would be little to distract her from the habitual patterns of her mind. Instead of tranquility, Fiona was soon confronting an old companion—the anxiety that was just below the surface.

She came into her first interview with me in a very agitated state. "I want to be calm and peaceful," she told me in a frustrated voice, "but I can't stop my mind."

"Where does your mind go?" I asked.

"Everywhere!" she cried, exasperated. "What I need to do with my work situation when I leave. How to have a better relationship with my boyfriend. Why I get so nervous around people. You name it. I try to quiet it down, but it just won't quit." As she talked her voice became increasingly shrill. Her body fidgeted with restlessness.

The thoughts spinning around and around in our minds can be very convincing. We build elaborate scenarios of failure and chaos and believe them to be true. This may be very creative, but it's not conducive to happiness! Worry is a very real kind of mental suffering. I know because I come from a lineage of worriers myself. My mother used to joke that when she couldn't think of anything to worry about, she'd *really* get worried. "It was my way of making sure I was taking care of things," she says.

The Problem with Worry

"New solutions and fresh ways of seeing a problem do not typically come from worrying, especially chronic worry. Instead of coming up with solutions to these potential problems, worriers typically simply ruminate on the danger itself, immersing themselves in a low-key way in the dread associated with it while staying in the same rut of thought."

—DANIEL GOLEMAN, FROM *Emotional Intelligence*

This approach reminds me of another story about the wise fool Mulla Nasruddin. Mulla's students find him one afternoon meticulously spreading bread crumbs around the perimeter of his house. After watching him for a while, one student finally asks him, "Mulla, why are you placing those crumbs like that?"

Mulla responds, "To keep away the tigers."

The confused student answers, "Tigers? There aren't any tigers for hundreds of miles!"

"Effective, isn't it?" Nasruddin replies.

Our minds can get stuck in worrying about phantom problems that we convince ourselves are real. As Mark Twain put it, "I have been through some terrible things in my life, some of which actually happened." Reasonable planning for the future can give us direction, but obsessing about what might go wrong puts us in a perpetual state of stress and rarely brings about positive results. Mindfulness interrupts the tape loop by bringing us back to the moment so we can respond to what is actually happening right now.

STOPPING THE SPIN

During her interview, as Fiona talked about what it was like to be caught up in the turmoil of her thoughts, I could see how painful it was for her. She said the chaos in her mind was like being "stuck in a labyrinth with no way out." I asked if she was willing to stop talking for a few moments and just be present.

"Can you feel your feet on the floor right now?" She nodded yes. "Can you feel your body making contact with the chair?" Again she nodded. "How about your breath? Can you feel it as your belly rises and falls?" Yes, she could. "Don't do anything for the next few moments other than knowing you're sitting and breathing." As we sat there quietly, she started to relax.

"Everything you need for the peace you're looking for is right here in this moment, Fiona. Whenever you notice that you're going around in circles, here is your instruction: Simply stop trying. Let yourself relax and ask, 'What can I be aware of that is actually happening right now?'"

Toward the end of the retreat I could see that Fiona had a smile on her face as she walked gracefully around the meditation center. Before she left for home, she wrote me a note:

> The one thing that is indelibly fixed in my brain is finally getting, "You don't have to figure it out." That would never have registered as an option before. Just today when I was doing walking meditation, struggling as my thoughts were going 'round and 'round, those words came into my mind. I stopped and closed my eyes and asked myself, "What is true right now in this moment?" And what was true was the rising and falling of my breath, and various body sensations coming and going. "The rest of life will balance itself out in its own time," I thought to myself. And I resumed my walking. What a revelation!

When you're caught in the spin cycle, one of the most effective ways to return to the moment is being mindful of your breath and your body. The body is always in the present, and pausing to pay attention to it opens up the space to notice what is going on in the mind. You can step back and ask yourself what is really true in this moment. It's like pressing "clear" on a calculator; no matter how complex the numbers have gotten, once you press that "C" button you have a fresh start. In the same way, coming back to feeling your body and breath helps you stop spinning your wheels. Instead of figuring things out, you can begin to trust that once you are in the present moment, your mind can settle you down enough to wisely deal with whatever is actually before you.

RELEASED FROM FEAR

Sometimes the most overpowering illusion the mind can create is fear. This is not the kind of fear that keeps you alive when a tiger is coming your way. In that case, fear is a signal to get the heck out. I mean the kind of overwhelming fear in the mind that threatens to eat us whole. You probably could find valid psychological explanations for why particular fears arise, but rather than trying to figure out the cause, the Buddha suggests directly addressing the fear with mindfulness in order to free yourself of its power. In his parable of the poisoned arrow, he uses a metaphor to illustrate his point. If you are shot with an arrow, do you start asking, "Who shot this arrow? Who made it? What kind of poison did he use?" No, instead you ask that it be pulled out as soon as possible. In the same way, when you find yourself trapped in mental fear, instead of trying to figure out why it's there, or spinning around in it, a wise and effective way of freeing yourself of confusion is to bring your mind back to the present. Recognize that you are caught in *thoughts* that are giving rise to fear.

I received some bad financial news, and found myself reacting with a familiar pattern of high anxiety. I went right into my bag lady fantasy and 'I'll-lose-everything-and-have-no-possibilities-in-life' pattern. But this time I was able to observe from a meta-level. I told myself that nothing bad was happening now, and that I didn't want to waste my life worrying. Amazingly I was able to shift into present time, which was actually quite lovely, and enjoy my daughter and the sunny day.

—A COURSE PARTICIPANT

During one of her first meditation retreats, Shoshana understood what Joseph Goldstein was saying about facing fear with mindfulness, but the terror she felt inside seemed very real—as did its cause. "I know it sounds utterly irrational," she says, "but I had a tremendous fear of—of all things—vampires." Late at night alone in the room set aside for walking meditation, she would hear autumn leaves crackling outside the window and fear the footsteps of something monstrous. The fear was so strong that night after night, she fled from the room. After days of this, Shoshana decided to do something about it. If Joseph was right, facing the fear with mindfulness would free her from what she knew was an illusion—at least she hoped so.

One night, about two o'clock in the morning, she bundled up against the cold and stepped outside the meditation center, into the Massachusetts winter. She recalls:

> Either there were vampires and I would meet my fate, or I would at last free myself from this fear by facing it directly. There was a lake across the street, and I set out to walk the three-mile loop around it in the full moonlight. I was certain

that a vampire lurked behind every tree. In the stillness, I listened for footsteps behind me. My heart felt like it would leap out of my chest, and the fear felt like electricity shooting through my body. But I managed to keep returning to awareness of my breath—which was really shaky—and to remain mindful of all those sensations. And I kept mindfully naming my experience, saying to myself, "This is fear. This is fear."

By the time she finished her long walk around the lake, Shoshana not only was freed of her fear of vampires, but she also had discovered the amazing power of mindfulness to cut through distress in the mind. And even now fear itself no longer seems as fearful. She says, "I don't think I've ever gotten so caught up in fear like that since, and when it comes up for any reason, I more readily remember 'This is fear,' and it doesn't carry me away."

A bumper sticker I see around a lot warns: "Don't believe everything you think." Whenever you find yourself lost in a swirl of thoughts, mindfulness of your breath and body can break the spell in the moment and even free you of mental patterns that don't contribute to your well-being.

WHEN EMOTIONS ARE OVERWHELMING

Many legends have been passed down about the powers of Milarepa, the great eleventh-century Tibetan yogi, who spent years meditating in a cave to purify his mind. In one of these stories, Milarepa returns from an evening walk to find his cave filled with a dozen demons. Cherishing his solitude, he tries to get rid of them. First he offers them spiritual teachings, hoping they will be appeased and leave. No luck. Then he scolds them, hoping his anger will frighten them away. They just laugh. He decides to make peace with them, saying, "It's clear that you're not leaving, so we might as well learn to coexist and live together." Well, that's no fun for a demon, so all of them leave, except a particularly nasty and terrifying one. In an act of complete surrender, Milarepa places his head in the demon's mouth, saying, "You are much more powerful than I. I will not resist you. Go ahead and devour me if that's what you want." In that instant the demon vanishes.

Overwhelming emotions, such as anger, grief, or sorrow, can feel like terrifying demons, and our automatic response might be to run away or

"Staring Back" at Thoughts

In March 2000, the Dalai Lama met with a small group of prominent neuroscientists, psychologists, philosophers, and Buddhist scholars to discuss the origins of negative emotions and the beneficial effects of spiritual practices. In his book *Destructive Emotions*, Daniel Goleman narrates the proceedings of this gathering, highlighting significant moments of dialogue. This excerpt is from Matthieu Ricard, who earned a doctorate in genetics in France and later became a Buddhist monk.

"At the beginning when a thought of anger, desire, or jealousy arises, we are not prepared for it. So within seconds, that thought has given rise to a second and a third thought, and soon our mental landscape becomes invaded by thoughts that solidify our anger or jealousy—and then it's too late. Just as when a spark of fire has set a whole forest on fire, we are in trouble.

"The basic way to intervene has been called 'staring back' at a thought. When a thought arises, we need to watch it and look back at its source. We need to investigate the nature of that thought that seems so solid. As we stare at it, its apparent solidity will melt away, and that thought will vanish without giving birth to a chain of thoughts. The point is not to try to block the arising of thoughts—this is not possible anyway—but not to let them invade our mind. We need to do this again and again because we are not used to dealing with thoughts in that way. . . . Finally a time will come when thoughts come and go like a bird passing through the sky, without leaving a trace."

resist them. But there's a problem with that. Trying to avoid or deny an emotion locks it in, repressing it but not releasing it. Not resisting the pain of negative states of mind is an act of bravery that allows them to dissolve. Like Milarepa, when we give up the struggle, when we stop trying to avoid our pain or get rid of it and instead allow ourselves to just be mindfully present with it, we begin to liberate ourselves from its hold on us. We begin to clear our cave of its demons.

Mindfulness is a tool you can use at any time to help keep you from getting lost in confusion. It can wake you up from the "bad movie" in your mind. And with practice, you can train yourself to be mindful even in the face of overwhelming emotions.

Fran has been a meditation student for many years, so she was well prepared to remain mindful when, on a long retreat, some of her deepest negative emotions arose. "A familiar heaviness of heart appeared almost as soon as the retreat started," she told me. Over the next few weeks she explored what she called "that energy in my life that's the hardest thing I've known—call it grief, contraction, depression."

In the silence and focus of a retreat, the deep mental patterns that arise can pervade the body and mind and feel overwhelming. I encouraged Fran to take the process of releasing intense feelings in small doses. "Start by allowing the feeling to just be there, and stay with it mindfully for a minute or two. Then you can take a break and regroup until you're ready to feel it again." By managing to remain present, even in small doses, with a very difficult state of mind, Fran was able to come to a new understanding:

> This feeling is very powerful and sticky for me when it arises. So I knew I needed to bring it into the light of awareness, to stay present with it—with the piercing pain in the heart—to bring compassion to it, to know the unstained awareness that can feel it and not be it, to call on a kind of warrior courage in allowing it, and to see how I habitually react to it. I don't know exactly what it will mean in my life to have done this work, but I know I had to do it.

Having the opportunity on a retreat to work so intensely released some of her negative mental patterns at a very deep level. But the basic process Fran was doing can be used to ease the mind, especially when emotions are overwhelming. Essentially she was recognizing what she was feeling without pushing it away, paying close attention to how the emotions registered in her body and mind, and realizing that the emotions were a passing phenomenon, part of being human. A convenient way to remember this process of working with difficult emotions is the acronym RAIN, a term first coined by meditation teacher Michele McDonald.

RAIN: A MINDFUL APPROACH TO WORKING WITH DIFFICULT EMOTIONS

R is for Recognize

In mythology a monster or demon has great power until its name is known. When the hero or heroine courageously names the demon to its face, the sinister force is broken, mastered now by the namer. Naming your emotions is the first step in weakening their power over you. For instance, in the midst of a heated discussion, you might recognize, "This is anger." Without condemning, resisting, or denying the feeling, this can keep you from getting lost in it. Or you might feel a kind of heaviness pulling you down and recognize, "Oh, this is sadness," and then do something to be gentle and nourishing to yourself. Even if you have no idea what you're feeling, you might simply realize, "I'm confused." At least this keeps you from doing a nosedive into chaos.

Ann, a participant in the Awakening Joy course, reported how honestly naming her feelings while in the midst of them helped her through a harrowing experience. One day her husband began complaining of chest pains. Not taking any chances, she drove him to the local hospital where he failed the stress test. Within minutes Ann found herself sitting in the waiting room while her husband was down the hall possibly having a heart attack. Remembering the instructions from the course helped Ann to remain present instead of spinning out in fear. She says:

As I sat there waiting, I was able to simply notice my emotions and think, "Okay, this is what anxiety feels like." Doing that kept me from getting carried away by the whole situation. I was somehow able to just be present, trading "what if's" for being okay without knowing why or what the future would bring. I just kept telling myself that this was a moment of life for me to meet.

Someone I know uses a rather creative naming strategy when she's gotten stuck and feels agitated and overwhelmed. She gets a cup of tea, goes out on her porch, and lets herself be what she calls "Pissed-off Buddha" for a while. After a half hour or so the energy shifts and, the storm past, she returns to being just Sophia sitting on her porch drinking a cup of tea. Then she can address with more balance and clarity the situation that triggered her strong emotion.

Labeling to Calm the Mind

Researchers in the Brain Mapping Center at the UCLA School of Medicine made a significant discovery about the value of using words to label fearful circumstances. When subjects in an experiment were shown faces with expressions of anger or fear, the fear centers in their brains showed increased blood flow, indicating that their own fight-flight responses were being stimulated. However, when the subjects were asked to choose a word to describe the facial expressions of anger or fear, the blood flow to the fear centers diminished. Additionally, parts of the prefrontal cortex—a brain area that regulates emotions—showed increased blood flow. The researchers conclude that the activity of labeling, which takes place in the higher regions of the brain, can regulate emotional responses, helping you to feel calmer.

A is for Allow and Accept

Allowing and accepting what you're feeling means letting go of any agenda for the experience to change. As soon as you start hoping for a desired outcome—*Maybe if I'm mindful, the feeling will go away again, like it did last time*—you're resisting what you're feeling and creating aversion in your mind, even if it's subtle. As we've seen earlier, resistance locks a feeling in rather than allowing it to undergo the natural process of change.

But just remaining present for a painful emotion can be very hard. We're so used to resisting unpleasant feelings. We want to distract ourselves or figure out a quick solution. *I think I'll go out for a drink, or maybe a movie . . . and maybe I'll meet someone interesting.* Not that you shouldn't give yourself a nourishing break if you're having a hard time, but if you want the long-term reward of being freed from the pain of habitual negative feelings, distraction won't do it as readily as saying, "No matter what, I'm going to stay here with this feeling." You may feel certain painful sensations in your body. You may go through states of mind that are really uncomfortable. Allowing your feelings means you remain aware of them, without pushing them away if they're unpleasant, not holding on to them if they're pleasant, not getting lost in them. For a few moments at least, you give the experience permission to be just as it is.

I is for Investigate with Interest

Once you Recognize an emotion and Allow it to be just as it is, you can then Investigate how it is expressing itself in your body and mind. Without trying to figure out or explain anything, notice what sensations accompany that emotion. What does sadness feel like? Heavy? Thick? Where do you feel it? In your chest? Your throat? How big an area is it? The size of a golf ball or softball or beach ball? Does it have a sharp outline or fade out at the edges? Notice if the sensations stay the same or change subtly or dramatically, from moment to moment. They might diminish. They might get more intense. Your job is to Allow and Investigate with a kind, nonjudgmental awareness, moment by moment.

You might also shift your awareness for some time to include the mental atmosphere associated with the emotion. Is the mood dark, swirling, heavy, tight, light, expansive? In the same way, let the experience be just as it is, and touch it with a kind, interested awareness. Then, after some time, come back to your body. Are the sensations the same as before? Have they changed?

While the idea of allowing and exploring an intense emotion, like fear or rage, might sound overwhelming, you will find that your awareness itself can hold whatever emotion is arising in the moment. When you are afraid, for instance, the part of your mind that is *aware* of the fear is not afraid. It is simply aware of the thoughts and sensations that make up the experience of fear. The same is true if you're experiencing anger. The *awareness* of anger is different from the anger itself. You can rest in the awareness of those emotions, rather than getting lost in them. In this way, awareness becomes a refuge that lets you safely investigate your actual human experience.

N is for Non-identification

When you identify with an emotion—*I am such an angry [sad, lonely] person*—you put yourself into a box. In actuality, a continual flow of thoughts and emotions passes through the mind. You can't point to any one of them and say, "That's me." Anger may come but you're not always angry. You may become frightened more than you'd like, but can you say you're a fearful person when you're laughing with a friend? Our emotions are all arising in the field of mindful awareness, doing their dance for a while, then changing into something else. Instead of thinking, *I'm such an angry person,* you can understand, *There is anger in this mind right now.* It does not define who you are.

Not identifying with an emotion is another way of saying, "Not taking it personally." From the perspective of Buddhist teachings, having a particular static identity is just not true. No emotion is you, nor is any emotion unique to you. Emotions are human experiences arising in response to certain conditions. Your anger or sadness isn't so different from my anger or sadness. Understanding the commonality of our experience leads to a profound shift in how we relate to our mental activity.

Instead of thinking of our thoughts and feelings as *my* mind, we can begin to see them as *the* mind, a shared human experience.

Using the RAIN process when you are experiencing difficult emotions can have extraordinary results. When you don't push your feelings away nor get lost in them, after a while you see that, like everything else, they change. They have a beginning and an end. This can make a huge difference in your life. You're not as apt to believe you'll be stuck forever and start pushing the panic button. And you can trust that you have the capacity to work skillfully with strong emotions.

I'm finding that when I'm open, compassionate, and curious about my suffering, it is greatly lessened. It's not a solid block of 'things always being wrong' but something that passes through. This has been opening up a lot of freedom and ease.

—A COURSE PARTICIPANT

RAIN

When you are in the midst of a strong emotion, take a few moments to try this approach:

Recognize what you are feeling and name it. Anger, fear, sadness, confusion?

Allow the feelings to be present, without pushing them away and without getting lost in them.

Investigate the feelings in your body and mind. Explore the landscape of the emotion with curiosity and interest. Where in your body do you feel it? How does it feel in your mind—heavy, tight, open, agitated?

Non-identification is the key to freeing yourself from the emotion's grip. Don't take it personally. What you are feeling is a human emotion that arises and passes away. It does not define who you are.

After thirty years of marriage, Robert found himself going through a painful divorce. Relating to his intense pain with mindfulness allowed him to get through some of the toughest times. He shared this reflection:

> Grief comes in waves. Sometimes I think I'm going to drown and can only chant "Help me, help me, help me." Using RAIN, I ride the waves. Each leads me to a variety of body and memory information. Paying respectful attention and not identifying, I ride the waves and they pass. My inner ship rights itself and sails on. I continue to feel awake and alert and radiant in the midst of this beautiful spring, and I have faith that I'm learning what I need to learn to go on in life. It's not fun, but on balance it feels like a rich adventure.

RAIN will help you move through emotions with more balance. What's more, the deep-seated tangles of stories and feelings will begin to diminish when you don't feed them.

USING SKILLFUL MEANS

Sometimes emotions are just too powerful to work with using the RAIN method alone. We saw earlier that even someone like Fran, who had been meditating for years, had to be gentle with herself and take breaks from being mindful of intense feelings. Wisely opening to difficult feelings includes knowing when you've reached the point where you're no longer balanced in the process. If you're struggling or feeling overwhelmed, you need to back off. Otherwise, you will end up closing down or getting lost in your thoughts.

In situations like this it's wise to find ways to work with your emotions using what in Buddhism are known as "skillful means." These are basically any methods that work to diminish your confusion and develop your understanding of how to relate to challenging circumstances. My philosophy is "Get all the help you can get." Listen to your intuition. Whatever supports you in your ability to stay present with the hard stuff in a constructive way is a skillful means. Reaching out to wise friends,

A Word on Depression

"It is important to recognize there are many helpful approaches to finding well-being, and you must find the ones that are best for you. This is particularly true for those suffering from clinical depression. While many of us can make choices that pull us out of negative emotions, the emotional exhaustion that seems to enervate physiologically depressed people makes that virtually impossible for them to do. However, Greg and I have seen a substantial group of people who report that they've chosen to pull themselves out of deep depressions. Their paths are torturous, but most of them talk about making mini-choices that start to build on themselves, like telling the truth, or appreciating some part of their lives, or giving to others. But we recognize that there can also be a value in using medications. In some cases, that seems to open up a door of opportunity for depressed people to walk through. They then can begin to make more happy and healthy choices."

—RICK FOSTER, COAUTHOR WITH GREG HICKS OF
How We Choose to Be Happy
[FROM PERSONAL LETTER TO AWAKENING JOY PARTICIPANT]

working with a good therapist, or taking medication if there's a chemical imbalance are all skillful means. One of the most important foundations for a healthy mind state is a healthy body. Besides working out or walking, holistic models of exercise, such a yoga or tai chi, can work wonders for the mind.

One of the primary values of mindfulness is that by directly feeling our difficult emotions, we begin to get to see and understand how they work. For instance, when we're in the midst of a strong emotion, it can seem like our suffering will go on forever. But just as physical pain is not a solid and unchanging experience, so too emotions, even very strong ones, have moments when the intensity shifts. Have you ever been sobbing in grief, and then suddenly everything inside you goes still, and you forget for a moment what you were crying about? Or have you been in the middle of being angry with someone, and suddenly you recall that you have something to take care of, and your entire focus shifts? Those pauses are like breaks in a storm.

My six-year old daughter, who has a very serious heart condition, was scheduled to see her cardiologist. The day before the appointment, I burned dinner and set off all the smoke alarms in the house, left the door of my car open which ran down the battery, and the battery in my cell phone died. The morning of the appointment, I burned breakfast, the car wouldn't start, and I completely flipped out. After seeing the cardiologist, however, as we were driving back home, a little voice in my head reminded me that everything changes, and even though at that moment things seemed really dire, this was not going to be the way it would always be.

—A COURSE PARTICIPANT

Sylvia Boorstein says this is like a slight shaft of sunlight peeking through the clouds in the midst of pelting rain. That sliver of light can give us the perspective to know all is not gloom and doom. In that moment we are reminded that everything—including very convincing feelings—will change. Even seemingly overwhelming emotions are not as solid or entrenched as we may believe. Your sorrow and suffering are not permanent, and no matter how bad things may seem, you will smile again, laugh again, and feel joy again.

If you need to, you can prevent intense emotions from snowballing by temporarily shifting your focus to something that distracts you. One of the skillful means suggested by the Buddha for dealing with disturbing thoughts and feelings is "forgetfulness and inattention." It may be surprising that one of the major advocates of being awake and attentive is telling us, "Just forget it." But the Buddha's methods are eminently practical, and when certain feelings are overwhelming, this is what works.

As a parent, I know the value of that method. Adam was a sensitive child and could be easily startled. One Saturday afternoon when he was four, his grandma and I took him to the Pickle Family Circus, an enchanting clown and magician show. In the middle of the performance, with no warning, a huge balloon suddenly exploded as part of the act. While the rest of the audience howled with laughter, that explosion launched Adam into a different kind of hysterics. His wailing wouldn't stop as I carried him out.

When we got outside, I glanced over at the concession stand twenty feet away and happened to notice his favorite ice cream. "Oh look, Ad," I said to my howling son, "they have Ben and Jerry's." In an instant the screams stopped as he surveyed the field to locate the treasure. I calmly and gratefully carried him toward the ice-cream stand, slowly letting out each word: "Oh, we're in luck. They have Cherry Garcia!" (His favorite.) Adam forgot he was having a meltdown, and as soon as he had the cone in his hand, he was completely cooled off.

Sometimes when we're overwhelmed and thrown out of balance by an emotion, we're like little children. In fact, often what we're feeling is directly linked to our tender "child self," and we can use some skillful

Overcoming Overwhelm

When you feel overwhelmed by an intense emotion:

- Look around you for something in the moment to appreciate.
- Engage one of your senses to return you to the moment. What do you see, hear, smell, or feel? You might listen to a favorite piece of uplifting music or take a relaxing hot bath. Let yourself sink into that experience.
- Imagine the frightened, sad, or confused part of you as a young child. How old is that child? Imagine holding him or her in a tender embrace. What would you want the child to know?

By shifting your focus from the intense emotion, you can wake up from the dream your mind is creating and wisely address what needs to be attended to.

parenting means. Be gentle with yourself and consider using the Buddha's forgetfulness method. Take a walk in the park. Go get an ice-cream cone!

Whether you pause because you've taken a few mindful breaths, or you hear a baby cry in the next room, or you suddenly hear a song on the radio that changes your mood, use that opportunity as a way to consciously turn your attention away from a strong emotion. With this kind of "forgetfulness," you are remembering not to feed the negative feelings. Then they can begin to subside and you can consider more wholesome choices.

Another way to shift your focus and "change your mind" is to nurture yourself or do something to discharge the negative energy: exercise, do some yoga stretches, take a walk in nature, speak to a friend, or give yourself a time-out in your room to let the feelings move through you.

What's most important in using skillful means is that you don't get lost in your suffering but instead use it to deepen your understanding of life, to act wisely, and to develop compassion. This openness will also most readily lead you back to joy and well-being. It creates the space to hear your inner wisdom, feel your kind heart, and get in touch with your aliveness.

After a shocking diagnosis of cancer, I learned to sit with my fear, and when it felt too big, to use skillful means and do something else. I learned I could move from one thing to the next—from hearing test results, to doing my pre-op prep, to lying on the gurney waiting to go into the operating room. When it was just one thing at a time, it was not overwhelming. I felt embraced by love with the outpouring of prayers and calls and emails. I think I truly realized that I am not alone. I experienced compassion for others going through similar experiences in a way I couldn't quite understand before. So the gifts were endless, and it was not an 'all bad' experience. Life was filled with richness, presence and, weirdly, joy at times as I lived closer to the edge than ever before.

—A COURSE PARTICIPANT

CALLING OUT TO SOMETHING GREATER

Often when our suffering is great we experience the pain of isolation—perhaps the most painful feeling of all. We feel like no one can understand or help us, even friends. If your feelings are too strong for you to be mindful of, and temporarily distracting yourself from them doesn't work, what do you do? You can reach out to something greater

Reaching Out to Be Held

Let yourself find that deep feeling of sincerity and innocence inside your heart, as if you are a child praying. Now from that place, call on the benevolence of life, however you conceive it, to guide and support you. Imagine a field of benevolent energy surrounding you and enveloping you, inside and out. Take that feeling in deeply and notice where you experience it in your body. Notice the state of mind it creates. If that benevolent field had a color, what would it be? Let yourself sink into and be infused by that soothing color. Allow yourself to be held by this field of benevolence. Relax into it. Feel its protection.

Return to this experience from time to time, and get to know it. This refuge is always available when you need it.

than yourself, you can call upon the forces of benevolence to help you. Whether you think of this as God, the Dharma, spirit guides, or some higher power beyond yourself, you can call out to that benevolence for the compassion and loving support you need.

We sometimes have to reach the depths of sorrow or pain before we finally turn to something greater than ourselves. This is a positive step, if for no other reason than it orients the mind away from fear, bitterness, and confusion and toward a healthy vision of possibilities. And there is a kind of innocence in this, like a child in prayer, as we get beyond our stories and dramas and humbly open our hearts in vulnerability.

SUFFERING IS GRACE

I once went to a talk by Julia Butterfly Hill, an environmental and social activist who spent two years living on a small platform in a two-hundred-foot redwood tree to protest logging of old growth forests. Her story was inspiring, and the power of her commitment to truth touched me deeply. During her first year, the powerful weather cycle known as El Niño brought in one of the wettest and stormiest winters on record. At times the wind was so fierce that Julia could do nothing but cling to the edges of the platform. Fearing for her life, she would pray for the strength to get through the ordeal. No sooner had she survived one storm than another even worse would come up. *Why isn't God listening?* she wondered. Then one day she realized that in fact she *was* getting what she was praying for. Precisely by going through those trials, Julia was discovering an inner strength and resilience that could meet any storm or challenge.

Two weeks ago my boyfriend broke up with me; I was devastated as I am deeply in love with this man. I was not able to see this as any kind of gift, but then I decided to try to cultivate an open heart, toward myself and toward him. This has been challenging and immensely rewarding, as I have found a deep well of love and caring that I thought was all about him. I've discovered instead it was all about who I am and who I can show up to be in the world.

—A COURSE PARTICIPANT

Neem Karoli Baba, a Hindu guru who has been one of my most beloved teachers, used to say, "Suffering is grace." When we're in the thick of it, suffering hardly seems like grace. Yet in my classes when I ask how many people have come to a spiritual path through suffering, almost every hand goes up. I would say they have been graced. Suffering shakes us out of complacency and motivates us to look for a happiness not dependent on circumstances. If we look honestly, we can see that even very challenging times have bestowed on us invaluable gifts.

A great twentieth-century sage known as The Mother, who with Sri Aurobindo founded the international spiritual community of Auroville in southern India, talked about how our greatest difficulties can in fact reflect our greatest possibilities. She said: "You carry in yourself all the obstacles necessary to make your realization perfect. If you discover a very black hole, a thick shadow, you can be sure there is somewhere in you a great light. It is up to you to know how to use the one to realize the other." If you've come to this search for happiness because of great suffering, you can know that you have within you a great light. Don't feel discouraged at the enormity of the task. Rather, know that you are likely to be even more motivated to find the true gems hidden in the darkness.

By opening to our pain, rather than simply enduring it, we deepen our understanding and access those qualities in us that are most noble. Helen Keller, completely unable to see or hear, found the grace and insight to conclude: "Character cannot be developed in ease and quiet. Only through experience of trial and suffering can the soul be strengthened, ambition inspired, and success achieved. . . . All the world is full of suffering. It is also full of overcoming."

As you go through hardships, keep in mind that you are developing courage and strength you probably didn't realize you had. As Julia Butterfly Hill found, the strength to persevere in the face of relentless challenges doesn't develop overnight. Patience and perspective unfold over time as priceless gifts. One of the most profound aspects of suffering as grace is that we learn we have the capacity to meet whatever life brings us and respond with wisdom.

When my friend Don Flaxman found out that he had incurable cancer, all his years of spiritual practice bore fruit. He had learned how to face the hard stuff fearlessly and with balance. As he shared the news of his diagnosis with me, I was deeply moved not only by his acceptance of the situation but by how he had turned it into an opportunity to deepen his love of life. He told me:

> I'm now in the richest period of my life. Now that I have less time, I'm more open than I've ever been. I'm amazed at how much joy is available just by smelling a pretty flower, seeing a hummingbird, or hearing a friend's voice. I don't waste my time complaining. Expressing love and gratitude is the most important thing I can do now.

A GIFT BEYOND WORDS

Nancy went through indescribable sorrow when her fourteen-year-old daughter, Julia, took her own life. I met Nancy on the first anniversary of that tragic event when she still felt she could barely find a reason to go on living. She had decided to come to a meditation retreat, seeking a way to cope with her pain. She found that meditation practice gave her a refuge and helped her remain sane in the midst of the swirl of emotions she was feeling. Each February she returned for another retreat, taking the time to sit with all the grief, anger, and confusion that were her constant companions. And each year she and I have shared a ceremony honoring the memory of her daughter.

Little by little, over the course of four or five years, Nancy learned to accept her daughter's tragic death and eventually to find the willingness to live again herself. During one of her retreats, Nancy shared with me an important realization. She understood that it wouldn't do her or anyone else any good to let that tragedy block all the love that was inside her. She knew that her daughter would much rather have her mother find happiness than freeze-frame her life. Nancy decided that being present for other parents facing the same tragedy would be the best way to honor her daughter. After that retreat she started volunteering as a support group leader for parents whose children have died—the same group she'd attended during her years of deepest grief.

One day a beautiful card appeared in my mailbox, with a note from her:

> I have received a gift that is beyond words. I've witnessed my deepest despair, the darkest, most wounded quarters of my heart, and learned not to flinch or back away. I rested in love and even tasted joy, all the while still knowing the sorrow of my loss. A few days ago I held a bereaved mother in my arms as she sobbed—she had lost her son to suicide. I held her to my heart as she held on for dear life. And as I rocked her it was as if I was rocking Julia, rocking myself, rocking the broken hearts of all beings. In that rocking, in that holding, we were all held in one heart. I have been so blessed.

Nancy had come full circle in that moment of being able to comfort someone who had gone through what she had gone through. Now several years later I see a radiance shining through this woman who has touched the depths of suffering and found something that sustains her and inspires anyone who meets her. She still has moments of sadness and grief, and she still misses Julia, but a joy and appreciation of life have emerged—a joy she thought at one point was no longer possible.

Psychiatrist R. D. Laing says that those who have traveled to the depths of despair are often the greatest healers. As Fran, the woman who chose on a retreat to face the pain and depression that had haunted her for years, puts it:

> What I can see already is that this ability to stay present with pain, with great awareness and kindness, is the heart of being able to be present in the same way with the pain of others—and that's a gift, for certain.

Nancy and Fran discovered one of the greatest gifts of suffering: the tender heart of compassion. When we open to our own pain with tenderness, we dissolve the armor that cuts us off from ourselves and life. When we relate to our pain like the mother who holds the child instead of scolding him, we develop the ability to offer a kind and caring refuge to others when they are in need. In Step Nine we'll further explore how remaining open to the suffering of others, and responding with compassion, leads to a profound sense of peace and well-being.

STAYING OPEN TO THE WORLD

Although we don't have to search for suffering, hiding from it in order to be joyful doesn't work. For me an important part of awakening joy is staying aware of what is going on in the world, letting my heart remain open to the pain as well as the joy. For example, while reading the newspaper is not considered one of the most uplifting practices, I do it every day. It reminds me of our shared humanity, deepens my gratitude for the blessings in my life, and motivates me to express my caring in tangible ways.

When you don't close your eyes to sorrow and suffering, it's easy to feel weighed down. You may wonder, "How can I possibly be happy when there is so much pain in the world?" Poet Jack Gilbert encourages us to have "the stubbornness to accept our gladness in the ruthless furnace of this world." Although the Buddha's teaching starts out by focusing on suffering, the goal is happiness. Likewise, the crucified Christ is an image of intense suffering, but the true goal of a Christian's life is to live in the joy of the Resurrection. Despite our awareness of suffering, we can remember that happiness is also a gift of life.

By following the practices offered in this book, you've already taken several steps toward living a more joyful life. You've discovered that true happiness lies in wholesome ways of being. You've learned the power of setting your intention and developed the tool of mindfulness to support wise choices. You've also explored how a grateful heart lets you see that life is full of blessings, along with the sorrows. And you've seen that fearlessly being with your sorrows keeps your heart open to all of life.

Step 5

THE BLISS OF BLAMELESSNESS

Speak or act with an impure mind
And trouble will follow you
As the wheel follows the ox that draws the cart.

. . .

Speak or act with a pure mind
And happiness will follow you
As your shadow, unshakable.

—THE BUDDHA, *The Dhammapada*

I REMEMBER THE MOMENT AS if it were yesterday, rather than a few decades ago. I picked the infant up and held him in front of me. Although I had doubted that he was actually mine, when our eyes met something in me knew it was true. It was like holding myself. As we looked at each other, his eyes innocent and filled with wonder, I could feel myself falling in love. My life with its new possibilities flashed before me. Since the age of fourteen, I had so many times imagined playing catch with my son.

Suddenly my reverie stopped short. I was twenty-two years old, it was the late 1960s, and I was just getting the hang of being on my own. This wasn't the life I had envisioned. Terror struck. Thoughts flashed through my mind like a lightning storm as I tried to understand what had happened and how this scene came to be.

About a year before, my neighbor's sister, Bonnie, had started dropping by from time to time when she was in the neighborhood. Gradually our visits of friendly talk had slipped into singing together, making out, and eventually finding our way to my bed. "Free love" was the philosophy in those casual and permissive days, and "If it feels good, do it" was my credo. I didn't stop to think about the consequences, beyond making sure that we were using birth control. When she stopped coming around at some point, I just figured that was that and got on with my life. And now here I was, holding a baby.

A few days before this, I'd received a Christmas card with a photo of an infant boy and a simple note on the back: "Hi. My name is Anthony. I'm your son. If you want to see me, call . . . " Stunned and paralyzed with disbelief, I'd gone into a tailspin. For the next three days it had all seemed like a bad dream, a nightmare that I'd hoped would somehow just disappear.

But then the doorbell rang, and there was three-month-old Anthony in his mother's arms. I remember Bonnie saying, "Here, meet your son," and passing him to me. Dazed and flooded with a swirl of emotions, I'd told her I needed some time to be alone with him and carried him into my bedroom.

Those first moments of letting that beautiful baby into my heart were short-lived. Confused and immature as I was, barely able to take care of myself, the thought of taking care of someone else was overwhelming. Apprehension shot through my body as I imagined how my life would be turned upside down. And then there were my parents. Telling them I had a son seemed impossible, as did introducing them to his mom, who was African American. They were set on me marrying a "nice Jewish girl." I began to panic. If I held this baby, my son, for another thirty seconds, there would be no turning back.

I carried him back into the living room and thrust him into his mother's arms. "I can't do this!" I announced. "Why didn't you tell me sooner?" I remember her saying something about being afraid I'd pressure her to get an abortion. My bewilderment flared into anger, and as we began to shout at each other, the tender infant in our midst started to cry. The spell was broken. Bonnie bundled Anthony up and stormed out of the apartment, slamming the door behind her.

I collapsed onto the couch as a potent mixture of shock, relief, and shame engulfed me. Over the next few days, these emotions gave way to numbness and denial. It would be twenty-nine years before I would see my son again.

When fear and confusion drive our actions we cause suffering to others, often not realizing that we ourselves also suffer. Because I chose not to participate in his life, that beautiful innocent baby became the victim of my fear. His mother was denied my emotional and financial support as she faced the daunting task of being a single mom. I would not realize until years later the sadness and pain I myself carried for abandoning my son.

LISTENING TO THE FRIENDLY GUIDES

Every choice we make has a consequence—this is the essence of what the Buddha referred to as natural law. Or as Jesus put it, "As you sow, so shall you reap." That's good news when we're sowing good seeds. It's the other ones that worry us. You probably can think of times when

Reframing Good and Bad

Living with integrity is a practical strategy for awakening joy. It's also considered a "skillful" one, because it makes our lives work better. In Buddhist teachings, thoughts and actions are not categorized as good or bad but rather as "skillful" and "unskillful."

- To be skillful means to think and act in ways motivated by the desire to enhance the well-being of yourself and others.
- To be unskillful means to intentionally think or act in ways that harm you or others.

you engaged in some kind of questionable behavior and later faced the consequences. It might have taken a while before your actions caught up with you and made you squirm. But you might also recall some of the immediate discomfort you felt when you first chose to do whatever you did—the turmoil in your gut, that sinking feeling, or the sense that someone was looking over your shoulder. That's an immediate and useful consequence. Becoming familiar with uncomfortable feelings like these and letting them inform wise choices are the underpinnings of a peaceful mind and joyful heart.

It's often said the body doesn't lie. No matter how cool we may want to appear, the blush of embarrassment on our face gives us away. Likewise, the knot in our stomach or constriction in our throat can tell us something's not right even as we think or say, "I'm fine" or "It's okay to do this." Marvin, a course participant, wrote about what happened as he paid attention to the actual experience of his body and mind when he was facing an ethical challenge at work:

> I was in a situation in which I was tempted to act in a way that was inconsistent with the best practices of my profession. For a while I thought I wasn't doing anything wrong, and most people would still agree. But whenever I thought about it, I felt uncomfortable, needing to hide my action. It was a gut-level discomfort that felt like a weight on me. Finally I decided, "Enough! This is not working for me, even if it feels legitimately okay for others. I need to stop doing it." I felt an immediate sense of physical release—my shoulders expanded, I took a deep breath and let it out with a big "Oof!" I felt physically light and mentally free of all that exhausting ethical juggling. Although many of my colleagues wouldn't understand what the big deal was, I know I got my integrity back in that moment of decision.

How do you feel when you've done an unskillful action? Responses from participants in the Awakening Joy course reveal in graphic terms the impact such choices can have on well-being:

- Sick to my stomach, haunted for days
- Anxious, stressed, distracted, my blood seems to race.
- Tight in my chest, almost panicked.
- At first triumphant, then, shortly after, dark and remorseful.
- Chest collapsed, eyes downcast, body tense and defensive.
- Cringing, dead inside.

One answer in particular vividly captures the feeling: "My body slumped and my mind went gray with regret and sadness."

Not such happy feelings! In my experience as a teacher, these are not the feelings of a few neurotic individuals but rather what anyone might notice when paying mindful attention.

How do you feel after you've done a *skillful* action? Responses from participants in the course reveal quite a contrast to the feelings noted above:

- Content and peaceful.
- Light and joyful, playful.
- Like there is a glowing in my chest.
- Connected.
- Large of spirit.
- Like a smile is welling up from within.
- A desire to mentally replay the experience and enjoy it more than once.

Besides this friendly feedback system in our bodies, we also have what we often call "the voice of conscience." This one is a little trickier. I grew up with Jiminy Cricket singing, "Always let your conscience be your guide," and I knew without question what that meant. While moral codes vary with culture and history, once we've learned "right from wrong," it's pretty well wired into our internal program. However, it's important to know the difference between the encouraging proddings of a healthy conscience and the undermining voices of habitual self-judgment. The first leads you toward those expansive feelings of contentment and joy, the second toward fear and anxiety.

When you pay close attention, you will notice that the finger-wagging, critical voice that says *You're going to blow it again* is filled with fear, and it pulls you down. The voices of wisdom that wish for your genuine happiness are, like the voice of a compassionate mentor, gentle reminders filled with patience, kindness, and love. They point you toward a new horizon. As you learn to listen to them, you will find the way to release yourself from negative conditioning and into a more easeful life.

The Buddha referred to the happiness of integrity as "the bliss of blamelessness," and he offered a set of guidelines to take us there. Once I truly began to follow these guidelines myself, I was on the path back to the deep and true connection I first felt with my infant son. It would lead me to finally give him the love and caring that was his birthright. And I would learn that it is never too late to set foot on the path of blamelessness.

Natural Law

For one who leads a virtuous life,
it is a natural law that remorse
will not arise . . . ·
For one free of remorse,
it is a natural law that gladness
will arise . . .
For one who is glad at heart,
it is a natural law that joy will arise.

—THE BUDDHA

THE DUBIOUS BLISS OF IGNORANCE

If we know that acting with kindness and integrity will bring us happiness, why do we choose to act in any other way? Growing up, we may have learned to think or act in ways that are less than wholesome, but

Remembering the Gladness of the Wholesome

Think of a time when you reached out and were kind to someone. Let yourself recall the pleasure you felt in your mind and body as you saw how happy they were. Or remember a time when you made a choice to be genuinely open and truthful. Even if it was hard to do, maybe you recall a sense of relief, clarity, and connection? Take these positive feelings in and let them motivate you to continue to choose skillful actions.

even when we know better, we often continue to do what is easy and most familiar. We might spend years exploring the wounds in our past that lay the ground for our behavior, yet still continue doing things that hurt others and ourselves. Why? Because we make bad choices—even when we know we'll end up feeling unhappy—out of habits based in confusion.

While we might think that what we're saying or doing will get us what we want, when we look deeper, we often see that we're motivated by fear. Afraid of being caught in a compromising situation, we lie to cover up our part. Afraid of not getting enough of what we want, we take what's not rightfully ours. Afraid of being hurt by a loved one, we launch a preemptive strike. It might look like it's worth it at the time—that's the promise that keeps a habit in place—but inside us, our joy and aliveness are being compromised.

That young man who turned his back on his son already had in place a history of habits based in fear that led up to that moment. While I wouldn't have considered myself an immoral person—I certainly didn't go out of my way to harm others—I knew how to conveniently disregard the effect my actions might have on another. I could feign helplessness or blame someone else when things spun out of my control. I could avoid responsibility by pretending to myself that I couldn't do a task at hand. I saw no problem in telling "white lies," concealing the truth from myself

Going on Automatic

When you have spoken or acted in ways you later regretted, what contributed to that choice? Participants in the Awakening Joy course answered:

- ▸ I was feeling tired or stressed.
- ▸ I wasn't taking care of myself.
- ▸ I was in a hurry.
- ▸ I was drinking alcohol.
- ▸ I was angry.
- ▸ I felt threatened or blamed.

When we're not taking care of ourselves, or we're lost in some strong emotion, we more easily act out of fear or get lost in blind desire. We go on automatic, and our unconscious habits take over.

or others to avoid being caught in unskillful actions. So although I found a spiritual path in my mid-twenties and committed myself to living a life of integrity, as the years went by, the momentum of habit supported my continuing choice not to find Anthony.

I rationalized I wouldn't know where to begin looking for him, but the truth is I was afraid—afraid of what he'd think of me, afraid of what kind of person he might have become, afraid of how my life might turn upside down if we actually found each other. Somewhere inside I knew my son was probably wondering about his father, and deep down there was a sense that my life wasn't whole. Each September around Anthony's birthday, a sense of shame and incompleteness would visit me. I'd wonder how he was, what kind of life he had, what sort of person he was becoming. And I'd wish him well in my heart wherever he was. Then I would conveniently forget about him until the next September.

"Ignorance is bliss" goes the familiar saying. Isn't it easier to just for-

The Bottom Compartment

"Even though we all desire integrity, we're hindered by unconscious factors that lie deep within each of us. When you turn awareness inward through meditation or relaxation, you find this dark recess of consciousness. I like to compare that to the lower compartment of the refrigerator. Imagine that you have a very nice clean house, a beautiful kitchen, a fancy refrigerator. But somehow a very bad odor is pervading the place. You wonder, 'What is going on? I cleaned under my toilet, I washed my dishes, I got new vegetables this morning. Where is this odor coming from?' But then when you open the refrigerator door, you realize you haven't looked into that bottom compartment for the last few months, and now there are lots of rotten vegetables in there.

"The unconscious realm is like that bottom compartment. It's in each of us. It's one reason why we practice meditation. Meditation is not about religious discipline but about becoming more and more aware of one's internal issues, so that nothing is hiding away from your awareness. We need to be courageous and honest enough to bring our awareness inward and see, 'Oh there is the psychological lower compartment of my refrigerator, and some rotten vegetables there smell pretty bad. But it's okay. This is who I am right now. But I must be fully aware of it.' Practicing awareness is the way to cultivate integrity."

—ANAM THUBTEN RINPOCHE
AT AWAKENING JOY COURSE, BERKELEY, 2008

get about the consequences of our actions, denying when our integrity might be slipping? But do we really forget? Do we really avoid suffering? From one September to another, I turned my attention to other things, convincing myself everything was fine. But inside I was unsettled by the dissonance between what I felt was true and what I didn't want to accept—between what I sensed was right and what I couldn't bring myself to do.

FACING THE TOP TWENTY REALLY AWFUL DEEDS

There's a price we pay by becoming more conscious: We no longer can pretend we don't know any better. We more readily see the ways we fall short of our ideals. As meditation teacher Ruth Denison puts it, "Karma means you don't get away with nothing, darling!" Because karma is not an easy teacher in delivering to us the consequences of our actions, the humbling process of waking up requires genuine compassion and kindness for ourselves.

That begins with forgiveness, but it's not always easy to forgive ourselves. What do we do with the guilty feelings? How do we resolve, in our hearts and in our relationships, the pain we may have caused? I am somewhat of an authority on guilt. Being Jewish, you might say it's part of my heritage. But I've learned that when we're stuck in guilt and self-condemnation, our capacity for joy is limited. To arrive at blamelessness requires facing the past honestly, doing what we can to reconcile with others, and forgiving ourselves by replacing guilt and self-judgment with compassionate understanding.

I am now at a place in my life where I can say with clarity and honesty that I act with integrity most days in most situations. I can also see areas for improvement every day. The fact that this is all a normal part of life (not a terrible shame, or secret, or crisis) brings me a lot of happiness.

—A COURSE PARTICIPANT

I had a crash course in self-forgiveness on one memorable meditation retreat. Sitting in silence, with my own mind as my only company, I came face-to-face with a string of actions from my past that made me cringe. With all those hours of meditation each day, any mental states that got in the way of a loving heart came to the surface. Many of the memories from my days as a young man made me wince with shame. No matter how much immediate gratification I may have derived at the time of those actions, they were certainly not bringing me happiness now. My body would shudder with guilt and sadness.

I'm not trying to let myself off the hook, but in retrospect, some of my misdeeds may not have been all that terrible. Ram Dass points out in his book *Be Here Now* that as we become more conscious and aware, our "impurities will seem grosser and larger" because we're seeing them more clearly. I'd like to think that's what was happening.

Whether or not my misdeeds seemed bigger than they'd actually been didn't really matter as much as the fact that it was very painful to recall them. This was a sign that I was a different person, no longer capable of hurting others the way I had in the past. But even though I was fast getting the lesson, the parade of unskillful actions continued replaying themselves. They eventually became so overwhelming I decided to make a list of the Top Twenty Really Awful Deeds I had ever done. I thought naming them might help me at least deal with them more consciously. To my immense relief, I was only able to come up with what I considered Seventeen Really Horrendous Actions. Nevertheless, my guilt and remorse felt as awful as if it were a bottomless pit of shameful acts.

Stanton Peele, a pioneer in the field of addiction treatment, talks about the "accumulated disgust" with our unwholesome behavior that crescendos into a moment of truth when we realize *This is not working for me anymore.* We become acutely aware in a new way of the horrible feeling inside when we lose our temper with our children yet again, overeat and overdrink, or exploit someone. When you see clearly that your choices lead to more misery, that's when you're ready to move in a new direction. However, you can't accomplish this by turning against yourself. You have to go gently, recognizing that you are in a process.

FROM SUFFERING TO COMPASSION

A wise parent understands the confusion of an angry child. She knows that whether the behavior is due to frustration, fatigue, or hunger for attention, what the child really needs is to be held in love and for the pain to be understood with compassion. Then the child can begin to calm down. In the same way, by tenderly holding with kind awareness the pain and confusion that gave rise to our own hurtful behavior, we can begin to transform our suffering into compassion.

On my "Retreat of Awful Deeds," compassionate understanding for myself at first felt impossible. All I could do, hour after hour, was acknowledge and accept the truth of all those actions I had done. Then a curious thing started to happen. Because I wasn't pushing away or denying those images and feelings, I found that my guilt and shame and sadness were diminishing. In their place a tender understanding of my ignorance was arising. I could see how confused I had been to think that any of my deceptions or betrayals or denials could bring me happiness.

The Buddha didn't consider evil to be a disembodied force. Instead he said that all harmful and negative thoughts and actions come from ignorance—not understanding the way life works. We think we're doing what makes us happy, but because we don't understand, we make choices that lead in the direction opposite to where we're aiming. We miss the mark, which is in fact the root meaning of the word "sin."

The ways I had hurt or mistreated others had arisen from this kind of ignorance and confusion, and my choices also reflected how unkind I'd been to myself. Trying to avoid the pain of remorse by simply forgetting about or denying my harmful actions had disconnected me from being fully open to the love and compassion I yearned for.

During that intense inner process, my self-judgment was transforming into understanding, not only of myself but of others as well. I could clearly see that whatever anyone does makes sense to them at the time. We are all shaped by a multitude of circumstances, and some of them can give rise to a distorted perspective on reality. Sometimes our misdeeds are unintentional, but when we consciously hurt others, it is most likely

Forgiving Yourself

Think of an incident from your past that you still regret or feel guilty about. Consider what conditions, inner and outer, might have motivated your words or actions. Was fear a part of what motivated your choices? Now imagine yourself as a wise and kind being who understands and forgives you. Notice if there is any change in your body or mind as you take in that forgiveness. Is there any way you might act differently if a similar situation presents itself in the future?

because we ourselves were hurt, and that unprocessed pain is affecting our actions.

I once saw a poster that conveyed this point in heartbreaking terms. The picture of a sad-looking boy was the backdrop for this statistic: "A child raised in a home with domestic violence is seven hundred times more likely to become involved in domestic violence as an adult." When we recognize that every action has a cause, which is itself part of a long chain of cause and effect, a great compassion for ourselves and all others arises.

WISE REFLECTION

Looking back at myself as a frightened, immature, self-absorbed twenty-two-year-old, I can see now why I was unable to accept responsibility for my son Tony. It doesn't change the fact that my actions created pain for him and added undue pressures to his mother's life. It doesn't change my sadness that he didn't have me as a loving dad as he grew

Wiring Up the Positive

When you're trying to break a habit that doesn't serve you, instead of thinking about how poorly you've behaved, focus your attention on what you want to do and how you want to feel. Rather than getting caught up in self-judgment, recall the light and joyful way you feel when you *do* choose wisely, and let that feeling motivate you to continue. Research in neuroscience indicates that it can take several months for the neural circuits that would carry your new habit to consolidate fully. Sustaining a new way of being and acting over that period of time will help ensure that you've wired it into your brain.

Integrity feels good. When I act outside of integrity, there is a trace of pain that follows me around. When I act with integrity, I feel lighter in my body, and I can simply go on to the next thought or action. There are no second thoughts about what I've said or done.

—A COURSE PARTICIPANT

into manhood. But insulating myself from ever feeling that pain would have prevented my heart from opening enough to feel my love for him, forgive myself, and eventually be open to reconnecting with him.

How you deal with your mistakes either compounds the problem or helps you grow. Rather than heaping on the guilt, you can reflect on what happened and learn from each situation. Recently I heard a Baptist minister, Reverend Welton Gaddy, define forgiveness in a fresh and insightful way. In a television interview he said, "Forgiveness is not about wiping away consequences. Forgiveness is about creating possibilities." That applies to both forgiving others and ourselves. The times when we fall out of integrity can serve as springboards to more skillful choices in the future. This process takes lots of patience and kindness. When you've practiced unwholesome habits for a long time, you need clear intention and real determination to wake up and change. Saints are few and far between, but there are lots of people committed to waking up. As long as you're heading in the direction of more ease and peacefulness, that's what counts. In each moment, you are either deepening the ruts of sorrow or the grooves of joy based on what you choose to think or say or do. Why not choose joy?

HABITS FOR HAPPINESS

As part of his direct path to happiness, the Buddha offered a set of guidelines for building positive habits that get us in the right groove. These precepts, as they're called, recommend healthy and skillful choices in areas where we can easily go astray. The principle underlying all of them is the same—if you want to be happy, don't intentionally cause suffering to yourself or others. Every spiritual tradition—whether a religion or a philosophy, such as humanism—has a code of ethics. Virtually all of these guidelines are based on not harming others and some version of the Golden Rule, to treat others as we would wish to be treated.

The basic Buddhist version, which will look familiar to anyone who knows the Ten Commandments, is made up of five precepts or promises: to refrain from killing, stealing, sexual misconduct, lying, and using intoxicants. However, rather than being strict directives, the precepts are viewed as guidelines, ways to support well-being and peace of mind.

For the path of Awakening Joy, I've reframed the five basic precepts as five habits you can actively develop to bring more happiness into your life. They are meant as inspiration, not as a measuring stick that ends up thrashing you with guilt. As you try these out and explore the layers of understanding in each one, you will learn more about yourself as well as the connection between acting consciously and inner peace.

1. Honor all life.

At the heart of all these guidelines is reverence for life, traditionally expressed in the first precept as refraining from killing or harming other living beings. The image of St. Francis of Assisi, with wild birds resting on his hands and the animals of the forest gathering around him, exemplifies the gentleness and purity of heart that is the essence of harmlessness.

The capacity to feel reverence for life is a natural part of us. Children, unless they've been harmed or taught to harm, often feel a deep caring for all living things and want to protect them. When I was about six years old, my uncle invited me for an exciting adventure—he was going to teach me how to fish. I was thrilled . . . until I pulled up a sunfish on the end of my line. At the sight of the poor creature struggling on the hook, I imagined having a hook in my own mouth. Feeling sick to my stomach, I begged my uncle to throw it back in. Only when I saw the fish free again did my discomfort go away.

We are faced daily with choices about how to honor life and yet stay alive ourselves. You're probably going to take antibiotics when the choice is between you and some bacteria. When you're barreling down the road at seventy miles per hour, your windshield is a lethal weapon for flying insects. Although like many Buddhists I'm a vegetarian, some of my wisest, most respected friends are not. Tibetan Buddhists come from a high mountain terrain where fresh vegetables are scarce, so while they take the vow not to kill, they do eat animals. Eating meat does not preclude honoring living beings, as Native Americans and many hunters would attest. The intention with which we do any action is what has the most effect on our integrity.

We can develop the habit of honoring life in many ways in our daily lives. Respecting the ideas and feelings of others is a way of honoring the life within them. Protecting the environment, working for human rights, supporting organizations that serve those in need—all draw upon and awaken tenderness for life. Working at an occupation that contributes, directly or indirectly, to the health and well-being of others is a significant way to honor life. You might even see how it feels to help insects trapped in your house find their way outside. In this world filled with suffering, there are countless ways of reaching out to offer relief.

I've been having a very hard time at work. Something is really off. Every day I sit at my desk and do tasks I know must be hurting innocent people, and I'm reaching the point where I can't do it much longer. I don't know what I'll do for a job—I'm working for one of the few employers around here—but until I leave this place, I know I can't be happy.

—A COURSE PARTICIPANT

After a huge fire in our city, my husband and son and I decided to open our home to a family of three who had lost their own. It was pretty challenging for us—for weeks on end, we all had to keep stretching beyond our comfort zone. But what I recall most of all is the joy we felt in sharing with them as they struggled to deal with their displaced lives.

—A COURSE PARTICIPANT

2. Share your time and resources.

The second precept is traditionally stated as not taking what is not given. Like the Commandment "Thou shalt not steal," on the most basic level this guideline refers to not taking the possessions of others. However, we can take what is not ours in other ways as well. If you push into line ahead of others, aren't you taking something from them? Or if you get so involved in your own fascinating story that you don't realize your busy friends are trying to get out the door, aren't you taking what is not given? This guideline encourages you to take care that your pursuit of happiness is not at the expense of others.

Instead of just avoiding taking from others, you can increase your happiness by actively reaching out to be generous. As we saw in Step Three, sometimes that means consciously choosing to stretch beyond what you think you can offer. We are often bigger than we think, and when we stretch beyond our limits, we find our capacity for joy is also bigger.

Another level of this precept points to our relationship with the abundantly generous planet we live on. When we mindlessly take from her resources—depleting fossil fuels, harming delicate ecosystems, polluting air and water—aren't we stealing from the Earth? What is now known as the Deep Ecology movement goes beyond simply recycling or turning off a light. It holds that doing what we can to restore balance and health to the planet is an act of caring that deepens our connection to all of life and nourishes our spirit.

3. Take care with sexual energy, respecting boundaries and offering safety.

The common principle behind all five of the Buddhist precepts is a shift in perspective from "What's in it for me?" to "What can I offer another?" This shift in terms of sexuality can be life-changing. We move from regarding another as an object for our own pleasure to considering how we might bring greater happiness. Intimate partners can express their love by delighting in giving physical pleasure. In other relationships we can give the gift of safety in our presence by maintaining healthy boundaries. Traditionally stated as "refraining from sexual misconduct," this guideline ensures deep and true connection with another by advising us to offer the respect and safety that allows both of us to flourish.

Because sexual attraction is so powerful, it can easily lead to actions that can undermine our integrity and create a lot of suffering, for ourselves and others. Think of all the prominent public figures who have not only jeopardized their careers but deeply hurt their loved ones when they engaged in unethical

I recently almost had an affair with a married man, and while I felt intense desire, I also felt a profoundly awful churning in my gut which immediately told me that I couldn't do this. Because I tuned in to that churning feeling, I remembered again my commitment to try not to cause further harm in this troubled world, and I turned away.

—A COURSE PARTICIPANT

sexual conduct. You might recall in your own life some moments of regret that followed certain choices. We might lead someone on for our own gratification. We might mistake sex for love. We might take advantage of another or cross a line that harms others. Sometimes we're not sensitive to our partner's needs and wants. Maybe we rationalize that it would be okay to do one thing and say another.

The potent force of sexual energy can bring great pain or deep intimacy. As a sexual being, you can move from seeing what you can *get* to what you can *give* through respect and nonexploitation. In this way, you create the conditions for well-being and joy, in yourself and others.

4. Speak kindly and carefully.

The fourth precept is about speaking what is true and useful in a kind way. Traditionally, it is stated as refraining from lying and false speech. Most of us are all too familiar with the guilt we feel or the pain of retaliation when we blurt out something hurtful to or about someone. We also know the sweetness of offering and receiving words that convey love and support. Because speech is so much a part of our lives, developing the habit of using words kindly and wisely can be one of the most significant ways to increase happiness for ourselves and others.

Sometimes being both honest and kind might seem like a difficult combination. But the next time you're in a conversation that could become confrontational, try practicing wise speech. Notice what your intention is. Is it to be right, to control? If the heart of your intention is deeper understanding and healthier communication, the other person will often sense that.

We communicate with more than our words when we speak. Psychologist Albert Mehrabian, a pioneer in the field of nonverbal communication, formulated what has come to be known as the 7%-38%-55% Rule. His research revealed that only 7 percent of our feelings and attitudes are carried by our words. The tone of our voice constitutes 38 percent of the communication while 55 percent is conveyed by body language. When our intention is to be kind, our words align with the sound of our voice and the way we are using our body, and we are more likely to receive a kind response.

Not lying also means being honest and accurate in communication. While we pretty well know when we're not speaking the truth, we can easily slip into another form of deception—speaking in superlatives. *This was the worst day of my life. That was the most boring talk I've ever been to. I could've just died. I'm absolutely starving.* Even though we're being casual and know we don't mean those things literally, a habit of using words loosely can easily slide into reporting facts loosely as well. When we exaggerate, we actually disconnect ourselves from the truth, from what's real.

The other half of wise communication is compassionate listening. However unskillful another's communication may be, if you listen wisely, you can hear the suffering, fear, or confusion beneath their words. Instead of getting upset and reacting, listening in this way can help you choose to respond with openness and kindness. You're also more likely to stay in touch with your own best intention, so that your focus can shift from "being right" to more deeply understanding.

I'd get so frustrated during phone conversations with my father. He'd give me a minute-by-minute account of his day, and it was all I could do not to hang up out of impatience. During one call recently, I remembered that I was trying to bring more compassion and happiness into my life, and I said to myself, 'He's lonely. Just be here with him, for him.' I felt myself get so much bigger inside. I was more relaxed, and he sounded happier and more relaxed. I decided to try this out with other people and let go of grumbling to myself that I don't have time for them, or judging them for being so demanding. It has really made a difference in my relationships and in how I feel.

—A COURSE PARTICIPANT

Wise speech not only applies to your interactions with others but also to your relationship with yourself. Notice how you speak to yourself, the tone of thoughts in your mind. If they're harsh, see what it's like to change that to a kinder, more compassionate voice. Practice speaking to yourself as you would want others to speak to you, then consciously extend that same spirit of kindness and respect to your communication with others. Notice the effect on your level of happiness and ease.

5. Develop a clear mind and healthy body.

The fifth precept is typically stated as: "Refrain from intoxicants that cloud the mind and lead to heedlessness." Because drugs and alcohol so obviously affect the mind and body, some choose to follow this guideline by complete abstinence. Others interpret it as using substances in moderation so that the line from clarity to poor judgment is not crossed. Beyond the obvious pain of substance abuse and addiction, intoxicants can compromise our faculty of awareness and our ability to assess a situation and make wise and skillful choices. When this precept wobbles, so do all the others, making it more likely for us to cause harm to others and ourselves.

As a child of the 1960s, I'm no prude. I understand very well the appeal of changing one's consciousness—the temporary good feeling that helps us forget our pain and feel "loose" or creative. Our brains are wired to pursue what is pleasant, but the paradox is that what we think will make us happy can sometimes perpetuate our suffering.

We all experience hurt and frustration in our lives, and a quick fix of immediate pleasure can look like a good way to deal with the pain. Getting high on drugs or alcohol, overeating, smoking cigarettes, shopping—all numb the pain but don't address it. As we saw in Step Four, the way out of our suffering is by facing it head on. The path to wholeness requires honestly feeling our pain. Though this may seem like the harder route, it is a surer path to abiding happiness than what temporary pleasure offers.

During a workshop I was teaching, one of the participants, David, told me about a time when he had to face head on what he was doing to himself. He said he'd been on a steady regimen of drugs and alcohol and was on the verge of losing everything dear to him—his wife, children, job, home. One night, shaken to the core when he realized where he was heading, he struck upon the words that turned his life around and have become his guiding principle for happiness ever since: "Act with integrity in the moment of choice." I was so struck by the power in these words that I pulled out my notebook and wrote them down. Years later I still refer to them. As you honor your body and mind in the "moment of choice," by being conscious of what you take in, you develop the clarity that helps you make wise choices in all areas of your life.

For those who meditate, clarity of mind has the added benefit of aiding the power of concentration. When the mind is concentrated and still, an inner happiness not dependent on external circumstances becomes

Cultivating Habits for Happiness

Choose one of the five habits or precepts that you would like to cultivate as a way to bring more joy and well-being into your life, and commit to doing it for one week. Brainstorm ways you might act in alignment with this guideline. Write them down and place the paper in a prominent location where you can readily see it every day.

Your old habits may rebel and struggle for dominance. Each time you are faced with the moment of choice, take a breath, and choose integrity. Whenever you do choose to think and act in alignment with integrity, notice how you feel. Is there a sense of relief or ease? What kind of response do you receive if others are involved? When you later recall your choice, how do you feel about it? These reflections will help anchor your new habit as it develops.

At the end of the week, notice if it has become easier to make positive choices. See if your level of well-being and happiness has increased.

available to us. Not only are these joyous mind states pleasant in themselves, the concentrated mind leads to deep purification and wisdom, cutting through and releasing old patterns that cause harm to ourselves and others.

Remember that these guidelines for behavior are not supposed to induce guilt but rather help wake us up to ways we can bring more happiness into our lives. If something "feels off," whether it's in your job or in how you are relating to others, keep in mind you have a choice. Take an honest look at what you can do differently. Sometimes the choice for integrity can be difficult, but knowing that you're making a choice for your own well-being can give you the courage to take a challenging step. No matter how far you've strayed from integrity, you always have the capacity to turn around and begin again. Aligning your life with your values is a process of development that requires patience, compassion, and continual commitment. But the reward is the bliss of blamelessness. What could be better than that?

A COMPLEX AND REWARDING ADVENTURE

Living in our world with integrity can be a complex adventure, and sometimes there is no simple answer. Grappling with this led course participant Cindy to some wise reflections:

> In my experience, it's possible to get really entangled in choices that take multiple variables into account. *Should I buy food that is organic but non-local, which supports organic farming but has a big impact on the environment by requiring that produce be trucked long distances? Or should I buy local but non-organic, which might be supporting the pesticide industry and compromising my health?* At some point, getting caught up in too many considerations makes virtue an intellectual exercise rather than a felt-sense in the body, and then it's no longer helpful. We cannot come up with a perfect answer! This is not easy. What is "right" is created afresh each moment.

The bliss of blamelessness depends upon listening carefully to the ring of truth inside. While often choices in any given situation are not black and white, if you pay close enough attention, the feeling of tightness or ease in your body can pretty well guide you toward actions that are best aligned with your intention to live with integrity. As you refine your ability to hear the voice of wisdom, you increasingly choose behaviors that are healthy and make you feel genuinely alive, invigorated, and big-hearted.

A SECOND CHANCE

For me, a major shift in my life began with a phone call that came one hot August day in 1999. A woman's voice asked if I had ever known

Holding to the Truth

"In 1971, during the first year of our marriage, I helped my husband, Daniel Ellsberg, release to the press the top secret documents that came to be known as the Pentagon Papers, confirming that Congress and the American public had been misled into entering the war in Vietnam. Even though he faced going to prison for the rest of his life, Dan felt compelled to reveal the truth.

"We had both been inspired by the teachings of Gandhi, who lived with a deep respect for all life and a commitment to non-harming and non-violence, even toward those he would call enemies. He called the principle behind this *satyagraha,* 'holding to the truth.' The power that arises from this practice was known as Truth-Force or Soul-Force.

"I remember the day Dan and I stood in front of a bank of cameras and shouting reporters, and he took full responsibility for the release of the papers. We were holding hands in the middle of that chaos, and it was as if we were in an electrical current of great power. I believe this was an experience of Truth-Force.

"There is a dimension of integrity that comes from recognizing our oneness and interconnection with all life. Each of us can access the power of Truth-Force when we act with that kind of integrity. Wholesome states, such as kindness, compassion, and service, open us to that power."

—PATRICIA ELLSBERG
AT AWAKENING JOY COURSE, BERKELEY, 2008

someone named Bonnie with whom I might have fathered a child. After a silence, I quietly answered yes. *Who was this woman and what did this mean?* My breath caught, and I could feel the blood rushing to my head. "Yes,"

I replied again, "it's possible." My mind flooded with different thoughts and scenarios. *My son has found me! What is he like? He's in trouble and is turning to me for help. Maybe he's a drug dealer and wants to make sure I pay for my actions.* In the midst of my fears and concerns, I could almost feel the woman on the other end of the line begin to smile. "Oh, if that's so, you are very lucky," I heard her say. "I'm a friend of his, calling for him. Tony is one of the most wonderful human beings I've ever met."

A mix of emotions surged through me—gratitude, relief, curiosity, fear, guilt, excitement. "Have him call me as soon as he's ready," I heard myself say. When I got off the phone, I knew in the stillness of that August afternoon that my life was about to dramatically change. Shock intertwined with infinite possibility. I was being given a second chance.

Within a few hours, Tony's call came. During those first awkward moments our conversation was tentative, but by the end of the call we had made arrangements for him to fly up the following weekend for a visit. Over the next few days, I felt overwhelmed with both trepidation and excitement. *How would this work out? How would Adam feel about suddenly having a big brother? How would my own life change? What would Tony and I say to each other? Who was this "most wonderful person" and what would he think of me? Could he possibly forgive me?* Whatever was going to unfold from this opportunity, I was prepared to take full advantage of it. I had learned through years of practice that healing comes from directly facing the truth of whatever life presents me.

Over the course of that weekend, Tony and I both realized how fortunate we were that he had found me. I was struck by how much he reminded me of my father—the person who most taught me how to love. The sparkle in his eyes, the dimpled cheek, the infectious smile all radiated the same goodness I knew so well and had greatly missed since my dad had passed away fifteen years earlier. Tony's heart of gold dazzled me, and beholding this young man was like a rerun of that moment with him twenty-nine years earlier when I had mysteriously known him as my flesh and blood. Only this time I wasn't running away.

Tony too saw someone quite different from what he feared when his fiancée Leesa was first tracking me down, spending many hours on the Internet. Instead of encountering an uncaring and insensitive father who had betrayed him, he had found, despite what had happened, someone he could admire and feel an easy, natural connection with.

NEVER TOO LATE

Four months after that first reunion, Tony came to my weekly meditation group in Berkeley. In the back of a room crowded with students, he sat quietly and anonymously. The stunned group listened as I recounted our story and the recent events of our reunion. It was a story that outlined my confusion, fear, and shame as well as the gratitude I felt for this second chance. I talked about the love I felt as I got to know this son of mine for the first time. I shared my awe and wonder at the mystery of life, and the joy I was feeling at both of us finding this missing piece of our lives. Finally, I expressed my hope that at some point Tony would truly forgive my confusion and let me completely into his heart.

Then, to the surprise of everyone in the room, I invited Tony to join me on the stage where I introduced him. As we sat there together in front of my silently marveling community, Tony reached out to me and whispered, "I forgive you, Dad," and suddenly burst into tears. The microphone picked up his voice, and the room filled with raw emotion and tenderness as everyone witnessed this amazing turning point between us. Words cannot describe the power of that moment for me as my heart took in his love.

Tony's reentry into my life has given me many lessons. He has conveyed the pain and hurt he experienced by my absence, and his anger over being abandoned. These deep wounds have certainly left their mark on him. Although I've forgiven myself, this is something I have to live with for the rest

I finished graduate school, took a job based on my course of study, and then realized that I didn't want to do it. As I work through the huge emotional response to this situation, I am aware that by leaving the job I didn't want, I acted with integrity toward myself. I did what was right for me, even if it was against what I had spent three years working toward. Now, as I try to figure out what to do next, I am trying to be more honest with both myself and my friends about the challenges, confusion, and sadness that are coming up, and I am working toward finding a wise livelihood that is in line with who I am, who I want to be, and what feels right.

—A COURSE PARTICIPANT

of my life. At times I consider that perhaps all of this is part of a bigger picture we just can't understand. It certainly has taught both of us a great deal about what is important in life. And because of what I've gone through with Tony, I have been able to help others choose wisely when faced with difficult decisions.

This story has continued with unimagined blessings. Adam has been thrilled, not only at having a big brother he feels close to, but one who is a musician to boot. Jane and Tony have an affectionate relationship, and she's happy he's in our lives. At Tony's wedding I walked down the aisle with my mom, who's crazy about Tony and is his greatest admirer. It's like they're long-lost friends who've found each other. I've met with Tony's mother, Bonnie, and expressed my sorrow for not being there for both of them when they needed me, as well as my deep gratitude for all the love and caring she gave Tony. Bonnie now considers my mother one of her friends, and she and I have a warm connection, occasionally spending time together at Tony's house when we're both visiting. Tony has taken my last name and has blessed me with three stunning granddaughters, Jordan, Sydney, and Taylor Baraz. He turns to me when he needs someone to talk to who will understand. As Tony has let me into his heart, and I've let him into mine, the hole created by all those missing years has filled with sweetness, laughter, and love. Like any family, we've had our challenges, but we also hold them in the context of all these blessings.

Having deeply experienced the consequences of my actions informs how I live now. Rather than focusing on what the immediate effect of any decision might be, I imagine how it will feel six months or five years from now when I look back on the choice. This long-range view of well-being has been a great ally in wise decision-making. The Buddha's words about a life of integrity leading naturally to joy are not merely theoretical. I know the truth of that teaching from direct experience, and I use it as my North Star.

We can choose at any time to enter a life of integrity. It may be tempting to stay asleep, to continue sliding over all those little—or big—infringements we've gotten used to. But as my younger son, Adam, who spent a college semester in India studying Eastern philosophies, wrote in one of his essays for the program:

When I mess up, I am again stuck with that altogether too familiar bad feeling. The voice in my mind chides, "And don't pretend you didn't know better!" When these moments start to feel truly excruciating, I pity myself and daydream about the peace I could have if I didn't know better. "How sweet it would be to go back to the bliss of ignorance!" But much farther down in my gut I know the truth. There is only one bliss. And in life, when given the choice between the short-lived pleasures—the Bliss of Ignorance—and the long-term fulfillment—the Bliss of Blamelessness—hopefully I'll choose the latter.

BEING TRUE TO OURSELVES

Sometimes the hardest area of integrity is being truthful with ourselves. Are we telling ourselves the truth when we berate or put ourselves down? Is it true when we say, "I don't have the capacity to handle this"? Are we acting with integrity when we betray ourselves by not developing our gifts and talents?

Integrity is not just about following guidelines for morality. On a deeper level, it's about being true to yourself. If you are in touch with your heart and your deepest impulses, you will make choices that do not harm yourself or others. It's not always easy to follow that "still, small voice inside," but it's worth listening carefully enough to hear it.

As part of your integrity practice, you might focus on being uncompromisingly honest with yourself. Not brutally honest, but honest in a

A North Star

If you're facing a decision that could compromise your integrity, imagine how you will feel five months or five years from now looking back on your choice.

The Fragrance of Morality

"In Buddhism we talk about the fragrance of morality. It means that when you practice integrity, it's almost like you have an extraordinary divine scent around you, and you magnetize everything you are searching for—all the goodness, virtue, joy, freedom, even enlightenment if that's what you're looking for. Integrity is the first step toward the highest goals you are trying to actualize in this human existence.

"When we practice maintaining integrity and demonstrate it through our actions, our speech, the way we treat other people, we become extraordinary examples to inspire others. It's like how one candle can light hundreds of candles, and those hundreds of candles can light thousands of candles. Can you imagine such an enlightened society? But we must start with ourselves. When you practice integrity, you will see the reward immediately. You'll discover that you're happy, that your friends and family members are happy, and even your dog is happy too. That is because of the fragrance of morality."

—ANAM THUBTEN RINPOCHE
AT AWAKENING JOY COURSE, BERKELEY, 2008

kind and caring way that genuinely supports your intention for greater happiness. Try asking yourself, "What do I really need to do right now that would bring me greater well-being?" Then listen with care to your deepest wisdom—feeling it in your body, hearing the supportive and resonant voice of clarity in your mind.

You can actively practice the "bliss of blamelessness" by paying attention to the uplifting feelings that arise in your body and mind when you choose to act with integrity. As you pay attention to the pleasant visceral sensations, you are training yourself to make the choice for happiness. Rather than looking to avoid suffering, you become motivated by the "gladness connected with the wholesome."

When we walk the path toward the bliss of blamelessness, our goodness overflows. The joy you're looking for starts with being aligned with your values. As you act with integrity, you become a clear vessel for goodness to move through you and touch others. That not only makes you happy in the moment, but the goodness that radiates out will come back to you many times over.

Step 6

The Joy of Letting Go

He who binds to himself a joy
Does the winged life destroy;
But he who kisses the joy as it flies,
Lives in Eternity's sunrise.

—WILLIAM BLAKE (1757–1827)
"SEVERAL QUESTIONS ANSWERED"

Let's say you've been enthusiastically following the steps of the Awakening Joy course. Some old patterns that used to get in the way have lost their power, and some new practices have proven valuable in keeping the channels open to joy. "Great! I've finally figured out how to be happy," you declare. "This is the way life is supposed to be." Then one morning you wake up feeling lousy, or something happens that's not quite so pleasant, and you scramble to get back "your happiness." The more it fades away, the harder you try to hold on to it, and the very holding on squeezes out the joy.

We can't hold on to happiness any more than we can hold on to anything or anyone. As we've seen in previous steps, trying to hold on in a constantly changing world is futile, and it pulls us out of the moment. Yet we do it all the time. To begin with, we hold on to our material goods. There may be a lucky few of us who live simply and without a lot of things, but if you're at home, look around you. You've probably got a ton of reasons for hanging on to most of the objects you see.

That's just the external world. Our inner world is even more filled with stuff we hold on to—our ideas of what we think life is about, who we think is right (usually ourselves), how things are supposed to be. When any of these important things are threatened, our world can feel like it might crumble. *There's a scratch on my new car!* Or, *Why isn't it like it was when we first met?* Or, *Why did you do that?!*

It's natural and healthy to care about things or people or ideas. They are the stuff of life. Giving and receiving love and appreciating beauty and pleasure are some of the most fulfilling and joyful aspects of our lifetime. But caring too much can have a subtle, or not so subtle, quality of holding on. Relationships change, favorite things break, pets die. Trying to hold on to the way we want life to be only leads to frustration and disappointment.

The Buddha decided to teach when he realized that, although all human beings want to be happy, they continue to think and act in ways that create more suffering. He defined the cause of this suffering basically as hanging on to the way we want things to be. We want life to always be pleasant for us. And when it's not that way, we think something's wrong, and we struggle to set it right.

On my first meditation retreat, I learned an unforgettable lesson about this with the help of my teacher Joseph Goldstein. One afternoon I'd fallen into a most exquisite state of mind. A calm, easy presence and feeling of completeness had engulfed me. It was as if there were no separation between me and the rest of life. I was breathing in as the Universe was breathing out. The Universe was breathing in as I breathed out. I was so happy, and I didn't want that sweet state of mind to ever end. Of course it did. Over the next two days I tried everything I could think of to recreate the experience. *Maybe it was the way I was sitting on my meditation cushion. Maybe it had to do with what I'd eaten for lunch. Maybe I needed to more diligently pay attention to my breath.* But somehow the harder I tried, the more elusive that state was. In place of calm and presence were disappointment, agitation, and confusion.

Disheartened, I went to Joseph to tell him how frustrated I felt because I'd "had it" and then I "lost it." He smiled knowingly and told me a story. During his extended meditation practice in India, he had experienced a sustained period of bliss. For several weeks, every time he sat down to meditate, his mind was clear and his body was filled with light. When he had to return to the States to see his family and take care of some things, Joseph left this tremendously pleasurable experience behind, figuring that when he got back to India, he'd pick up with the bliss where he left off.

But a couple of months later, back on the cushion in India, "instead of bliss, my mind was like mud and my body felt like twisted steel," he told me. Speaking slowly to let his words sink in, he went on. "I spent nearly two years trying to recapture that blissful state. Even though my teacher told me to let things be just as they are, I kept trying to make my experience different." Then Joseph leaned forward to drive home the point: "*I* was the dummy. Now *you* don't have to go through that. What you need to do is let go of the way things were and just be with what's happening now."

Truly letting go doesn't come easy to a control freak like me. But what comes to mind when letting go is the memory of being a child again and sledding in a quiet place I discovered. It was a long, steep hill with many trees, and I felt the wonder and thrill of letting go and just flying down that long hill, steering around the trees, and landing safely at the very bottom. It was a feeling of utter peace.

—A COURSE PARTICIPANT

Circumstances change, we change, things change, and letting go of what we're holding on to can be a great relief. It is also the road to happiness. The Buddha taught that the end of suffering—the highest happiness—comes from developing "a mind that clings to naught." That's a tall order. But even loosening our grip just a little can bring about a lot of happiness. Letting go to any degree is not easy, and I don't want to sound flippant about it. Sometimes life asks us to let go of more than we think we can bear—our homes, our jobs, our loved ones. However, while we can't deny the suffering, holding on to what is already gone only adds to our pain.

I once saw the great Thai meditation master, Ajahn Chah, give a simple and profound teaching about letting go. One day a local villager, who was in the group gathered before the master, asked him if he could explain the teachings in a way that would be easy to remember every day. In response, Ajahn Chah reached for his ceramic cup and held it up. "You see this cup? It was given to me as a gift," he began. "It is pretty to look at. It holds my water. I enjoy it. If I can see this cup as already broken, I won't cry when that happens. In this way, I can fully appreciate it while it's here. Letting go like this is how I can truly be happy in a world where everything changes."

Letting go is about freeing ourselves from that which complicates and confuses our mind. That covers a very broad spectrum. When I ask Awakening Joy participants what they let go of during this step in the course, the answers have included:

- Ingrained ideas of having to say or do something perfectly.
- Love letters from my college boyfriend.
- My youth as I let go to the signs of aging.
- A certain kind of friendship with my children as they go off to college and don't want a lot of interaction with me.
- Independence and self-sufficiency due to a physical injury.
- Fear of being abandoned by my partner, who is actually very steady.
- The need to be right.

What are we really holding on to? Most fundamentally, it's the illusion that we have control in a world of change. This attempt to control keeps us bound in fear. And unless we let go as circumstances change, we end up suffering.

One of the secrets of happiness is learning to distinguish what we want from what we truly need. Wise letting go leads to joy when we realize we don't have to hold on to extra baggage, whether it's in our garage or the closet of our mind. We put down an unnecessary burden—the attachment that comes from grasping on to what we think will make us happy.

When you stop holding on so tight—to ideas, beliefs, objects, or beings you cherish, and precious concepts of who you are—you begin to live in a way that lets you flow with life. You can meet what life brings you and respond creatively, in trust, and with generosity of heart. You discover that letting go is something you do *for* yourself, not *to* yourself. Happiness doesn't depend upon what you have or what you hold on to. Rather, by learning the art of letting go, paradoxically we get what we really want. You step into the contentment and ease of a relaxed mind.

Letting Go

If you let go a little, you will have a little peace. If you let go a lot, you will have a lot of peace. If you let go completely, you will have complete peace and freedom. Your struggles with the world will have come to an end."

—AJAHN CHAH, FROM *A Still Forest Pool*,
COMPILED BY JACK KORNFIELD AND PAUL BREITER

THE STORY OF STUFF

Friends have told me about the Dalai Lama laughing in one of his talks as he recalled a particular week he spent in Los Angeles. He has always loved scientific gadgets, and each day on his way to give teachings, he would stop to look at items on display at a nearby electronics store. He said that by the end of the week he wanted things he didn't even know the use for. He wanted them just because he'd seen them.

That's one of the ways the mind works—often what we see is what we want. This is fertile ground for the U.S. advertising industry. Annie Leonard's amazing short film, *The Story of Stuff*, portrays how we in the United States are basically drowning in material goods.

Among a number of disturbing statistics, the film notes that:

- The average US person now consumes twice as much as they did fifty years ago.
- We each see more advertisements in one year than people fifty years ago saw in a lifetime.
- In the US, we spend three to four times as many hours shopping as our counterparts in Europe do.

In the film, economist Victor Lebow is quoted in order to explain how this glut of consumption came about. He was writing just after World War II had ended, and what he had to say was prophetic:

Our enormously productive economy demands that we make consumption our way of life, that we convert the buying and use of goods into rituals, that we seek our spiritual satisfaction, our ego satisfaction, in consumption. . . . We need things consumed, burned up, replaced, and discarded at an ever-accelerating rate.

Of course desire is going to arise in response to clever advertising. "Bet you can't eat just one," the famous potato chip ad challenges us, summing up the strategy to get us to want more and more. We end up believing that the next new thing is going to make the difference in our life that will make us happy or healthy or lovable. We get a little thrill of excitement at the promise and again at the purchase. Fearing we might not have enough, we hold on to things we don't need, just in case . . . And

Sustainable Contentment

"When you are living in contentment, you automatically start to have a lighter footprint, a lighter use of resources. You don't have to keep adding more and more to your life. In fact, it feels really good to want what you have, to take care of it, and to be aware that everything you're using is a representation of energy. You feel more and more as if you are a part of a family and that you don't want to gorge yourself at the table, taking ten times your share. Contentment chills out the desperation of accumulation, which the culture hammers you with. If you are saying, 'I'm quite content now, and adding on all of this stuff complicates my life,' then you are automatically moving toward being part of the solution. Your life is the expression of that."

—CATHERINE INGRAM
AT AWAKENING JOY COURSE, BERKELEY, 2008

where does this get us? Environmentalist Bill McKibben, in his book *Deep Economy*, writes: "In 1946, the United States was the happiest country among four advanced economies; thirty years later, it was eighth among eleven advanced countries; a decade after that it ranked tenth among twenty-three nations, many of them from the third world."

John D. Rockefeller, when asked how much money would be enough, replied, "Just a little more." When does "enough" become satisfying? In *Hooked*, a collection of essays edited by Stephanie Kaza, Buddhist monk Ajahn Amaro quotes one of his colleagues, the noted Thai Buddhist economist and scholar, P. A. Payutto. Writing about the principle of moderation, Payutto says:

> It is an awareness of that optimum point where enhancement of true well-being coincides with the experience of satis-faction. Consumption . . . must be balanced to an amount appropriate with well-being rather than to the satisfaction of desires. In contrast to maximum consumption leading to more satisfaction, we have moderate, or wise consumption leading to well-being.

Getting and holding on to more and more stuff doesn't raise our level of happiness. In fact, quite the opposite. We can feel overwhelmed by all the papers, objects, toys, clothes, and other things that fill our closets, garages, storage rooms, and homes. When our goal changes from quelling desires to enhancing our well-being, we have a helpful guideline for choosing what we need over what we want.

When course participant Cynthia noticed she was doing "a little too much spontaneous buying," she decided to try an experiment:

> I made a commitment for a period of time not to buy anything other than groceries and necessities. When the impulse would arise to buy something extra, whether that was Starbucks cof-fee or a spiritual book, I would just jot down the item in a little notebook, notice my feelings and reactions, and move on. Invariably I would discover that I had managed to survive

and be happy without having made the purchase. It was quite liberating. I found that letting go is being at peace with what is and what one has—quite the opposite of "the more you get the better."

Happiness comes from being engaged in life, not in acquiring more stuff. As you explore the revolutionary idea of having enough, you might try getting more involved in activities that don't have to do with buying or acquiring. Spend time just talking with a loved one or sitting down to listen to one of the CDs you already have in your collection. Go out for a bike ride or learn something new. An important key to greater well-being is spending time rather than money on what you love.

LETTING GO INTO TIME

Imagine having a schedule that gives us time to rest, play, and cultivate our happiness in our daily life. How many of us have that? Yet in the Bible, even God took a break after work, and commanded us to "remember the Sabbath and keep it holy." I don't mean to say that you can't be joyful when you're in the midst of lots of activity. I love being fully engaged, often in a number of projects. But when I get lost in the swirl, I get spun out of balance.

We live in a 24/7 culture, and if it *feels* to you like you're packing in more than you used to, you're right. In their essay "Consuming Time," Professors David Loy and Linda Goodhew reported in the year 2000, "The husband and wife in an average U.S. household are now working five hundred more hours a year than they did in 1980." Add email, phone calls, the basics of life, the next exciting adventure, the latest movie, and lunch with a friend, and you're stressed out and far from joyful.

My colleague Patricia Ellsberg, who leads guided meditations at the Awakening Joy course in Berkeley, likes to speak playfully to participants about a condition prevalent in our society—FOMS, Fear of Missing Something. Besides all those movies, concerts, lectures, meetings, friends, etc., we have sixty-plus television channels at home and endless amounts of important and fascinating information on the Internet. No wonder we're afraid of missing things—we have so many choices that we miss almost everything available to us every day! The Beatles movie *Yellow Submarine* that came out in the late 1960s was prophetic in featuring a character whose mantra was: "Ad hoc, ad loc, and quid pro quo! / So little time! So much to know!" He was called "The Nowhere Man." Being happy means recovering from FOMS and arriving at the *somewhere* in time that is this moment. It means being present for our lives in a balanced way and letting the rest go without regret.

Too much on our plate gives us indigestion. But sometimes the way we handle our overcrowded schedules is like trying to cure indigestion by eating even more. Course participant Beverly finds that her busyness feeds on itself. "If I get out of balance—too little sleep, no quiet time—the loop starts looping wildly, and I get busier, trying to make up for lost time." In written Chinese the characters for "busy" are "heart" plus "killing." Besides the physical diseases stress is known to cause—strokes, heart attacks, diabetes, and ulcers, among others—it also closes our heart spiritually and emotionally.

We might pack a lot into our schedules but, like eating a diet of junk food, we remain hungry because we lack real nourishment. When another course participant, Norma, looked at how she was spending her time, she realized she was involved in a lot of activities that, while seeming important, were actually unsatisfying and kept her from doing things that would contribute to her well-being:

> *Normally I race right through some of the things I have to do with my young son—picking up toys, getting him ready for bed. But the other day I discovered something that was delightful. I actually stopped to enjoy fully the happiness in his eyes and the smile on his face. I felt it with my whole body. I don't even remember exactly what we were doing, but I can instantly bring back the feeling of joy I had during that moment.*
>
> —A COURSE PARTICIPANT

I realized that my favorite excuse for not doing things I would enjoy has been, "I don't have time." Letting go of that belief has been really powerful for me. Whenever it comes up now, I look at what really matters, and I change those words in my mind to, "I am making the time to enjoy life."

Just as we can be greedy for things, we can be greedy for experience and activities. Being interested in life is one of the ways to awaken joy, but you can do so without feeling compelled to do or have a multitude of experiences in order to be happy. Letting go means being right here with your life as it unfolds instead of continually reaching out for more. It is a shift toward simplicity, not complicating your life or your mind with a clutter of things to do. Peace Pilgrim, in her eponymous book, shares the wisdom she developed during the twenty-eight years she spent walking across the country to deliver her message of peace. She writes:

> If your life is in harmony with your part in the Life Pattern, and if you are obedient to the laws which govern this universe, then your life is full and good but not overcrowded. If it is overcrowded, you are doing more than is right for you to do, more than is your job to do in the total scheme of things.

I once heard a decluttering expert advise being wary of the word *just*, as in "I'll *just* do this quick errand before my next appointment," or "I'll *just* check my email one more time before I go." *Just* is an unrealistic belief that things won't take time. Then we find ourselves rushing and hurrying to catch up. You will never get to the end of your "to do" list. As is sung in the celebratory song "Circle of Life" from *The Lion King*, "There's more to see than can ever be seen/More to do than can ever be done." What really needs your attention and is most important to your well-being? My motto regarding all the undone emails and tasks waiting for me is *"Behind is just a state of mind."* If you're too busy to enjoy your life, then perhaps you're too busy. What can you do with your time that will nourish you and make life more worthwhile? Take a walk in nature. Play some music. Spend more time with your kids or loved ones.

Taking some quiet time for yourself is a good way to bring more joy into your days. Even a few minutes of down time can help you tune into what you really want to do in "your one wild and precious life," as poet Mary Oliver puts it. Trimming down your calendar may feel awkward at first, but eventually your time can be filled with quality rather than quantity.

Habits of busyness and the mindset of "more" are not easy to break. It takes a strong intention to change. Whenever you do "give yourself time," remember to pause and pay attention to how good it feels in your mind and body. This will help support your shift to a happier life.

GETTING OUT OF THE MIND TRAP

Like any other skill, the ability to let go develops over time. When you first begin, you may find that instead of feeling freer, you're battling previous habits that don't want to give up. One course participant wrote to say: "The more I try to let go of habits that don't serve me, the more resistance I feel and the more I struggle."

It helps to remember where that struggle is taking place. As we have

Letting Go of Busyness

What can you let go of in your schedule—or put into it—to have more ease and fulfillment in your life? What do you believe about yourself or about life that makes you do more than you are healthy or comfortable doing?

If you tend to overbook yourself, try this: For one week, if you add something to your schedule, see if you can delete something else. At the end of the week, notice if you have felt more spacious or balanced. What did you "do" with the extra time in your schedule?

Sometimes it's not possible to pare down a schedule. In that case, give yourself "mini-breaks." Take a brief moment, between dropping off one child at daycare and getting the other to soccer practice, to pause, close your eyes, take a deep breath, and feel what it's like to be "out of time." Even if you've just dashed down the hall at work from one meeting to another, stop for a few seconds before you open that next door, close your eyes, let your body relax, take a breath, and come back to yourself. Chances are you won't feel quite so *busy* after a mini-break.

seen in each Awakening Joy step so far, our mind is the main arena where our lives are happening. Life keeps changing around us, but the mind can dig in its heels. Another participant writes: "I find that my mind attaches itself to a particular problem or situation and keeps bringing me back to it." It can feel almost impossible to let go of fear, resentment, negativity, or compulsive behavior, especially if you've been practicing them for a long time.

I am working with being more patient and open to empty slots of time in my schedule. I have found that I can really enjoy doing nothing when I allow myself that pleasure.

—A COURSE PARTICIPANT

In Asia there is a clever way of trapping monkeys that offers a helpful clue for getting out of a rut in the mind. A coconut, hollowed out and with a hole in one end, is filled with sweets and tied to a stake. The monkey comes along, smells the sweets, sticks its hand in and grabs a fistful. Though the hole is big enough for an open hand to get through, it's too small for a fist full of sweets to get out. Even as the monkey hears

Letting Go of Expectations

Having a plan is useful as a guide, but if it becomes a rigid expectation, you could be setting yourself up for disappointment. Choose a particular activity that you do regularly, such as a task at work, or cooking a meal, or having a conversation with a friend or one of your children. For one week, each time you are about to begin that activity, notice if you have an expectation of how it's "supposed to" turn out. Experiment with letting go and just being open to whatever happens. This doesn't mean letting go of accomplishing the task, getting the meal on the table, or bringing up certain topics in conversation, but rather being open instead of closed in your approach.

As you engage in the activity, notice how you feel in your body and mind when you let go of your expectations. Does letting go have any effect on your enjoyment of the experience?

the humans coming and starts to panic, it holds on tightly to its prize. All that monkey has to do to be free is let go of the sweets and slip out its hand. As Joseph Goldstein likes to put it, "It's a very rare monkey who figures that out."

When you can't seem to get out of a difficult state, and negative thoughts play themselves over and over in your mind, the first step is to recognize them simply as thoughts. The reason they seem so convincing is because we believe that they are real. Often they have to do with who we believe ourselves to be. If you're trapped in resentment, for instance, it's most likely because you've identified with having been wronged. Maybe you were, but as one course participant puts it: "So what? I realized I was storing resentment in my body and heart. When I let it go, I felt light, free, happy." Like the monkey in the trap, all you need to do to be free is relax your grip. Even if it's hard to let go of all that righteousness, if the choice is between hanging on or being happy, which do you choose?

OPENING UP YOUR OPTIONS

When you let go of thinking that things should be a certain way, you open yourself up to the fact that there are usually a number of options

Lightening Up

Even a few minutes of mindfulness meditation each day carries over into your life, teaching you how to swim *with* rather than against the current of life. During meditation, each time you notice that you're thinking, no matter how interesting or important the content of the thought may seem, practice letting it go. Don't worry if the same thoughts keep coming back. That's common. Just keep letting go each time. Little by little you'll feel less rigidly attached to your thoughts in daily life. Try it and see.

that you hadn't considered. I've learned over time to pay more attention to that anxiety in my gut that's really trying to tell me: "Wake up. Something's off here. Get your bearings straight." When I slow down to acknowledge it, it usually helps me remember what my true aim is and how I might accomplish it. This recently happened when I set out for the airport one Friday afternoon, proud that I'd given myself plenty of time to park my car and board the plane. It would be a short flight to San Luis Obispo, about 250 miles south, where I was going to teach a retreat.

Two hours after leaving home, I was still creeping along in traffic that had turned the freeway into a parking lot. It would be a close call, but I was still confident I'd make the flight. I had my pre-printed boarding pass, no baggage to check, and a good book to read. I was all set. When I finally got to the airport, thinking I'd made it just in the nick of time, the parking garage was full. The attendant directed me to a lot at some distant location, and anxiety kicked in. The signs were not marked clearly enough for my nervous eyes, and I ended up circling the airport three times, sure I'd stumbled upon the Bermuda Triangle of parking lots. I was getting more agitated by the moment. *They've been planning this retreat for a year. Fifty people will be very disappointed. I've got to get there.*

My pleasant little journey was turning into a real mess—until suddenly I realized I was simply not going to make the plane. The moment I let go of my idea of what should be happening and accepted the situation exactly as it was, the agitation and stress went away, making way for a new idea. *Wait a moment. This car I'm trying so desperately to park can actually take me there.* I felt waves of happiness as I turned out of the airport and onto the freeway, heading south. I spent the next five hours singing along with my favorite songs, enjoying my own company, with no email, chores, or tasks to be done. And I arrived at the retreat feeling happy and at ease.

My husband and I have been working on letting go of taking offense when no offense was intended. Example: 'Why did you put that there? No offense. I'm not saying you are stupid for putting it there. I'm just curious.' Letting go of the need to be right is wonderfully freeing.

—A COURSE PARTICIPANT

When you let go of how you think things should be, you can respond to challenging situations with openness and flexibility, imagining options and alternatives that can't arise in a contracted mind. We may have a tendency to see ourselves as the center of the world, but life manages to remind us that it's otherwise. Recognizing that you are just one part of an interacting system with others who have their own reality can be a great relief.

The ability to let go is critical in relationships because that's where we find ourselves continually coming up against the fact that things just aren't always the way we want them to be. Especially with those closest to us, it's easy to fall into habits of reaction when they don't conform to what we expect. Pamela was exploring what letting go meant as part of the Awakening Joy course when the perfect opportunity arose to try it out. One particular morning she woke up in a peaceful state, feeling full of gratitude. But when she went to the kitchen and opened the refrigerator, she saw that a bowl of chicken broth she was saving for soup had been tipped over and was dripping into the vegetable bins and onto the floor. "I knew my husband had done it while looking for a late-night snack," she wrote. "I felt the anger rise in me, along with the usual grumbling, as I went to get paper towels to clean up the mess." But then another possible response occurred to Pamela:

> I realized I could let go of all of that and, in fact, that was what I wanted to do. I cleaned up the mess and didn't say a word to my husband. It was not a stifling or even an *effort*—those feelings were just gone. I was grateful for my husband, grateful for the abundance of food in my refrigerator, grateful to be able to get up in the morning, to be alive and well, to see how inconsequential the mess was. After that little bout of turbulence, my mind had returned to that clear and serene state I'd awoken in, just from choosing to let go of my usual reaction. Beautiful!

Pamela could have responded in a number of other ways, but the point for her was letting go of a state of mind that would have left her, and likely her husband as well, feeling closed down and unhappy. If your intention is to be genuinely happy, you may find yourself shifting around some priorities. When you see yourself with the fisted hand in the coconut, you know how to get out of the trap.

WHAT STORY AM I BELIEVING RIGHT NOW?

One evening during the break at an Awakening Joy class, I heard a cheerful voice which I soon connected to the middle-aged man buoyantly striding down the aisle to greet me. "James, I have to tell you something!" When he came closer, I could see it was Daniel, the accountant I had seen once for spiritual counseling, who was now taking the course. "It worked!" he beamed. "And I just want to say thank you." ·

He must have known by the look on my face that I was sorting through my memory bank to find out *what* had "worked."

He reminded me of the time months ago when he had asked for my advice about reacting negatively to feedback from his wife. Whenever she'd suggest something, he'd take it as criticism. "I know she loves me and means well," he told me at the time, "but my mind says, 'There she goes again, trying to control me,' and I withdraw and get distant. I can see I'm being reactive, but I can't seem to do anything about it."

"What would you need to change inside so that you wouldn't react so quickly?" I'd asked him.

"If I didn't jump to those negative conclusions, I'd probably be much better off. But they're so deeply ingrained that I don't think it's possible to change."

I could see that Daniel had convinced himself of a particular way of looking at himself and his relationship. This was the story he told himself, over and over. Stories of some kind are happening all the time in our mind. They arise from our past experiences, and are reinforced through associations with present experiences. Mostly they go on outside our conscious control. A song from your teenage years comes on the radio, and there you are back at your first kiss. A bird chirping outside your window carries you to some idyllic place in your mind . . . or reminds you that you're stuck behind your desk all day. The reaction is automatic.

Even a single word can activate a stream of associations and emotional responses. Pause for a moment when you read this next word: *Trouble.* Notice if any particular images or memories associated with that word arise. Are there any particular feelings in your body? Maybe tightness or heaviness? Now take a few breaths to erase "trouble" from your mind, and pause when you read this next word: *Kindness.* Any images or associations? How does your body feel? Light or spacious?

If a single word can tangibly affect the mind and body, imagine the effect of the full-blown stories we carry around. Some of our stories are healthy and inspiring and contribute to our well-being. *I deserve to enjoy my life because I'm doing good things in the world, I'm kind to myself and others, and I'm learning to be open to the joy when it arises.* Or you might tell yourself: *Exercising regularly and eating well helps me live up to my full potential.* As we have seen, the more you feed these kinds of positive beliefs and conclusions, the more likely you are to be happy.

It's the negative stories that become a problem. You find yourself in a funk, and you feel compelled to explain why it's happening. There could be lots of reasons, but often the mind goes toward those based in fear or disaster. Patricia Ellsberg talks about how she sometimes wakes up in the night with feelings of free-floating anxiety or sadness. Immediately she wants to figure out why. She says:

> The stories may be different at different times, but they almost always make me feel worse, as I perseverate over why I feel this way or how I can get rid of the feelings. And the more I resist or try to escape from them, the more they persist. Most of the time the bad feelings just go away, especially if I just accept them with kindness. But if I had persisted with the story, I could have been caught in them all day.

The stories that limit you or free you are really all in your mind, and you can change them. I often give students a "prescription" to help in the process. Sometimes I write it down on a piece of paper and suggest they carry it in their wallet. "Whenever you find yourself getting reactive, withdrawn, or confused," I tell them, "remember that you have a prescription in your pocket that will relieve your pain." The prescription

I write? "What thought or story am I believing right now?"

That was the prescription I'd given Daniel, all those months ago, when he'd come to see me for that counseling session. He had taken the medicine, and it had worked. "I still get caught," he said, "but when I remember to ask myself what story I'm believing, it makes all the difference in my relationship with Jean. We're getting along better than ever."

LETTING GO OF STORIES THAT LIMIT US

Some of our most debilitating stories—those that limit our capacity to live full, rich lives—have their roots in our childhood. During our early experiences, we came to conclusions about ourselves and about life, and until we become conscious of these conclusions, they secretly control us. This was so clearly what Marian was caught up in when she came to talk to me during a meditation retreat I was teaching many years ago. I had known Marian for some time, and in all my interactions with her, she'd always seemed cheerful, and I'd sensed a genuine warmth. So I was a little surprised by what she started telling me when she came in for her scheduled interview.

"I know now why I don't feel love, for myself or anyone else," she began. "I've known why for years, and it's about time I just face the fact that that's the way it's going to be."

"What do you think the reason is?" I asked, aware of how isolated and alone she must be feeling.

"It's because I was never loved as a child. My parents were not emotionally available, and there was no model for me to learn how to love. So, of course I'm incapable of giving or receiving love as an adult. I think at this point it's too late in my life to change the pattern. That's how I'm wired."

Although I could see Marian was convinced

Several times a day I've been asking myself that question: 'What story am I believing right now?' especially when my energy is low. For example, is this the story about how I have way too much to do and always feel tired and never get a break? Or is this the story about how I deserve to kick back and relax after a good day's work? Is this the story about how my body isn't perfect and my sister is thinner than I am? Or is this the story about how I've been working out consistently for two years now and actually feel pretty cute in those jeans I like?

—A COURSE PARTICIPANT

of her story, I didn't buy it. Obviously she wasn't seeing something in herself that others were. And I was sure she had been loved by someone.

"Was there no one in your life when you were growing up who showed you love?" I asked.

"No one," she sadly replied.

"Marian, perhaps it's true that you've never been loved. If so, I'm terribly sorry. It seems that this belief about your childhood has had a big effect on you for some time." She nodded, sorrow written all over her face. "But before we assume that's so," I continued, "I want you to think back to see if there was *ever anyone* who loved you as a child. Close your eyes and take your time. Think of all the teachers, relatives, friends from your past. Was there anyone from whom you received kindness?"

After about a minute of holding fast to her position, Marian's face started to relax and then brightened into a smile. "Oh my! There was someone," she said sheepishly. "My brother. I never counted him, but he was really always there for me."

I grew up in a culture where women were supposed to get married and have children. Every morning, I would wake up with a voice in my head that told me I was a woman who had not been chosen. My mum and my sister have said some very indirect unkind things to me around that. This morning, I woke up and answered back. I said, 'That is a story I don't have to believe.' I realized that my mum and sister have been repeating the story that someone told them. I appreciate the freedom of naming it.

—A COURSE PARTICIPANT

"Do you think he loved you?"

She paused; then, speaking slowly, she said, "Now that I think of it, he always stuck up for me and wanted me to be happy. I guess he really did love me."

"Well, I guess you'll have to change the story that you were never loved," I said softly.

With that, Marian began to sob, realizing she could let go of the limiting belief that had kept her from recognizing that she was capable of loving. Fifteen years later she still speaks of that moment as the beginning of seeing herself as the loving person she clearly is. It was also the beginning of a profound transformation toward real well-being and joy in her life.

Recognizing the stories you're caught in is the first and major step in freeing yourself of their power. Building on that insight is what supported Marian in making a real change in her life.

You can't just say "abracadabra" and change such deep and long-abiding stories. Therapy, retreats, and other forms of self-exploration all help in changing beliefs and behaviors that undermine our happiness.

TRYING OUT A NEW STORY

It's true that Marian didn't receive as much love as she deserved or would have liked, but that doesn't have to define who she is nor fuel the belief that she *never* received love. In paying attention to misleading beliefs, watch for the words *always* and *never*. Those non-provisional words keep us locked into one perspective. Like the proverbial blind men, each trying to say what an elephant is based on the one small part they are in touch with, we take one part of our experience and proclaim it to be the whole truth.

While getting a broader perspective on your past doesn't change it, it

---

Letting Go of Your Story

The negative stories we tell ourselves are a major source of our suffering. Take some time to reflect on and write down responses to the following questions:

- ▸ What story do you believe about yourself or others that keeps you from experiencing well-being and joy?
- ▸ When you think of this story as being true, how do you experience it in your body and mind?
- ▸ Imagine for a moment what it would be like if you took it as just a story, didn't believe it, and could let it go. How does it feel in your body and mind when you do that?

Whenever you find yourself getting caught in an inner struggle, ask yourself, "What story am I believing right now?" You might even write that question on a piece of paper and carry it in your wallet. Pay attention to how you feel each time you let go of the story.

does allow you to be less controlled by a story that no longer serves you. I discovered this in the midst of a dark time in my early twenties. Lying in my bed in the wee hours of a February morning, I was contemplating the sorry state of my life. Things never worked out for me, it seemed, and people didn't like me—well, certain people . . . namely, *girls.* (That's what we used to call women at that time.) I was listening to my favorite alternative FM radio station, and the soothing voice of deejay John Zacherley began to ease my troubled mind. He was telling me and the rest of his 2:00 a.m. audience to remember that, even though life is sometimes hard, we're all fortunate to be alive and why not make the best of it while we're here? Then, as if to underscore his point, he followed his words with a cut from the song "You Can All Join In" by the rock group Traffic. It was as if the lyrics were sent to me from above as a healing message:

> Make your own life up if you want to
> Any old life that you think will do.

Could I really make up "any old life" that I thought would do? What would that look like? And how could I get out of the life I was stuck in? Contemplating my predicament, I picked up a pad of paper and started doodling. I found myself drawing a circle, around and around, and suddenly realized that this was an image of exactly how I was stuck. I was putting out to others the message: *I'm a loser. I'm not likable. You don't want to waste your time with me.* What did I expect would come back to me from that line of thinking? Prom King?

What if I did make a different life? One where I believed things would work out, where girls would like me, where I was lovable and, as the Traffic song went on to say, could make a difference in the lives of others by just being myself? I watched as my hand drew a tangent off that endless circle, moved across the paper, and started an entirely new circle. I began to imagine what it would look and feel like to know I was lovable and that people actually enjoyed being around me. In my mind's eye there was an image of me radiating positive energy, and I could feel the experience completely filling my body. It was a landmark moment.

I made up my mind to try an experiment. For the next week I would

Letting Go of the Soap Opera

"One area where we tend to hold on is that of our personal story, the running narrative that tells you who and what you are. We rehearse it and habituate to it as the character we know ourselves to be. We wake up in the morning, and here comes the story, like a long-running soap opera. One of the easy ways to begin letting go is to notice how debilitating it is to be carrying this story, to be obsessed with the wants and desires, the loves and the hates of this character. Simply notice how contracted that story feels, how old and tired it feels.

One of the ways you let go is to stop paying so much attention to everything that is arising and passing in the mind. Then you start to become more and more interested in just being right here, in the freshness of now. And you start to feel more and more a mystery to yourself. As you stop giving yourself a narrative, you become more and more of a surprise to your own self. You experience yourself as a vibrancy, a floating awareness, sometimes as an emanation of love or curiosity or wonder. This becomes so delightful that it's very easy to become disinterested in all the neurotic material and extraneous thought."

—CATHERINE INGRAM
AT AWAKENING JOY COURSE, BERKELEY, 2008

project the image of that confident, lovable young man I had just met inside me. I would let go of the story that things wouldn't work out and try a new one. What did I have to lose?

During that week I discovered that exuding confidence and assuming the best would happen made me less preoccupied with wanting validation from others; and what's more, I was able to actually be interested in who they were for themselves. This, of course, made them able to feel more at ease with me and enjoy my presence. Although it would take lots more work to fully embody this new way of perceiving my life, I had opened the door of my self-imposed prison.

Once we let go of the limiting stories we've created about ourselves, a whole new world of possibilities opens to us. The old stories may still come up from time to time—those constellations of thoughts and beliefs carry the momentum of years of practice. Even though the stories are dysfunctional, because they're comfortable in their familiarity, we tend to hold on to them. But with mindful attention, over time the healthier perspectives can get integrated and lead us in a new direction.

THE JOY OF GENEROSITY

Generosity is an active form of letting go, and it is a sure avenue to happiness. You're not only giving away something, you're connecting lovingly with others through the act of sharing. The Buddha actually recommended that when you are in the midst of a generous act, say to yourself: "I am being generous." This is not to build your ego but rather to "gladden the heart" as you reflect on the good feeling that accompanies a wholesome action.

Generosity not only releases the hold of the wanting mind, but also recognizes our interconnectedness. What you share of yourself and your resources deepens your connection with others. No matter what may separate you in time and space, the wholesome bond of generosity endures. If you take a look around your house, you are likely to see evidence of that generosity everywhere. Every time I use the ceramic cups Jane and I received as wedding gifts, I think of our friends Roger and Frances. And there are doubtless a number of households where you are present through what you've given.

One of the best ways to develop a generous heart is by stretching it a little. Sheryl, a participant in the Awakening Joy course, said that most of her life she'd thought of herself as stingy, holding back in situations where she felt something was needed or asked of her. But as she became aware of how small and closed down this was making her feel, she decided to follow a suggestion from the course and see what it would be like to respond by giving when the situation arose.

The big breakthrough in her experiment happened during an appointment she had for a massage. Her massage therapist, Consuela, was supporting her two kids as a single mom and had just returned from Colombia where she was visiting her own mother who was dying of cancer. As she and Sheryl talked, Consuela said she hoped she might get back there in a few months to see her one more time. Sheryl asked if the airfare was expensive. Consuela said she wanted to do it anyway, even if she had to put it on a credit card. Sheryl writes:

> I thought of all the frequent flyer miles I'd accumulated and decided right in that moment that I wanted to use them to buy her a ticket. I felt so excited to be able to do this. When I told her my idea, she started to cry with gratitude. Doing this has filled me with so much joy. That day ranks up there with some of the best moments of my life. I still feel a fullness in my heart when I remember doing it. I'm seeing how good it feels to give. I love it!

When we give to others—whether a beautiful or useful object, our time, or a word of encouragement—we get at least as much as we give. Jesus said: "Give and it will be given to you; a good measure, pressed down, shaken together, and running over will be poured into your lap" (Luke 6:38). This is a beautiful image of abundance when you imagine the overflowing measure of grain he was talking about. When we give to others, we don't get back an equal amount, we get back in abundance. You may have to let go of certain expectations to receive back in kind—you may give someone beautiful objects, and the recipient may give you back love in other forms. If you look for the joy inside yourself in the act of giving, your reward is already in good measure.

The value of giving is one of the underpinnings of Tibetan culture, in which generosity and happiness are seen as two sides of a single coin. Each winter thousands of Tibetans, in exile from their land, travel to the village of Bodhgaya, India, to the site where the Buddha attained enlightenment. There they have the opportunity to hear their spiritual leader, the Dalai Lama, speak specifically to them. Knowing how deeply

Feeling Generous

For one week let yourself act on each generous impulse when it arises. Be aware of the various sensations in your body and the thoughts in your mind as you take action. When you walk your dog, let yourself feel what you are giving. When you open the door for someone, feel the wholesomeness of the impulse. If any limiting thoughts arise, just mindfully notice them without judgment. Breathe into your heart and let go to the spirit of generosity. Pay attention to the good feelings that accompany contributing to the well-being of another. Feel the joy of generosity.

---

ingrained the quality of generosity is in these pilgrims, the beggars in this poorest area of India also converge on the village. I have seen even the neediest Tibetans there happily stretch to share what they have, more readily in fact than most of the well-heeled Westerners who visit. A common Buddhist teaching is that if you knew the value of giving, you would not partake of even a small morsel of food without sharing some of it. Deeply understanding this, these pilgrims see their generosity not as a sacrifice but as a source of happiness.

We can consciously develop the quality of generosity. The Buddhist scriptures speak of three kinds of giving. Step by step, they point the way to increasing happiness through opening the heart. The first is known as "beggarly giving." Perhaps you have something in your closet which has been gathering dust for eons and, after some deliberation, you finally decide to pass it on. Even though it's clearing some space for new clothes, you still feel a twinge of concern that you might need it some day yourself. The second kind of generosity is called "friendly giving." You have enough of something you value, or it wouldn't really hurt to let go of something you enjoy using, so you give it to someone. This giving is rather fun and easy with no feeling of sacrifice. The most noble generos-

Receiving Generously

Be sure to include yourself in your generosity practice. If you feel too depleted to be generous with others, take that as a cue to take time to nourish yourself. Whenever anyone is generous or thoughtful with you, receive their kindness fully and graciously. When you know yourself how good it feels to be generous, you can remember that by receiving you're allowing that other person to experience the joy of giving.

ity is called "kingly or queenly giving." You give what you prize highly, even if it's a sacrifice on your part. It's the kind of generosity I've seen in some cultures when I've traveled. I learned quickly not to admire objects or articles of clothing, because no matter how poor the owner, I was likely to be the immediate recipient.

In practicing generosity, the teachings suggest starting wherever you are on this continuum. If you're cleaning out your closet to give things to Goodwill, and you're berating yourself for being a "beggarly giver," you can instead tune in to the positive feeling of sharing something someone else might need. If you are obligated to volunteer time at your kids' school, even if it's a burden, perhaps you can discover the moments when you do feel good about what you're contributing. Little by little, as you focus on how good it feels to give, you reinforce and strengthen the power of generosity. Remember, however, to be kind to yourself and give in ways appropriate to your resources.

GIVING TO LIFE

The Buddha had a number of wealthy patrons who were earnest spiritual seekers. One of them, Anathapindika, listened carefully as the great teacher taught his monks about the virtues of letting go of attachment to worldly goods. Moved by this idea yet puzzled, the rich man went to the Buddha and asked if he should give up all his wealth, renounce the world, and become a monk. The Buddha replied, "A person who possesses riches and uses them wisely is a blessing to humanity," encouraging Anathapindika to honor his own destiny. You don't have to give away all your material wealth in order to be generous. You can use it in such a way that you become a channel for good. The Gates Foundation has done a tremendous amount of good, primarily by enhancing health and education around the world. If Bill and Melinda had decided to become monks, all that good might not have happened.

Whether we have great material wealth or very little, we all have personal wealth beyond material goods. Psychologist Martin Seligman makes the point that true happiness comes from understanding our strengths and sharing them with the world. He refers to traits such as enthusiasm, diligence, and leadership as "signature strengths" we can offer.

Whatever talents or skills we have, sharing them is an important form of generosity—and one that requires letting go of the false stories that may hold us back. As Marianne Williamson so aptly puts it in her book *A Return to Love:*

> We ask ourselves, who am I to be brilliant, gorgeous, talented, fabulous? Actually, who are you *not* to be? You are a child of God. Your playing small does not serve the world.

Sharing any of our gifts is a form of generosity that multiplies beyond what we might even imagine. Williamson sums it up: "As we are liberated from our own fear, our presence automatically liberates others."

When you let go of all the ifs, ands, and buts that keep you from doing what you're called to do, you can step into the joy of giving freely of what you have to offer from your own unique resources. In this way, as the Buddhist sage Shantideva says, you can be "lifted above poverty into the wealth of giving to life."

As we've seen, there are many dimensions of letting go that lead to a joyful heart. Letting go is a shift toward simplicity, uncomplicating our mental and physical environment—releasing what we don't truly need, like material stuff, crowded schedules, expectations, stories that don't serve us. Experiencing this letting go, this cleaning out, brings a great sense of well-being. We see how good it feels not only to put down the extra burden but to share what we have. Letting go is like weeding. When you get rid of the weeds, it makes room for more of the beauty to be seen and enjoyed. In the same way, when we let go of our extra stuff—whether material or mental clutter—it gives space for our creativity and full potential to flower.

Let It Go

Let go of the ways you thought life would unfold;
the holding of plans or dreams or expectations—Let it all go.
Save your strength to swim with the tide.
The choice to fight what is here before you now
will only result in struggle, fear, and desperate attempts to flee
from the very energy you long for. Let it go.

Let it all go and flow with the grace
that washes through your days
whether you receive it gently
or with all your quills raised to defend against invaders.
Take this on faith: The mind may never find
the explanations that it seeks,
but you will move forward nonetheless.

Let go, and the wave's crest
will carry you to unknown shores,
beyond your wildest dreams or destinations.
Let it all go and find the place of rest and peace,
and certain transformation.

—DANNA FAULDS, FROM *Go In and In*

Step 7

The Sweetness of Loving Ourselves

Searching all directions with one's awareness,
one finds no one dearer than oneself.

—THE BUDDHA
THE RAJA SUTTA

WHEN I WAS a child, a strange fantasy troubled me from time to time. I imagined myself before birth, along with countless souls on rows of shelves, waiting to be selected for life on Earth. A giant hand—of God or His right-hand assistant—was reaching out for the soul next to me but by mistake plucked me up instead. So I was the ultimate fraud, not meant to be here at all, making it only by accident. Each time this image arose, I was left haunted by the feeling that I would be found out and sent back.

Although I grew up in a loving home, inside I often felt lonely and afraid. Being the quiet one in a family of extroverts didn't help calm my fears. My sister was very pretty with a sparkling personality and wit that lit up a room. By contrast, I was chubby, wore glasses, and was shy and insecure. A familiar childhood memory is of watching my father, mother, and sister all boisterously engaged in witty repartee. Many a time, I would quietly mumble a contribution to the conversation, no one would seem to notice, and I would retreat into the bathroom in tears, wondering why no one listened to me.

As a teenager I had such a poor self-image that I actually winced when I looked in the mirror. Adults called me "cute," which was the last thing

I wanted to hear. My sister kindly tried to assure me that I'd be fine and well-liked, but I wasn't convinced. No matter how much positive feedback I received from others, fear of being exposed as "not good enough" remained a familiar companion into my early adulthood. I felt like a loser with no chance of turning into the hip guy I dreamed of being. In short, I didn't like myself. If somebody had told me it was possible to truly love myself, I wouldn't have believed it.

In my experience of working with thousands of students and clients, rarely have I encountered those who easily love themselves. Most commonly I hear: "If only I were . . . " followed by some variation of "thinner, stronger, kinder, smarter, calmer, more successful." Our assessment of ourselves is usually in comparison to others or to some ideal or standard we've adopted. If we have curly hair, we want straight; blue eyes, we want brown. If we tend to be quiet, we wish we were the life of the party. If we have a short fuse, we're convinced we'd be lovable if only we were calm and patient. On top of assessing ourselves as falling short, we add yet another layer of suffering. We close our heart to ourselves. This is the predicament we're often stuck in: We resist accepting ourselves as we are, yet this is what we've got. We can't be somebody else, no matter how hard we try.

In my early years of teaching meditation, giving talks alongside some of the wisest and most gifted teachers left me wracked with painful comparisons. Joseph Goldstein would inspire the students with depth, wisdom, and clarity. Then Jack Kornfield would weave his magic spell, enchanting and moving them with poignant stories and stirring words. Sharon Salzberg would bring them to tears with her guided loving-kindness meditations. Then it would be my turn. I knew full well that if I was a student, I would be wishing this kid would get off the stage so that the senior teachers could speak again.

In desperation I tracked down my sometime-mentor Ram Dass to see if he had any advice. He did. "Don't try to be another Joseph Goldstein," he said. "There already is one. Just be the best Jamie Baraz you can be. There's only one of those, and you're it. What if you just let yourself be who you are and see what you have to offer those students? Who knows? You may even like what you see."

There's only one of *you*, and if you let yourself be the best one of

You're the One

Imagine meeting someone who laughs at all your jokes, has similar tastes, and really grasps your take on things. This person understands all your hopes and fears. In short, this is someone who really *gets you*. How would you feel? Probably ecstatic! There is only one person in this world who completely fits that description, and he or she is right inside your own skin. This is someone you can learn to love.

yourself possible, you may also like what you see. In time you may even love yourself.

For many of us, the idea of loving ourselves may seem out of reach. But if you know how to love someone else, you have what it takes to love yourself. Think about what it's like to love someone. For instance, when I think of our son Adam my heart naturally begins to open. I become aware of that distinct combination of traits I sense as his essence—his insatiable curiosity about how the mind works, his mischievous spirit, the "edge" as he calls it that is a counterbalance to his tenderness, his charming personality, the genuine goodness that radiates from his heart. Even the quirky traits that sometimes drive me crazy can seem endearing when I hold them in the broader context of his goodness and potential. If I were to focus only on the negative, I would lose touch with all the amazingly good stuff. My love for him is there no matter what. The secret is to offer this same kind of love to ourselves—to love and accept the whole package.

The capacity to accept and love ourselves doesn't necessarily happen quickly or easily. Those negative voices from siblings, teachers, sixth-grade bullies, and disenchanted lovers still play in our mind. No matter how much positive reflection we've had, our brains are "like Velcro for negative experiences," as Rick Hanson puts it. Even seemingly insignificant events can leave deep impressions that color our self-concept and our ability to embrace who we are.

Learning to love yourself is a process that evolves over time. It begins with letting go of self-criticism and forgiving yourself for being who you are. In Step Five, we looked at forgiving ourselves for past actions and the confusion that produced them. Here we are forgiving ourselves for habits and behaviors we continue to get caught in that are less than wholesome. We forgive our bodies for how they look or for how they function; forgive our minds for being scattered or not being smart enough; forgive our personalities for not being witty or interesting enough.

As you stop focusing on what you don't appreciate and start seeing yourself as a unique, mysterious, changing being, you allow your best self to shine through. And the joy of that radiates out to the world.

CATCHING LOVE

Meher Baba, the great Indian master, says, "Love is essentially self-communicative; those who do not have it catch it from those who have it." Our capacity to love is awakened in us through having received love from others. Even if we're convinced we've never known the experience of love, as Marian in the previous chapter believed, for very few of us is that true. Most of us—even those who had to build personal defenses in order to survive fearful circumstances in childhood—somewhere along the way received love from someone, whether that was a parent, a caring teacher, a kind relative, or a loyal pet. But until we are willing to recognize and accept that love, we block our capacity to give it to ourselves.

For me, a turning point in my ability to "catch love," and really take it in, happened during one of those "experiences" common in the sixties. I was in my apartment in Flushing, New York, and it was 1969, the height of the psychedelic revolution. Like so many in that era, I was seeking change, release from the pain of being me. I longed to belong to something bigger, something filled with love and joy, and the social-spiritual revolution of the counterculture gave me hope. In that era, before meditation and other more grounded ways to explore the mind had entered our culture, chemistry seemed to hold the key to what I was looking for.

One evening, without a great deal of thought or preparation, I "dropped acid," eager to find out where it would take me. Unfortunately, that was to the brink of hell. While this experience was a turning point in my life, I would say it was a dicey strategy for transformation. Compared to others I know, I was very lucky. I managed to return from hell—but I didn't do it alone, and that opened me to an important revelation.

That night I wouldn't have been able to put my private nightmare into words, but looking back I remember that everything—inside and outside—was spinning around so fast that there was no ground anywhere. I was in uncharted territory with no guidance or wisdom to draw upon. I felt like I was teetering on the edge of the Void, about to be overwhelmed by something horrifying and incomprehensible. I knew I was about to lose my mind. When people talk about "abject terror," I can honestly say I know what that is like.

Not knowing if anyone could hear me, I started screaming for help, and my roommate and his girlfriend, who were in the next room, arrived as my saviors. Taking my hands, they sat on either side of me for what felt like an eternity.

"Don't leave me! Don't leave me!" I'd cry out from time to time.

"It's okay. We aren't going anywhere," they'd tell me again and again.

As they kept assuring me that they were present and would stay, something unfamiliar began to happen inside me: I let myself gradually open to their caring and attention. Instead of feeling awkward and unworthy, I let myself take in the warmth and support they were offering. At some point the thought occurred to me that here were two people I knew and respected, taking their time to be with me. At that, something switched inside me, the resistance stopped, and the love and connection began to feel natural. Even more remarkable, I stopped feeling like I didn't deserve it—a radical turnaround for me.

The next day, after the impact of the drug had worn off, I was faced with a sobering but delightful insight: For the first time in my life I directly questioned my belief that something was wrong with me and that I was unlovable. If that was true, then how could these friends have cared so much?

Taking in the love of my friends actually awakened a little love inside me for myself. Later that day when I passed by the hallway mirror, I stopped to take a look at the person reflected there. I still wasn't exactly thrilled at what I saw, but something was different in the way I was reacting to that image. A tiny smile seemed to hold the faint message that maybe I wasn't so bad after all. Maybe there was something there to at least *like* a little bit. That was the beginning.

SHIFTING THE FOCUS

All of us can find something in ourselves to at least *like*, but it may be a long step from like to love. What's the difference and how do we take that step? Over the course of a few years I've watched a young woman, Alexa, gradually make that shift. I first met her when she came in for a scheduled interview during a meditation retreat. I was immediately struck by her vitality and sparkle. When Alexa told me she'd been in theater, I could easily imagine her feeling at home in the limelight. I had no idea, at the time, of the pain that accompanied her enjoyment of being on stage. As Alexa continued working with me as her meditation teacher and spiritual counselor, I came to understand how deeply self-judgment had penetrated her life.

Over the next few years, as part of her healing process, Alexa kept a journal and eventually wrote a thesis for her master's degree tracking her journey. There she reflected:

> I'm realizing that all my life I've compared myself to everyone else. Fatter, prettier, smarter, more creative, less intuitive, the list goes on and on. I have hated myself so much that I've clung to make-believe personas and addictive substances and behaviors. Anything to avoid the depths of my self-hatred.

Alexa told me she hadn't always felt that way. Until she was seven years old, her childhood had been "silly and sacred." But when her parents divorced, she was left with "an emptiness I couldn't name. I began to do what most people in our culture do. I began to search for ways to fill the empty void." Part of that meant turning to food for comfort, which didn't really work.

"I began to view my body as my enemy," Alexa wrote in her journals, "and as the years leading up to high school went on, my self-loathing worsened." Unless she weighed one hundred pounds and looked like a Calvin Klein model, she hated her body. Unless she got top grades in classes, she concluded she wasn't smart enough. Less than the starring role in a play must mean she wasn't talented. By the end of her freshman year in high school, Alexa was so stressed and felt like such a failure that she began to binge and purge, and starve herself. Always a litany of self-judgment ran through her mind: *I hate my stomach, I'm too aggressive, I'm always depressed, I loathe myself.*

You might not feel as self-deprecating as Alexa, but perhaps you have your own litany of perceived shortcomings. Maybe you feel shame at how impatient you are with your partner or child. Or your face is covered with acne. Or the brilliance of a friend or colleague leaves you feeling worthless in comparison. From there you can easily build up a case against yourself and end up, like Alexa, focusing only on what's wrong.

The good news is: We don't have to like everything about ourselves in order to love ourselves. Ajahn Sumedho, the American who became a monk in Thailand, says that as you learn to love yourself, you don't have to "pretend to feel approval toward your faults." You just don't want to "dwell in aversion to them." Instead of getting caught up in judgment and self-hatred, which only feeds a negative state of mind, you can begin by shifting your focus to more positive ways of regarding yourself. For Alexa that kind of shift was the beginning of opening to let the love in.

As the retreat went on, one morning Alexa came in for an interview, looking dejected and hopeless. "I know I'm supposed to be practicing kindness toward myself," she began, "but I just can't pretend I love my body. I don't. I wish it were different. And I feel so stupid that I just can't get past that."

I knew that feeling very well myself and the prison she felt locked in.

"Alexa," I said softly, "you don't have to pretend anything, but if you focus only on what you don't like, you cut yourself off from seeing all the beauty and goodness that are also part of you."

I shared with her one of my favorite stories that my colleague Jack Kornfield likes to tell. The Babemba people in southern Africa have an approach to dealing with the personal shortcomings of tribal members. When someone acts recklessly, he or she is brought before all the villagers. Everyone stops working and gathers around for a ceremony that can typically go on for days. As Jack tells it in his book *The Art of Forgiveness:*

> Then each person in the tribe speaks to the accused, one at a time, each recalling the good things the person in the center of the circle has done in his lifetime. Every incident, every experience that can be recalled with any detail and accuracy, is recounted. All his positive attributes, good deeds, strengths, and kindnesses are recited carefully and at length.

When the ceremony has ended, everyone celebrates and embraces the person as once again part of the tribe.

When I finished with the story, Alexa remained silent and thoughtful. After a few moments, I said, "What if you were to do some version of that for yourself and shift the focus to all the good things there are to appreciate about yourself?"

I asked her to close her eyes and let an image come to mind of herself just as she is.

"Now let yourself be one of those villagers and tell Alexa all the good things she has done in her brief lifetime. And tell her about all the good qualities you see in her." After a few minutes I could see a tenderness come over Alexa's face. Tears flowed down her cheeks as she spoke.

"She's so sweet, and she just wants to see everyone happy. She's kind, and she's creative."

"Let yourself take in those good feelings, and when those thoughts of hating your body arise, see if you can shift the focus just a tiny bit. As you practice this perspective, you might begin to see this person as worthy of your love."

Giving Genuine and Effective Appreciation

"Saying to yourself, 'You're wonderful. You're great,' may not be the most effective way of loving yourself. A little voice inside says: 'Not always,' and underneath there's a gnawing feeling that you'll get found out. Effectively appreciating yourself is about acknowledging the specifics of *how* you are great. The more specific you can be about what you appreciate, the more you get in touch with the gifts you have to offer others and the resources you have to tackle challenges.

"In her book *Mindset,* Stanford University psychologist Carol Dweck talks about what she calls a 'growth mindset' in contrast to a 'fixed mindset.' When we say, 'I'm so great and wonderful,' we are encouraging a fixed mindset, which means we believe we're supposed to know it all already. Therefore we give up easily when faced with a challenge. We avoid negative criticism that might be helpful. We negatively compare ourselves to others. When we hear about amazing people doing amazing things, we feel worse. We end up looking at what's wrong with ourselves instead of what we appreciate.

"With a growth mindset, when you're faced with a challenge, you say to yourself, 'I'm still learning. I may not do this perfectly, but I'm learning how to do it.' When we hear criticism, we say, 'Thanks for letting me know, because I can get better based on what you're telling me.' We're inspired by people who are doing great things, 'because they're giving me something to go toward. I can try to do that too.' As a result, people with a growth mindset tend to reach more of their potential.

"If you want to appreciate yourself, or encourage others to appreciate themselves, this is what you can do: *Praise efforts, choices, and strategies,* and do it with specifics. When you do this, you're telling the brain: 'Do more of this. This is important, remember this in the future.' You're learning a lot of strategies in the Awakening Joy course. Whenever you use one of them, appreciate yourself, remind your brain, so you can continue to choose good strategies in the future."

—M. J. RYAN, AUTHOR OF *Attitudes of Gratitude*
AT AWAKENING JOY COURSE, BERKELEY, 2008

Even the tiniest opening of seeing the goodness in ourselves can begin to break through a lifetime of self-judgment. By inclining our mind toward looking for what is good and wholesome in us, we stop feeding the negative and start bringing our positive qualities to life. As we do this, we cultivate a new way of regarding ourselves, so that over time the old voices inside that belittle us are replaced by others that are kind and supportive.

PLANTING SEEDS OF LOVE FOR OURSELVES

One of the participants in the online Awakening Joy course wrote: "What I truly want to feel is the love of a holy person, like Dipa Ma, a love so vast it can forgive and embrace every storm everywhere." Dipa Ma was a simple and renowned meditator and spiritual teacher living in Calcutta. She radiated such a powerful field of compassion that in her presence one did feel loved without limit. But this great teacher herself would say that we are all capable of such love. If we are to be the ones to give this kind of love to ourselves, rather than waiting for someone else to come along and do it, how do we begin?

As Dipa Ma taught, the capacity to love that is inherent in every

Seeing What You Like

Spend a little time in front of a mirror, looking deeply at the image you see reflected there. Notice any judgments or habitual reactions that may arise. Instead of believing or feeding them, just acknowledge them and let them go. In a heartfelt way, say aloud or to yourself at least three specific good qualities you know you have. For instance you might say, "You really care about others," or "You're a terrific dancer." Don't try too hard. Even a glimpse of self-appreciation is a good start. As you acknowledge your positive attributes, notice the feelings that arise in your body and mind. Be sure to pause and take them in.

one of us can be awakened and developed through the practice of lovingkindness or *metta,* which refers to a state of mind that radiates kindness, wishing well without wanting anything in return. It helps you awaken love when you're not feeling it, and deepen and amplify it when you are. We begin with ourselves and continue opening our hearts to eventually include all beings. Traditionally, the practice is done in meditation, directing loving thoughts to ourselves or others by silently repeating certain phrases. Typical phrases for sending lovingkindness to ourselves include: *May I be happy, May I be peaceful, May I live with ease.* Each time we say these words, we are planting seeds that will eventually blossom into love.

When I first learned lovingkindness practice, I was taught that, in addition to repeating the phrases, it's helpful to engage the imagination in relevant ways. As you say a phrase such as *May I be happy,* you might visualize an image of yourself with a glowing heart. With *May I be peaceful,* you might imagine yourself on a hike in nature or relaxing on a sunny afternoon. As each image arises, I imagine that the thoughts and feelings linked with the words I'm saying are being splashed over that particular image of myself. Whenever a strong feeling of genuine well-being arises, let yourself sink into that feeling. Take in the love you are offering yourself.

The more fully we can embrace the meaning of these simple good wishes, the more effective they are. When we open and take in the good wishes we are offering to ourselves, the transformation can be profound. At Awakening Joy courses, I introduce participants to lovingkindness practice by gently speaking various phrases, encouraging them to repeat the words to themselves, and to feel and take in the meaning. After one class, Sandy sent me a note relating what had happened to her during that simple meditation:

> As the phrases were spoken, I let myself deeply feel each one. There was no analysis, no thinking about it, just a simple nurturing message I was giving to myself. A strong sense of compassion for myself arose, and then compassion for others. Since that time, whenever I say the words to myself, which I

often do, I feel the same nurturing, compassionate, and happy feelings, like a warmth throughout my being. The experience that one night has changed my life.

JUST BE AS YOU ARE

The practice of lovingkindness is often preceded by self-forgiveness. This helps clear anything that might block warm feelings we could have for ourselves. When I ask participants at a course what they need to forgive themselves for, I receive lots of responses. People seem to readily know their faults. Good thing this is asked in the context of learning to love themselves! Some of the responses include:

- Being unkind to myself in those moments when I most need kindness.
- Chickening out sometimes, giving up before I start.
- Being so opinionated.
- Blowing up at others.
- Stuffing my emotions with food.
- Making bad choices.
- Not being perfect or even good enough.

It's striking to see how often that last one comes up. The tendency to perfectionism is merciless, but forgiveness allows us to let go of any ideal standard we measure ourselves against. You can't be anyone other than who you are right at this moment, and that's where you have to start if you want to forgive and love yourself. On my Really Awful Deeds retreat, that realization that all of us are doing the best we can showed me what a huge misunderstanding this drive to perfection is. If any of us could have grown into different people, "more perfect" human beings, we would have.

Back in seventh-century China, the Third Zen Patriarch said that to live "without anxiety about non-perfection" is the key to genuine happiness. We don't have to get rid of our shortcomings before we love ourselves. Seeing non-perfection as part of our shared humanity, we don't have to take our flaws so personally, although we can take them as a gift to learn from. While granting ourselves forgiveness takes patience, as we practice lovingkindness, we plant the seeds that will flower in their own time.

Embracing the totality of who we are means having compassion for our difficult-to-accept aspects. What we're doing is pulling out the second dart talked about in Step Four: When we're angry, not getting angry at our anger; when we're afraid, not being afraid of our fear; when we're jealous or petty, not getting caught up in condemning ourselves. Of course you'll make mistakes, but you don't have to throw out the baby with the bathwater. With understanding and compassion, let yourself be just as you are. Forgive yourself as you'd forgive someone else who is trying to do the best they can.

THROUGH THE EYES OF LOVE

Although opening up to receive my friends' love many years before was a major milestone, its main effect had been to diminish my self-judgment. As important as that was, it was just the beginning. It's one thing to not beat yourself up; it's quite another to truly delight in who you are, and I still had a ways to go. The door to self-love had opened a crack, and eventually I would find the way to throw it open wide.

Once again the significant change happened on a silent retreat, this one focused specifically on the practice of lovingkindness. Hour after hour I sat in the stillness of my room earnestly following the instructions, beginning with sending caring wishes to myself: *May I be safe from harm. May I be happy. May I be healthy. May I have inner peace.* I knew that days later we would be moving on to sending thoughts of lovingkindness to others, and this would be the foundation.

After three days of continued repetition of the lovingkindness phrases, I had to admit that I was experiencing a kindly self-acceptance and friendly appreciation for myself . . . but nothing more. "Well," I thought, "as the Supremes sing, 'You can't hurry love.'" Though I noticed a slight frustration over the lack of juice, I trusted that with each phrase I was planting the seeds of lovingkindness for myself, and that they would eventually bloom. What I didn't know was that those days of mechanical repetition had led me to the doorway I was looking for—and it was right around the corner.

As I sat there, the fall sunlight making its way through the leaves into my room, I found myself musing about the fact that others often can find us lovable far more readily than we ourselves can. *If only we could see what others see,* I thought to myself, *it would be so much easier to love ourselves.* I decided to try an experiment: *What would I see if I tried looking at myself through someone else's eyes?*

Who really loves me? I asked myself. Immediately the image came to mind of a certain friend whose love for me was strong and never in doubt. I could see his smile of delight as he beheld me, and feel his open heart beam me with affection. As I took in that love, I began to experience a buoyancy and uplifting in my own heart.

Continuing the experiment, I asked: *Why does he feel that way about me? What exactly does he see?* I imagined being him and looking at myself from his perspective. Without any effort, I became aware of the kindness that so wants to be there for others, the playful spirit that loves to sing and have fun, the good heart that enjoys seeing others shine, the years of earnest and sincere spiritual practice. Without any squirming or pretending, I took some time to drink myself in, to really "get" what my friend was seeing.

Intellectually I knew those things about myself; the particulars were not surprising. But as I saw myself through my friend's eyes, there were none of the "yes . . . buts" that I would typically throw at myself. All at once I got the essence of *who I am.* The unique expression of "Jamesness" became apparent to me in a way that it never had before. I wasn't just a collection of good qualities and "yes . . . buts"; the whole was greater than the sum of its parts. And I began to understand and see for myself that James, this person my friend was looking at, was enough—more than enough just as I was. It was a moment of genuine and deep self-love, completing the circuit of an impulse that had been set in motion that fateful night twenty-seven years before when I'd finally opened up and let in the love of my friends.

I could also see and understand that loving myself in this way wasn't being on an ego trip. While I had made certain choices that allowed me to

Seeing Yourself with Love

Bring to mind someone who genuinely loves you. Imagine yourself as that person, and look at yourself through his or her eyes. What qualities do you see in yourself from that perspective? Pause a few moments to fully take in what you see.

Now shift your perspective back and feel what it is like for you to have those qualities. Appreciate them, delight in them. Write them down in your Joy Journal and share them with your Joy Buddy or with a trusted friend. For one week remind yourself each morning of the qualities you saw in yourself through loving eyes.

develop ways of being that I appreciated, I couldn't take credit for the raw material. Essentially "being James" was something that had happened as a natural unfolding of life. I had broken through self-assessment and understood the beauty and wonder of my true nature, the same true nature that is the essence of everyone. Each of us is a unique and beautiful expression of creation. Huang Po, a ninth-century Zen sage, said that "in a flash" it's possible to comprehend what and who you are, and it is so much bigger than what you might have expected.

Staying in contact with the qualities I had seen through my friend's eyes, I let my consciousness slowly move back inside me. Now those hours of planting seeds of love were bearing fruit, and a sweet loving energy fueled the phrases as I said them. I was sincerely sending myself kind thoughts of well-wishing, and at last feeling fully deserving of them.

Oliver Wendell Holmes wrote, "A mind stretched by a new idea does not shrink back to its original dimensions." Something shifted that day which has remained ever since. For years I had been looking for love and fulfillment outside myself—loving others, looking for love from others. I now understood that no matter how much love came to me from "out there," until I could truly love myself, I couldn't really take it in.

In the Awakening Joy courses, I invite participants to do the same exercise I did on the retreat. Just the process of recognizing a few of their good qualities is challenging for some people, but the real stretch happens when I then ask them to turn to one of their neighbors and share aloud those good things they saw. At first there is a lot of discomfort. Many people squirm at the thought of saying such positive things about themselves to another. After a few minutes, though, the room begins to light up with enthusiasm.

THE TAPESTRY OF OUR LIFE

After that transformative experience, I had to reorient the way I thought of myself. Instead of my self-concept being "I am flawed and there's some good stuff in me," I knew instead that "I am good and there are some flaws." In time, this warm and tender love would also learn to hold, as we hold a suffering child, those aspects of myself that are harder to accept.

All those little blips of "what's wrong with us" can so easily get magnified into what seem like glaring faults. They suck all the oxygen out of the room of our psyche, and we come to believe that's who we are. By seeing yourself through the eyes of love, all the "buts" become like little clouds passing through a vast sky.

Embracing the totality of who we are is not about loving only our goodness and disregarding the rest. And it's not about being fond of just that part of us that is always sweet and kind. True love comes whole and unconditional. Loving the whole package means leaving nothing out. Unless we can do that, our love and joy are compromised. You might think, "I love 85 percent of myself, but if only I could somehow get rid of that other 15 percent." That thought keeps a lid on your joy. The love that embraces the whole package encompasses both compassion for the confused parts and love for the goodness.

An image from the brilliant PBS nature series *Planet Earth* sticks in my mind as an apt metaphor for the naturalness and perfection of all aspects of ourselves. The scene features a watering hole on a vast African plain. At various times we see the approach of giraffes, antelope, zebras, elephants, wildebeests, lions—some prey, some predators—all of them bound together by one simple fact, the need for water. Within each species are mothers and fathers, babies and the elderly. Watching them, I realized how it would make no sense to say, "Too bad that antelope is not a zebra," or "If only that giraffe were taller it would look better," or "That elephant is too old, it would be more beautiful if it were younger." Each animal comes to the watering hole with its own distinctive character and life.

Endless variation is part of the way life expresses itself. All of us, as human beings, are part of a vast and changing movement that is greater than any one of us. Just as sickness and death, volcanoes and earthquakes are part of what we might call the overall perfection of life, our confusion and ignorance are part of the totality of what it means to be alive. To feel wrong, bad, or not worthy of love because you're an elephant and not a giraffe is to see reality from a limited perspective. Even the tiger that attacks and eats the gazelle at the watering hole is not bad or wrong but simply part of the whole process, part of the way things are.

In the Eastern philosophy of Taoism, everything is part of the tapestry of life. And that includes you with all the unique qualities that make up who you are. Our tendency to believe that we, among all the other "elephants and giraffes," have something wrong with us and aren't good enough is—to borrow a phrase from Albert Einstein—"an optical delusion of consciousness."

TAKING GOOD CARE

In saying good-bye to someone we love, we often use the phrase "Take good care." This phrase holds a clue to cultivating love for ourselves. Love is taking good care—of your body and your mind, nourishing them with healthy foods, kind and effective healing methods, enough exercise, adequate rest and quiet time, creative self-expression and play. But the key to awakening joy is *how* we do that.

Loving ourselves by taking care of ourselves doesn't necessarily mean we always feel a lot of love while we're doing what we have to do. A devoted parent isn't deliriously happy about working long hours, shopping, cooking, cleaning, driving, supporting, and helping in all the countless ways necessary to raise a family. If the actions are done with resentment, they can leave everyone feeling confused, closed down, and disconnected. Remembering, even for a moment, that you're doing all these things because you love that child opens the way for joy.

The same is true when caring for yourself. Doing it out of love instead of obligation has immediate benefits. Before I go to the gym to work out, a little voice inside sometimes (or often!) says: *Do you really want to do this? Why not kick back and take it easy?* At that point I can either force myself to go and get onto the weight machines because "it's good for me," or I can remember that I'm doing it because I love and appreciate my body. One way can make me feel a bit resentful, at least until the endorphins kick in. The other can open my heart to make room for even a little glimmer of joy. When you take care of yourself out of love, your love for yourself increases.

When I ask participants in the Awakening Joy course what it feels like to be kind to themselves, their answers include:

- Relaxed and contented
- Spacious and light
- Grounded
- A welling up of joy in my chest, sometimes tears of joy
- Like I'm in the key of C
- Like I'm holding a baby in my arms—me!

You can bring this kind of tenderness and harmony into your own life by paying attention to what you need in order to really nourish yourself, and letting yourself have that—even if it means getting over that little hump of resistance and going down to the gym to work out. Pay attention to how good you feel when you're done, and acknowledge yourself for taking good care.

SPEAKING KINDLY TO YOURSELF

Alexa's struggle to move from self-hatred to self-love went on for several years. One day she came to me to ask how it could be possible to treat yourself kindly when you see so much wrong. Where do you start?

"I'll share with you one of my practices, one I did for nearly two years," I answered, hoping to assure her that she wasn't the only one who felt that way. I asked her to close her eyes and let one of the negative thoughts she had about her body come to mind.

"Not hard to do," she answered with a wry smile.

"Now place your hand on your cheek and gently caress it as if that hand belonged to the kindest grandmother, or some other wise and compassionate being. Silently say to yourself in the most tender voice possible, 'That's okay, dear. It's just a judging thought.'"

Though Alexa was at first skeptical and resistant, after giving it a try, she began to let herself feel the kindness coming through her hand. As it melted her frustration, compassion arose, and with it tears filled her eyes.

We all long for kindness and care, and we are the ones who can give that to ourselves at any and every moment. Cathleen, a course participant, said she was learning to pay attention to herself in the same way she is used to paying attention to other people. "That means I let myself notice the little thoughts and feelings I might have about something I need and take them seriously rather than dismissing them," she wrote. As Cathleen recognized, being kind to ourselves includes not condemning ourselves for the feelings that arise. It doesn't make sense to say, "I shouldn't be feeling what I'm feeling." Feelings arise in response to a complex of conditions. You don't say, "I could go for some fear right now" or, "How about a little self-hatred for a minute?" It's not like you have a choice about what pops into your mind. But you do have a choice as to how you *respond* to the fear or self-hatred when they're present. And that's where you can either deepen your suffering with self-criticism or hold the suffering kindly.

As discussed in the guideline for wise speech in Step Five, speaking kindly to

I'm finding myself naturally slowing down and seeing that I'm easily present, because I'm not on 'high alert.' My pace walking down the street to work is slower; I drive at a more relaxed pace, meaning with the flow of traffic and leaving plenty of distance between vehicles instead of rushing up on the car in front of me. Even my cardio workouts are done with an ease that is independent of the actual pace/speed I'm running. Now that I think about it, being kind to myself actually is a reduction of internal violence. Stress and tension are a form of self-inflicted harm.

—A COURSE PARTICIPANT

yourself is one of the most important ways to bring more joy into your life. A dear friend of mine often exclaims, "Oh, I'm so stupid!" when she makes a mistake. Every time I hear it, I cringe at how painful that must be for her. Learning to recognize the harsh voice of judgment inside your head, and in its place cultivating the gentle voice of compassion and support, can help you stay in touch with what you need in order to love and care for yourself.

LISTENING TO YOUR HEART

Jill said that when she began bringing a kind attention to herself as if she were a beloved child, her life began to change. One Saturday she awoke ready to do her normal routine: "a very full day of shopping and cleaning and working." As she was stretching out her breakfast with a final cup of tea, something inside called her to stop and take a bit more time that day to connect with herself. To her surprise when she just let herself relax and listen to her heart, a message came through loud and clear. Instead of doing a list of chores, she wanted to visit the Humane Society. For seven years Jill had been considering adopting a dog. That day she realized that being kind enough to herself to stop and listen opened her to a new, more joyous phase of her life:

> I needed that permission and "free" time to realize I could have something I wanted sooner rather than later. I could choose the happiness of living with a dog, instead of the more familiar belief that getting happiness takes a long time, and maybe I'm not ready enough or worthy enough to have it right now. Making that choice was a way of taking care of myself that has brought me tremendous joy.

An important way of caring for yourself that can get overlooked is developing your unique gifts and talents. Like a gardener lovingly tending a beautiful garden, we can delight in appreciating what we've been blessed with and bringing our potential to fruition. Whether your natural abilities lie in music, art, logic, intelligence, a sense of humor, kindness, connecting with people, or working with animals, great joy is found in identifying these gifts and sharing them with the world. This is not a matter of inflating your ego or falling into the trap of grandiosity. It's about honestly recognizing your particular gifts and abilities and expressing them. This is what leading a fulfilling human life is about.

Having doubts about our abilities doesn't mean we don't have gifts or skills. Nor does trying to get over our doubts mean that we're deceiving ourselves. Everyone has some special abilities, and allowing them to blossom is the true expression of self-love. In her book *The Life and Work of Martha Graham*, choreographer and dancer Agnes de Mille relates a conversation she had with Graham, the renowned pioneer of modern dance. De Mille, who as a child had been told she wasn't pretty enough to be an actress and didn't have the right body to be a dancer, was questioning her own talents, despite a recent success in choreographing a show. In response Graham offered her this wisdom and advice:

> There is a vitality, a life force, an energy, a quickening that is translated through you into action, and because there is only one of you in all time, this expression is unique. And if you block it, it will never exist through any other medium and it will be lost. The world will not have it. It is not your business to determine how good it is nor how valuable nor how it compares to other expressions. It is your business to keep it yours clearly and directly, to keep the channel open.

There are many ways to take good care of ourselves, and we can offer them to ourselves as we would to someone we are deeply in love with. This begins with shifting our focus away from what we think is wrong with us and toward a genuine appreciation of our very existence. It was this shift that led Alexa to a major turning point. One day, after all her efforts to let go of her self-criticism, something inside shifted, and Alexa saw herself at last:

> I just sat there, silently weeping. I wept for the sadness I've carried, the shame, the unworthiness, and I wept in painful joy

and visceral gratitude. . . . I am grateful to my body and my muscles and my lungs, my beating heart . . . I am falling head over heels in love with myself.

WHO'S DOING THE LOVING?

How can our little fragmented and conditioned self manage to get big enough to offer ourselves unconditional love? In truth, it can't. Einstein wisely said that a problem can't be solved on the level at which it was created, and to embrace ourselves fully requires realizing we are bigger than who we think we are.

Howie Cohn, a fellow teacher of mindfulness meditation, tells a tender personal story about how he came to know who is really doing the loving. During one of the many retreats he attended before he became a teacher, Howie found himself feeling unusually restless. He sensed that the pervasive feeling of discontent meant some deep discomfort was rising to the surface of consciousness and would have to be faced. As the days went by, a great feeling of isolation and loneliness came over him. The more intense the feeling, the more restless he became, wanting to do anything other than sit and be present with the pain.

One afternoon in his room as he was finishing a session of silent meditation, Howie opened his eyes and looked around. Neatly folded in one area was a large pile of his fashionable sweaters. His first impulse was to admire the collection and pride himself on his good taste, but he found himself instead wondering, *Why do I have all of these sweaters?* Then he began to notice all the stuff he had brought along to the retreat—handsome shirts and trousers hung in the open closet, several upscale toiletries lined the shelf above the sink, and a few gadgets he'd brought along that had seemed so essential covered the bedside table.

As he recalled the hours and hours he had spent searching for that "thing" that was just right, he began to understand. All around him was inescapable evidence of his futile attempts to run away from the feeling of emptiness that always lingered somewhere in the background—and was now filling every moment. This time he couldn't go out shopping to escape the great void. Added to that was the pain of self-judgment:

Why is comfort such a big deal for me? Why do I need so much stuff? Now, here in the safe container and silence of a retreat, he knew there was only one way to respond to that emptiness, and that was to go into rather than away from it.

As Howie stayed present with the loneliness, he could feel the deepening ache in his heart, the bottomless hollow in the pit of his stomach. When the pain crept through his entire body and loneliness turned to fear, Howie found himself curling up on the floor and sobbing. "I felt like a desperate child," he recalls. "I put my arms around my body and started rocking myself." Surprisingly soothed by the loving energy of this caring action, Howie began to notice a curious shift taking place inside him. Now he was no longer the small frightened child needing to be held but rather the compassionate and wise one doing the holding. He was literally embracing the part of himself he had been so afraid to face. And he knew that what he felt wasn't "Howie's love," it was unconditional love itself, able to accept and hold with compassion every part of who he was in that moment.

As we've seen before in this course, running away from difficult feelings doesn't make them go away. When Howie let himself stay in touch with the painful loneliness, he found himself carried through it to a new perspective. While Howie had the supportive atmosphere of a retreat, the transformation he went through in loving himself unconditionally can happen in other ways as well. Psychotherapist Linda Graham points out that if you've never felt loved, the presence of an "empathic other" can serve to awaken the loving presence inside you.

In whatever way you begin this process, you will come to understand that what you experience as "negative emotions," when addressed with wisdom and support, unfold into a broader knowing of who you are. You are not just the loneliness, anger, fear, or envy that might be overwhelming you. You also have within you the benevolent presence that can tenderly hold your confusion like a mother holds a child.

I think of this presence as our basic nature, as goodness itself. We all get glimpses of it in a moment of gratitude or generosity, or in the joy we feel when we hear about or witness a noble action, or behold an object of beauty. When we quiet down enough and listen carefully, we find it

On the Lookout for Goodness

Be on the lookout for those moments when something good expresses itself through you—a spontaneous urge to call a distressed friend, an impulse to give a donation to a charity. Be sure to pause and let those thoughts, feelings, and sensations register in your awareness.

is there all the time, beneath the confusion and static in our minds. The way I see it, this pure force is the impulse inside us that wishes for our happiness, that roots for our well-being. The process of learning to love ourselves means accessing and then empowering this force, so that it directs our choices and our life.

LOVE FINDING ITSELF

Your ability to love yourself evolves as you evolve, but when you finally love yourself, you have passed a watershed point in your spiritual practice. You no longer are trapped in looking to others to prove that you are okay. When you are unhooked from that need, you can simply open to the love coming your way from others without feeling unworthy or deflecting it. You can just let it join the love inside you.

In *Awakening Through Love*, writer and teacher John Makransky suggests a practice of being present for all the acts of kindness that come your way each day. When your partner gives you an affectionate hug, really take in the love. When a co-worker expresses appreciation, she is sincerely sending positive energy your way. Be there for it. When a dear friend greets you with genuine delight, he's communicating his love for you. Don't miss it. A stranger holds a door for you or smiles as you pass on the street. That is a communication filled with warmth and friendliness. Let yourself feel it. As Makransky puts it, if you're looking for all the small and large expressions of goodwill, you'll see that life is letting you know how deserving of love you are. If you're really present for all this kindness, you will be continually nourished by the benevolence around you. The more you open to receive all that love, the more you attract it to you. And you'll find that you become both a beacon and a magnet for love.

Following my own path has led me a long way from the adolescent wincing at seeing himself in the mirror. Over time the glimpses I've had of loving myself have become more of a consistent outlook. It's true that if the right button is pressed, I can still find myself back in the third grade, a mass of insecurity. But those thoughts don't last very long anymore, nor do they run my life, and I'm not so dependent upon the feedback of others to prop up my self-love. Even when stressed and confused, before long I can find my way back to that sense of compassion for my own humanity.

Loving ourselves means not only remembering who we are, but appreciating our particular way of being as one of life's infinite expressions. It means understanding that all the confusion and pain and shortcomings are part of the process of waking up. Alexa, who had been so deeply caught in self-hatred that she thought there was no way out, beautifully articulated this realization:

> On some days I am so full of love for myself and everything around me that it is all I can do to stop my heart from exploding with joy. I honor my pain, I bow to my capacity for change and growth that has manifested by pushing through the difficult times, and I rise in pure joy for the gift and blessing that is my life. As I rise in love for myself, I open to the myriad blessings in the universe and on Earth.

Step 8

The Joy of Loving Others

*It is important to understand how much your own happiness
is linked to that of others. There is no individual happiness
totally independent of others.*

—THE DALAI LAMA

WHEN I WAS twenty-five, I fell in love for the first time. Maria was my nurse in the hospital where I'd landed with a bad back. While being stuck in traction could have been depressing, I felt like I'd died and gone to heaven. Maria was the woman of my dreams. I'd never felt more at home with myself or so open and connected with another human being. And what was even more amazing, she felt the same. After so many years of wondering what love really felt like and whether I'd ever experience it, it had finally happened. Unfortunately, the relationship didn't last. The pain of separation was excruciating for me, but I had tasted something I would never forget—the joy of love.

Our most prized possessions don't compare in value to loving and being loved. Whether the juicy romantic love I felt for Maria, the natural and unquestioned love between a parent and child, the deep bond that forms between good friends, or the unconditional love we can have for life when we feel connected to everything around us, the essence of the experience is the same: to be held in a powerful, mysterious force, a living presence that allows us to be part of something greater than ourselves. We humans long for love, pray for it, die for it, live for it, and feel deep happiness or deep pain over it. Central to our lives is this capacity of the heart to know another, to feel understood and accepted, relaxed and connected, to be cared for and to care, to be delighted by and to delight.

Would anyone doubt that when our hearts are full of love we're happy? When we've got it, it feels like "this is what life is about!" Yet while we yearn for connection, relationships are often a source of hurt and disappointment. Friends can let us down. Our beloved children behave in ways that give us pain. Marriages begin with such promise, but nearly half end up in divorce court. From epic films and novels to country and western music, the *pain* of romantic love is almost a truism. How does that happen? How can something as beautiful as love be a source of so much bitterness and pain? In the face of such challenges, how can loving others become a reliable avenue to joy?

Relationships can bring us so much joy, yet can so easily occasion anger, disappointment, sorrow, and unhappiness. But as we've seen throughout this course, what is happening *inside us* is far more important than what is happening "out there." We can't control circumstances or other people, but we can train our minds to see clearly and our hearts to remain open, even in the face of pain. All the tools previously presented in the Awakening Joy course are brought to bear in Step Eight. The intention to be happy can be a guide and touchstone for how we relate to others. Mindfulness is the tool that helps us be truly present for and with others, as well as for the love that flows between us. Gratitude allows us to appreciate the lovely qualities in others that touch us. We learn to work with our pain and sorrow when things don't go our way or people disappoint us. Integrity is the basis of trust and respect so vital to the foundation of any relationship. Letting go of the stories and the expectations we place on others allows us to see them for who they are. Loving ourselves is the prerequisite for loving others and remembering that they too want to be happy.

Relationships of any kind can be challenging, but marriage and intimate partnership often seem like the ultimate test. When Jane and I decided to get married, my friend Sylvia Boorstein (who recently celebrated her fiftieth wedding anniversary) gave me some sage advice. I confided in her, as my first (and only) wedding day approached, that along with my excitement was some nervousness. I knew I'd found the right partner, but I wasn't sure how good I'd be at the institution of marriage. She looked at me with a twinkle in her eye and said with great compassion, "Don't worry, dear, you'll be fine. It's the first fifteen years that are the hardest. After that it gets easier." We both cracked up.

Jane and I have been married for almost thirty years now. She's my best friend, life partner, and the most important person in my life. There's no one I enjoy laughing with, playing with, creating with, loving with, and sharing life with more than her. She tells me the same is true for her. And there's no one with whom I more often lose my patience, feel frustrated, get angry, or feel disappointed and hurt by. When you feel such an intense connection with someone, what he or she says or does really matters.

From the beginning, Jane and I agreed that we're together to help each other wake up and to realize our full potential. Our wedding vows explicitly stated that we'll use our relationship as a vehicle to deepen our trust, respect, understanding, and love. When things get sticky or there's a messy situation, we have an agreement to use our marriage as a catalyst to deepen our love and connection. Of course this isn't always easy to remember when we're in the thick of it. But that commitment to help each other grow is the container that helps hold those difficulties. They become like a grain of sand that irritates the oyster into producing a beautiful pearl.

In his Hierarchy of Needs, noted psychologist Abraham Maslow posited that after our survival and biological needs are met, the "need to belong" is our highest priority. This is true whether you're a spiritual seeker who wants to feel "at one with everything" or an inner-city gang member who will do almost anything to be accepted by his homies. This connection with others is one of the most important sources of joy. The Buddha recognized this as well. When his attendant, Ananda, speculated that it seemed that having good friends was half of the holy life, the Buddha replied, "Not so, Ananda. Having good friends is the *whole* of the holy life."

For most of us, that means connection with other humans, although some people find the company of animals far more delightful, and some find their deepest relationship with a divine being. In our society, however, isolation and disconnection are all too common. The truth is, the world is filled with potential relationships of all kinds. If you put all your eggs in one kind of love-basket and think that love can only be found in romance, you undercut your own happiness. And as so many know, you can feel just as lonely and isolated in a marriage as in being single. If you feel too alone and on your own, this chapter may inspire you to develop new ways of connecting with others and awakening love.

Keira got divorced ten years ago and hasn't found a new partner, yet her life is full of connections through friends, service organizations, and work. She went through an initial period of feeling lonely and disconnected, and eventually realized she could choose to reach out and make connections. As a result she has discovered a life that's very rich. She now says, "If a special relationship comes along, I'm not going to turn it down, but having or not having one is not going to define whether or not I'm happy." Love is love, wherever it's found, and it starts inside each of us as we let the barriers to connection dissolve. Rather than expecting relationships to make you happy, if you focus on getting in touch with the joy inside, you will create happier and healthier relationships of all kinds.

Just as we saw with gratitude, we don't have to wait for love to strike. We can develop the capacity to awaken the love inside us by practicing loving. In this context, all those difficulties that arise can be seen as opportunities to grow in our ability to love. In Step Six, Ajahn Chah was quoted as saying, "Let go a little and you will have a little freedom. Let go a lot and you will have a lot of freedom." For this chapter we might paraphrase that quote to read: "Love a little and you will have a little joy. Love a lot and you will have a lot of joy." Step Eight explores many flavors of love and how we block their expression, and it offers various practices to help cultivate the joy of a loving heart. When it comes to the joy of connecting with others, I think the Beatles got it right: All you need is love.

LOVE LOST—AND FOUND

The summer after my relationship with Maria ended, I traveled to Boulder to study at Naropa Institute. There I sought out my hero, Ram Dass, for advice. As I sat in his office, surrounded by pictures of various spiritual beings smiling their beneficent smiles, I told him my sad tale. I had somehow lost the love that was meant for me, and my world had fallen apart. We talked for a while about how Maria and I might have fulfilled our part in each others' lives and that we were ready to go on. Maybe that was so, but it didn't stop the pain I felt. Maria had awakened a feeling of love in me that I'd never known before. And now it was gone.

"What am I supposed to do about that?" I asked, still distraught.

"Perhaps her gift to you is showing you that you had the capacity for love," Ram Dass offered.

"Yeah. Loved and lost."

Ram Dass looked at me with compassionate eyes. "Did you really lose it? As long as we think someone else is the cause of our feeling love, then when they go, we think we've lost that love. But I don't believe that's how it works."

"What do you mean?"

"While it's true that someone can awaken that love," I remember him saying, "it can never be lost, since it's been right inside us all along waiting to be activated." He went on to explain that our beloved is merely the catalyst that allows love to come alive. The experience of love is so wonderful that when we think that other person is the cause, we want to hold on to them. We get afraid to lose them, we resent them if they do something that "makes us stop loving them" for the moment, or we get possessive and jealous at the thought of their possibly awakening love in someone else. What we call the pain of love arises from mistaking unhealthy attachment for love. It looks like love but it's very different. Love is a movement of the heart that opens and radiates out. Attachment is contraction of the heart as it closes in fear. "Love is not painful," Ram Dass said with a wise smile, "and now that you know the experience of it, you know what your heart aspires to. That's what Maria gave you."

While it would take a while longer for the wound to heal, Ram Dass's words managed to start unwinding the knot in my heart and opened me up to understanding what love was about on a deeper level. The personal love between two people was a taste of a universal love that exists in everyone, and it shines on everything without conditions. I've seen this kind of continuous unconditional love in a few holy men and women. To develop that in myself is an aspiration I'm still working on. This kind of pure love is pure joy.

RELEASING THE AGENDA

Most of our "love" comes with some level of the kind of attachment that's painful. We want the people we love to think and act in ways we think are best for them. We want them to do and say things we like. When my son Adam was a teenager, I could see our relationship was changing. He didn't always agree with what I thought was for his own good, and he wasn't shy about letting me know it. And I certainly had an agenda for his behavior—getting homework in on time, contributing around the house, getting home by midnight on weekends. I found a great book, *Uncommon Sense for Parents with Teenagers,* by "teen-expert" and psychologist Michael Riera. He advises parents to move from the role of manager to consultant as their children mature—and he admits that it's easier said than done.

Once I was sure that Adam wasn't self-destructive, I tried to let go of thinking he needed to be a certain way and stepped back a bit to the

Feeling the Love

Think of someone you love dearly. (Pets are fine too.) As you imagine that person or being here with you, notice what happens in your body. Maybe your chest feels warm. Maybe a smile comes to your face. Let your attention rest on the feeling of that loving energy. Where did it come from? Does it belong to that person? A beloved one may awaken that experience of love, but the love is *inside you.* You can cultivate a loving heart by strengthening that feeling through mindful attention.

consultant role. This meant I picked my battles. And most importantly, I focused on letting him know I respected his judgment. I noticed that the more he felt my respect and confidence in him, the more he sought my advice. When he tripped up, rather than judging him by how he was or wasn't matching up to my expectations, I had to remember first and foremost that I loved and respected him. That helped loosen up *my* agenda for *his* happiness.

When we love someone, we want that person to be happy. It requires a lot of surrender to trust that they will find their way there by a different route than the one we think is best. This kind of letting go is needed in all

What's the Difference between Attachments?

In Western psychology, "attachment" has a positive connotation and refers to the theory that a secure connection with primary caregivers in early childhood is the basis of healthy social and emotional development. If we experienced adequate love and nourishment early on, we are likely to be resilient, have healthy relationships, and feel worthy of love. If we did not, we tend to be anxious or withdrawn, have difficulty in relationships, and feel uneasy in the world. Secure attachment is a solid basis on which to build a happy life.

Attachment in Buddhism, on the other hand, is defined as the cause of suffering. It is the futile attempt of the mind to hold on to or cling to anything or anyone in this ever-changing world. When we want things or people or ideas to be a certain way, we are *attached* to them, and when they're not the way we want, which is often the case, we suffer. It is the holding on that leads to "the pain of love."

To playfully sum up the difference between the two types of attachments: In general, a baby is supposed to be attached to its mother; an adult is not.

relationships but is especially true with our children. We fear something might go wrong, and in the process, sometimes we forget that the reason we're so concerned is because we love them. Not that we shouldn't look out for their safety, but being overly attached to what we think is best for them can turn our love into worry instead of joy.

Edith was concerned about her eldest daughter, who was six years old. She often found herself wondering if the girl was happy, watching to see if she was okay. Sometimes she felt helpless and unsure what to do to protect her from suffering. Although Edith knew her worrying wasn't helping, she didn't know how to stop or what else to do. Taking the Awakening Joy course inspired her to try a different approach. She decided to start focusing on the joy she could see in her daughter rather than on what might be wrong, and she sent an email relating what happened: "We have since had some beautiful moments together when I've shared her joy and aliveness. I let that resonate with me and felt happy, and I got the impression that my happiness in turn was resonating with her. I feel this is strengthening and nurturing her, much more than the worrying mode was doing."

What we think of as love can sometimes end up being a strategy to get our loved ones to behave in ways we think are "right," or to give us what we think we need. In doing so, we're seeing them only through our own filter, and it can cut off a genuinely loving connection.

I'd known Phyllis for a number of years as a meditation student, and I could see she had a deep commitment to getting through the ways in which her heart was closed. When she came in for an interview during a retreat I was leading, she felt open and trusting enough to share a profound insight she'd just had about herself.

"I realize that with people in my life I really care about, like my children, my husband, and close friends, I try to anticipate their needs, then do things for them to help them out and show them I care. I realize I'm trying to *make* them love me. And I'm seeing now how draining that is. It just doesn't work."

"How do you know it doesn't work?" I asked.

"Because they often tell me that I'm trying too hard. And they're right. But I don't know what else I can do. I really want them to love me."

I asked her to imagine putting herself in their place. "How would you feel about someone who was trying to make you love them?"

"Awful," she said. "I'd want some space."

"And how would you want that person to relate to you?"

Phyllis thought for a few moments. "I'd just want them to let me be who I am. I'd want to feel their love and support without them wanting anything in return."

"There's your answer. Just let them be who they are. Get in touch with what you love about them, and stay focused on that rather than what you want to get from them."

A key element in sharing a loving connection with others is shifting the focus off ourselves. If we're preoccupied with ourselves, we can't truly be present for others. We're too busy wondering how we're doing or what we can get from the interaction. *Do they like me? Am I boring? Do they notice how (intelligent, attractive, anxious, depressed, etc.) I am?* When you see yourself as the center of the world, you assess everything and everyone around you based on your likes and dislikes, wants and needs.

Say, for instance, Jane, my wife, walks into the living room. Without stopping to find out how she is or what might be on her mind, I launch into some item on my list—our plans for the weekend, whether Adam or Tony called, the latest news about a friend . . . It might take a few moments to realize that she could have her own reasons for coming to see me, or maybe she was coming in just to say hi and I missed it. Of course we need to communicate with others about the ten thousand things that make up our lives. But once in a while, if we can pause and simply recognize a beloved friend or family member not as a satellite to our world but as someone we love, we can feel our connection with them in a fresh way.

Without a self-centered agenda, we're curious and want to understand and know what another person's reality is like. To relate to others in this way—allowing them to be who they are and to be at ease with themselves in our presence—invites true intimacy. This is the basis of the joy of love and connection. Rather than assessing how others can satisfy our needs, we can appreciate their unique expression of life as it relates to our own.

From Agenda to Love

Bring to mind someone you love—a friend, a child, or perhaps a pet. Focus on how much you care about his or her well-being and happiness. Notice how good it feels to simply love that being.

Now turn your attention to something you *want* from him or her—attention, reassurance, affection, a certain behavior. Notice if the feelings in your body and your state of mind shift from openness to contraction, from a sense of fullness and connection to pulling back and closing down. Before you finish this exercise, let your thoughts return to the love and positive feelings you have for that individual.

When you notice that you're closing down to someone you love, stop for a moment and ask yourself whether you are attached to a particular agenda for that person. You may have reasonable expectations of others, and you might be annoyed if they don't fulfill them, but even through the disappointment, stay in touch with the love.

OPENING A CLOSED HEART

During the course of the retreat, Phyllis came to see that wanting to be loved and doing everything she could to get that from her family was based in a pattern that began in her childhood. "Will it ever end?" she asked one day.

Feeling compassion for her pain, I asked softly, "Do you want it to end?" She nodded. We were at Spirit Rock, which is located on four hundred acres of rolling hills dotted with forests of oak and bay trees. I suggested that she find some place outside where she felt safe and comfortable and do a little ceremony to consciously let go of that pattern.

"There's a particular tree I feel really good sitting under," she said with a spark of hope.

"Good. Go there and let that tree be your witness. Let go of the thoughts that keep you focused on what you believe is missing in your life. Turn your attention to all the love that's there. You're starting on the

Forgiveness

Forgiveness does not change the past, but it changes the present. Forgiveness means that even though you are wounded, you choose to hurt and suffer less. Forgiveness is for you and no one else. You can forgive and rejoin a relationship or forgive and never speak to the person again."

—DR. FRED LUSKIN, AUTHOR OF *Forgive for Good*

next chapter of your life. Let go of the past and let yourself discover the joy of loving—your own self as well as others. And be open to receiving their love."

On the last day of the retreat, Phyllis came in to see me. She was beaming as she gave her report on what had happened when she did her ritual at the tree. "As I sat there, it occurred to me that we've all meant well and done the best we could. In that moment, I was able to let go of all the blame and what-if's I've been carrying around. I think I'm ready to learn a different way of relating to my family now. I'm looking forward to seeing what it's like to express my love for them without trying to figure out what I can get back."

My exchange with Phyllis had a profound effect on me as well. That afternoon I found myself reflecting on her story and looking at my own life and the subtle expectations I was bringing to some of my close relationships. I decided to practice what I was preaching and focus on the love I felt rather than what I was hoping to get or what I was expecting from the other person. Each time I've managed to do that since, I've noticed an immediate release as the pain of wanting turns into the joy of loving.

FORGIVENESS FLOWS FROM A HAPPY HEART

As the saying goes, "Forgiveness is giving up all hope of a better past." The past is gone, and even though we may legitimately know we were wronged, we are the ones who end up suffering when our hearts are closed in anger. The Buddha likened holding on to anger and ill will to picking up a hot coal to throw at someone, and ending up getting burned ourselves. When we're holding on to resentment, we feel closed down, disconnected, isolated. We might be right, but are we happy? As discussed in Step Seven, the way back to ease and openness, which is really what we're looking for, begins with forgiving others. According to the Dalai Lama, an essential component of compassion and forgiveness is realizing that the other person's words and actions are not about *you*, but about *their internal reality*, which has intersected with yours.

Karen's marriage got off to a very rocky start. Bob's addiction to pain killers, successfully hidden during their courtship, had soon become apparent. But it took a couple of years before Bob was willing to face the problem and enter a recovery program. Although she supported him through the process, the shock and disappointment had left Karen feeling very ambivalent about the marriage and filled with resentment. "I did lots of therapy and meditation and workshops, but honestly, when I look back, I see I was holding on tight to my hurt and anger, and I didn't want to let go of them." It was a distant marriage. "It reminded me of a dry and barren desert," she said.

A real change began when Karen signed up for the Awakening Joy course. After the first few sessions, she wrote me a note: "I'm guessing that all of the work I've done over the years created some of the conditions for joy to enter my being, but without this course, I'm not sure what would have happened. Within a month of following the guidelines, I was experiencing a joy and a freedom that I never thought possible for myself. It was the singing that first really opened up the 'joy channels.' But the other practices have kept them open."

By giving herself permission to experience joy, Karen was entering an expansive new life, and as her heart softened, her feel-

When my husband is angry and in a bad mood, it is really helpful for me to recognize that he is confused and suffering, and that he doesn't realize this is not the way to happiness. This completely changes my state of mind from blaming and criticism (and from becoming just as angry as he is) into compassion and acceptance. I have also found that I can just let him be mad and still be happy myself.

—A COURSE PARTICIPANT

The Benefits of Forgiveness

Learning to forgive is good for both your mental and physical well-being as well as your relationships. In his book *Forgive for Good*, Dr. Fred Luskin includes the following research results:

- People who are more forgiving report fewer health problems.
- Forgiveness leads to less stress.
- Failure to forgive may be more important than hostility as a risk factor for heart disease.
- People who blame other people for their troubles have higher incidences of illnesses such as cardiovascular disease and cancers.
- People who imagine forgiving their offenders note immediate improvement in their cardiovascular, muscular, and nervous systems.

ings for Bob began to shift. "I began to feel a love toward him that I simply had not thought I was capable of." But it was almost too late. Bob was still operating on the momentum of "the marriage in the desert," and one night he announced that he'd spoken to a mediator about a possible separation. "The course had tenderized me enough by then that I cried and cried all night long," Karen remembers. "Bob was a bit confused by my vulnerability, which I'd rarely shown him, and he lay next to me holding the space as best he could." Karen describes that evening as a "dark night of the soul" that led her to "a profound cellular experience of *knowing* that I *did* want this marriage and our life together." Looking back now, she says:

> It has been different ever since! I sometimes pinch myself and wonder if it's all a dream. Bob, understandably, is sometimes baffled by the profound shift in my openness and love. I am not so naive as to think that the rough times will never come,

as they always do. But my hard-core anger and resentment has dissolved into compassion and love, and the joy that I feel with my husband and with myself is unmistakable. Needless to say, it has transformed our household as well, and our two beautiful children feel the shift, though they don't talk about it. The change is palpable in our home.

However closed or wounded your heart may be, it wants to open. When you forgive, you're not just doing it for the other person but for your own healing. As Archbishop Desmond Tutu, who chaired the Truth and Reconciliation process in South Africa, puts it: "To forgive is the highest form of self-interest. I need to forgive so that my anger and resentment and lust for revenge don't corrode my own being."

True forgiveness is based on understanding what might cause someone to act in ways that hurt us. Whether it's someone close to us or politicians we read about in newspapers, we are all products of forces beyond our control—genetic makeup, upbringing, influences of people we spend time with, and life circumstances. Although someone's actions may seem bizarre from our perspective, they make sense to that person. The forgive-

Asking Forgiveness

Bring to mind someone you have harmed in some way. Imagine that person right here with you. Allow any feelings of remorse to arise. Reflect on the confusion or ignorance that may have caused you to act in that way, not to excuse yourself for your behavior but to awaken compassionate understanding. You might silently say, "I'm truly sorry for any harm I might have caused you. I ask your forgiveness." Imagine that person hearing your sincerity, taking in your words, and forgiving you. Notice how that feels in your body and mind.

ness we talked about offering ourselves in the last chapter we are offering to others in this step toward happiness. When you can see the truth of what Jesus said on the cross, "Forgive them, for they know not what they do," you can forgive the confusion that leads someone to do a harmful action. You might think, "They know very well what they're doing." But Jesus, like the Buddha, was conveying that ignorance—the misunderstanding of where happiness lies—is behind that behavior. Realizing this, we can replace our anger with compassion. As the Dalai Lama says, "If you want to be happy, practice compassion. If you want others to be happy, practice compassion."

If you're not yet ready to forgive someone, then forgive yourself for being just where you are, particularly if you judge yourself for feeling the way you do. We can't hurry up the process. Sometimes hurts take a while to heal. But know that you're the one who benefits most from forgiving another, so be open to the possibility of forgiving sometime in the future.

Offering Forgiveness

Bring someone to mind who has harmed you in some way. Imagine that person in front of you. Reflect on the confusion or ignorance that may have caused him or her to harm you—again, not to overlook the actions but to open your heart to compassion. Offer forgiveness by silently saying, "For any harm you may have caused me, intentionally or unintentionally, I forgive you. I forgive your confusion." Imagine that person taking in your words and feeling your forgiveness. Notice how that feels.

When you find yourself feeling resentful or angry with someone, and you want to find your way back to connection, it can help to imagine that person as a small child, afraid and confused. Let your heart soften, and feel the relief as you let go of the tight feelings.

DEVELOPING A LOVING HEART

Developing a kind and loving heart may be the most important thing we do in life if we want to be happy. The Dalai Lama, who is one of the best examples I know of a happy person, says, "My religion is kindness." One of Jesus' main instructions to his followers was to "love one another." But how do we do that? How do we make kindness our religion? Some may think the ability to love is like a special talent—you either have it or you don't. Sometimes we look at someone and say, "She—or he—is a very loving person," and we might believe we can't be the same. But the capacity to love is inherent, we all have it, and it can be developed. The practice of lovingkindness, introduced in the last chapter as a way to love yourself, is also a way to cultivate your ability to love others, well beyond what you might think you're capable of. By repeatedly evoking the spirit of love within you, you strengthen it, and become an even more loving person.

The same phrases we use to send thoughts of lovingkindness to ourselves are here turned toward others to wish them well: *May you be safe from harm. May you be happy. May you live with ease.* You can also use any other words that feel natural and genuine. There are several categories of people to whom you can send benevolent thoughts, starting with those who are easiest for you to love, then those who are challenging, and then those you don't know. Ultimately you practice sending love to all beings everywhere.

Since lovingkindness practice is typically done while sitting quietly in meditation, you might wonder if there is some kind of magical energy that leaps across time and space and into the hearts of those you are thinking of. Some say yes, others no. I tend to think our thoughts do have an effect. Have you ever been thinking of someone you care about, and suddenly they call or email you "out of the blue"? Perhaps there's more than meets the eye in how we are interconnected. What I do know for sure is that sending kind and loving thoughts to others definitely has a beneficial effect on *you*. And as your love grows, you and everyone around you becomes a beneficiary.

This practice doesn't have to be limited to times of quiet meditation. During any encounter you have in your day, you can practice lovingkindness by silently wishing others well. You'll find that as you send thoughts of well-being to others, your own well-being increases.

LOVING THOSE YOU LOVE

You begin getting in touch with your capacity to love by starting with those who are easiest to love. The first group of people you send loving-kindness to includes those you feel grateful to for enriching your life in some way. They might be parents, relatives, teachers, clergy, friends, or mentors—those who have been kind to you, shared their knowledge, helped you get through a hard time, or believed in and supported you in some way that has made you a better person. This doesn't necessarily have to be someone you know personally. Mahatma Gandhi was my childhood hero. When I read his biography, something about him moved me to want a good heart, wisdom, and courage like his, and thinking of him opens my heart. For some, other saints or holy people might do the same. Or you might open your heart in gratitude and send lovingkindness to public figures, past and present, who have inspired many to develop their skills and talents for the benefit of others.

Your good friends and others you easily and readily love are in the

Radiating Love

Bring to mind someone you love or feel deeply grateful to. Notice where in your body you register these feelings. Many people experience a warmth and swelling in their chest. You might also explore what happens if a smile arises. What is your state of mind as you tune in to your love for that person? Let these feelings amplify as you radiate out gratitude and loving energy: *May you be happy. May you be healthy. May you feel my love for you.*

I've been practicing lovingkindness by noting tiny positive things in strangers, like saying to myself, 'He has good posture,' 'She looks good in that color,' 'He's using his turn signal.' This minuscule adjustment in where I place my attention has big results. I'm happier overall!

—A COURSE PARTICIPANT

next circle of lovingkindness practice. This is a nearly guaranteed way to awaken love in your heart. Just thinking of certain people can bring a smile to your face. The people in this group probably love us, as we love them. As you feel their love for you, complete the loop by sending love back their way.

When you first start this practice, what is most important is that you choose those who awaken your love, so that you can get to know that experience in your body and mind, and learn how to strengthen it by offering that energy of lovingkindness to others. As you dwell in your open heart, you are deepening your capacity to love.

As part of your practice of lovingkindness-in-action, take time to be present for the people around you whom you are closest to. Try seeing them with fresh eyes, perhaps as if they were new friends you're just getting to know. Ask them what's really going on with them these days, and then really listen. Tell them what you like about them. Tell them you love them. And express your appreciation. All of you will benefit from the field of love you create.

SCATTER LOVE

Think of how many people you pass in an average day for whom you have little or no personal feeling at all. Probably most of them. These are the people in the next ring of the expanding circle of lovingkindness, the "neutral" category, those we don't know and may never get to know. As you send them lovingkindness, it becomes evident that you have the capacity to develop a warm connection with almost anyone.

On my first lovingkindness retreat many years ago, I decided to choose my new neighbor, Richard, as the neutral person I would send lovingkindness to. Jane and I had recently moved to the neighborhood, and I'd had very little contact with the family across the street other than a wave and a hi. I started my practice by picturing Richard coming out of his house and giving me a smile and a pleasant hello as he got into his car for work. Then I imagined him in tender moments with his daughters and wife. Next I saw him in my mind's eye playing with his dog. I reflected that, just like me, he had his sorrows and joys, disappointments and successes. And just like me, he wanted to be happy and safe and open to all the love in his life. It seemed to me that he was basically a decent human being, and I figured if he was happy, everyone around him would benefit as well. As I held those images in my mind, I wished him well: *May you be safe from harm. May your life be filled with ease and joy.* I did this continuously for the next two days. I had no idea the effect it would have on me when I met him again.

The first time I saw Richard after the retreat, I suddenly felt so happy. Here was the object of my well-wishing right in front of me! I immediately went over to him, gave him a warm hello, and struck up a conversation. From that moment on we've shared a sweet connection. Only years later, one day when we were appreciating our friendship, did I mention the lovingkindness retreat to him. How surprised he was to find out that our warm relationship had started with two days of me silently wishing him well.

There are endless opportunities to open your heart to the many "strangers" around you. Here are a few suggestions. As you try any of these, be sure to pay attention to how you feel in your body and mind as you reach out toward others with the spirit of good will. That is what anchors the feeling of lovingkindness more deeply in your being.

> *I have made an effort to be more consciously present with all of the 'service' people I encounter every day: the checkout guy, the bus driver, the security guard in the lobby of the office building where I work. I make sure to engage them in some way, thank them for their efforts (and mean it), and sincerely wish them a good day when I leave. It takes me out of my head, and I leave feeling more connected to the community of people I come in contact with.*
>
> —A COURSE PARTICIPANT

- Choose a "Person of the Week," someone you see regularly but don't really know, to receive lovingkindness from you, in thoughts and actions.
- When you're waiting in line at the grocery store or caught in traffic, send thoughts of kindness to those around you.

- Smile or say hello to people you pass as you walk around town.
- As you hold open the door for someone in a public place, silently wish that person happiness and well-being.
- Stop and talk with a homeless person on the street. Your act of kindness might mean even more than a few coins.

SEEING GOODNESS

Most of the people we get to know in life started out as strangers. This gives us a wide and fertile field for scattering love. In just about any situation we enter, we can have a positive impact by connecting with others in a kind and loving way. Doing this with a genuine intention to enhance the well-being of others, and not just to "win friends and influence people," means we are drawing upon our goodness and meeting their goodness. Nelson Mandela, imprisoned for twenty-seven years, was much loved by his guards because he made a point of doing exactly that.

Seeing goodness is something I have tried to do in my life. Forty

Looking for the Good

Seeing the goodness in someone brings something real, alive, and uplifting out of them. It allows trust to develop between people who scarcely know each other.

For one week, take on the practice of looking for the good in everyone you come in contact with. See in each person the desire to be safe, accepted, and loved. Even if you know someone's shortcomings, keep looking for the positive qualities—creativity, playfulness, a caring heart, intelligence, loyalty—any and all positive qualities you might admire. Notice what effect this has on how you feel toward other people and on your interactions with them. Notice the effect it has on your own state of mind.

years ago when I first read about Neem Karoli Baba, an Indian guru who influenced many Westerners, I was struck by something he said: "The best form to worship God is every form." To me that teaching was an instruction to see the good in everyone. I've found that the more I look for what is good and beautiful in others, the more I see of it. And when I do this, it seems to draw the best out of them.

How do you feel inside when you sense someone is judging you, looking for all your flaws? Probably self-conscious, if not downright flawed. But when you're with someone who, even if aware of your flaws, is seeing your inner beauty, don't you feel beautiful? It's as if shining a light on those parts of you gives them more life.

I discovered the transformative power of this perspective as a young elementary school teacher at P.S. 122 in New York. At the beginning of each year, I gave myself a personal challenge: Could I find the secret to each child's heart so they could all come out from their hiding places inside? If I could do that, they would have a good chance at taking that leap—a huge jump over a giant abyss for some. When you know your teacher loves you and believes in you, especially when you're eleven or twelve years old, you start to maybe love and believe in yourself.

Seeing the goodness in most of those kids was easy. My heart was melted by their joy and enthusiasm, their wit or cuteness or sweetness. But there were almost always three or four who became my special projects for the year, often the kids with mean streaks, perhaps because they were abused or were so used to getting attention by being yelled at for doing something stupid that they didn't know another way. So I tried to get to them little by little with my love. I'd spend time alone with them at recess, or give them some kind of responsibility in the classroom to show I respected and trusted them. In quiet moments, one on one, I'd ask what they loved to do and listen with genuine interest. Most of the time it worked, and by the end of the year the feeling in the class was usually pretty magical.

Love can work wonders, building bridges across the greatest chasms. I had another experience of this at P.S. 122. The school was located in Astoria, at the time a predominantly conservative neighborhood in Queens, New York. In fact, that area was chosen as the home site for

All in the Family, a TV sitcom featuring Archie Bunker, the outrageous stereotype of a narrow-minded and opinionated American. Into that setting in 1969 came Mr. Baraz with long hair and a beard. The first time I walked through the halls, I left behind a trail of gasps and laughter from the stunned students and faculty. The principal called me aside, said the school wasn't used to someone like me, and politely suggested that I get a cut and a shave.

But I liked the way I looked. It made me feel like I belonged to the hip counterculture movement that was afoot. And even more, maybe it would be good for people to get past their prejudices. I explained my thinking to the principal who, although impeccably dressed with his bow tie and suit, was not as rigid as I might have judged him to be. "Give me two weeks," I asked. "Maybe people can get used to someone different. If it doesn't work I'll shave off my beard and cut my hair."

During that time I intentionally "killed them with kindness." I opened doors for parents and students, greeted teachers in the hallway with a warm hello, and generally beamed everyone with love. The thing that made this work was that I really meant it. I could see how well-intentioned each of these people were, wanting the best for the kids. Although I started with an ulterior motive, in the process I genuinely opened my heart to them. And seeing their goodness established a real connection between us. In the end, I kept my hair, taught there for the next nine years, and ended up being a very popular teacher.

LOVING THOSE YOU DON'T WANT TO LOVE

You might feel as if your heart is about as full as it can get, with appreciating people who've enriched your life, loving good friends, and opening up to include your mail carrier, coworkers, and the children you pass on your walk each morning. But lovingkindness practice knows that the heart has no limits. The next category of people to include in your heart are those you have a hard time with. Classically referred to as the "enemy" category, this group can include ex-lovers, bad neighbors, political figures whose actions anger us, and loved ones we're having a hard time with. Jesus taught, "Love your enemies, do good to those who hate you, bless those who curse you, pray for those who mistreat you." Here's your chance to try that out in the privacy of your own heart.

Why would you want to do this? What could be gained by sending good wishes to those who upset you? Why would you want to "turn the other cheek"? As with forgiveness, you are first of all practicing this for your own well-being. As long as you're holding on to the hot coal, you're the one getting burned.

Another reason for stretching to include those we don't really feel a lot of love for, at least not in the moment, is that anger and ill will don't really accomplish much. "Hatred never ceases by hatred," said the Buddha. "Hatred only ceases by love. This is an ancient and eternal law." While it's true that protesting against injustice, for instance, can arise from justified anger, ultimately what solves the problem is some degree of compassion and communication. This is not to deny painful feelings or pretend they're not there, in ourselves or others. But we can start where we are and honor our feelings with the intention of opening our hearts in understanding. In the end, when we do this, we are the ones who benefit, and in the spirit of lovingkindness our actions have more power.

Sending lovingkindness to our enemies is a kind of alchemy, transforming our bad feelings into good ones. One year on a lovingkindness retreat, I experienced exactly how that happens. My practice had progressed to the "difficult person" category, and I knew just who I'd pick. Sheila was someone who had temporarily moved into the large shared household where I'd lived for a number of years. Although she was impeccable in following the house guidelines, it seemed to me she was always complaining about something: Others in the household weren't pulling their weight. House meetings were too long. Someone was playing music too loud late at night, etc. Whenever we encountered each other, which was often enough living under the same roof, I imagined judgments cascading one after another from her mind. (Of course, one or two judgments arose in mine as well.) Every time I thought about her, my body would tense and I'd immediately feel a wave of dislike. There was no doubt about it. Sheila would be the perfect "difficult" person for me to send lovingkindness to.

In doing this stage of the practice, you bring to mind the positive qualities of the person—maybe he's good with children, or she's very generous with donations to good causes. This helps you soften your heart and makes you open to wishing them well. However, every time Sheila came to mind, all I could think of were those complaints and attacks. After a day or two of continually directing phrases of well-wishing toward her—*May you be safe from harm, May you be happy*—the negative images subsided a bit, but I felt nothing remotely close to what you would call warmth or an open heart. I was holding the hot coal, and I didn't really know how to put it down. Then on the third day there was a breakthrough.

While I was trying to send Sheila kind thoughts, the Dalai Lama came into my consciousness. It occurred to me that he'd probably have no trouble at all doing this task that was so challenging for me. His love and compassion are so tangible that you can't be around him without having your heart touched, and you end up feeling full of good will. I'd seen him a few times in a setting small enough to watch him interact with people personally. He always welcomed each one with complete openness

Loving Even Them (Yes, Even Them)

Bring to mind someone with whom you have a difficult relationship. Think of some positive qualities he or she might have. Try to remember some kind action he did that might soften your heart, or perhaps imagine her as a young child who's had a hard time. Now silently say these phrases as you think of that person: *May you find happiness in your life. May you be at peace.* Notice how this feels in your body and mind. If you feel any expansion or warmth, take those feelings in and let them grow.

It's important not to try to force any particular feeling. If you're not able to feel kindness toward this other person, be kind with yourself by allowing your feelings to be as they are, without attachment or aversion.

and love. An image came to mind of a time when I'd seen him greeting a line of people coming for a blessing. As I watched the scene in my mind's eye, to my surprise, Sheila appeared, awaiting her turn. Compassion was emanating from the Dalai Lama toward the two people ahead of her, and then she stood before him.

What if I were to see Sheila through the Dalai Lama's eyes? I wondered. The scene unfolded in slow motion. First I noticed her openness and vulnerability. Then I became aware of all the pain and sorrow she'd gone through in her life that shaped who she was. I could see her good heart and how she so wanted to be loved. Suddenly Sheila became a radiant being, beautiful to behold.

The wishes for the health and happiness of my "difficult person" now came more easily and sincerely. Something that was tight inside me began to relax, and it felt like all the energy I'd been putting into keeping my heart closed to Sheila was releasing itself into caring and joy. In the teachings of several Eastern religions, the peacock is an important symbol of the ability to transform negative feelings into positive ones. This is based on the belief that this magnificent bird can eat poison and turn it into its splendid plumage. I felt like all that poison of ill will inside me had been turned into something beautiful.

DISARMING HOSTILITY

Sheila was basically a good person from the start. But what about difficult people who are mean or cruel? One might wonder about practicing lovingkindness toward those who intentionally cause harm to others. Why should we wish for their happiness? The poet Longfellow wrote, "If we could read the secret history of our enemies, we should find in each man's life sorrow and suffering enough to disarm all hostility." When we look at the background of those who commit violent crimes, we usually find great suffering in their childhood. Those who seem to get pleasure from another's misfortune are themselves the unfortunate. Stuck in the prison of their contracted minds, they have little genuine love coming back to them. If your wish for their well-being were to come true, and they'd understand where happiness really can be found, they would no longer intentionally cause harm to anyone. So we send lovingkindness to them, not as a reward but as a prayer. And again, when you can wish for your enemy what you wish for your friend, another tight place in your heart will have softened into compassion.

When I did see Sheila again after that retreat, I felt a lot softer toward her. Somehow I could hear some of her remarks differently, not as complaints but as legitimate observations, and she and I have shared a warm connection since.

It's clear to me that the way we think of others certainly affects the way they relate to us. Hal has a difficult relationship with his mother, so he chose to direct his lovingkindness practice to her. He wrote:

> I noticed a marked difference in her responses. On days when she was just after me no matter what, I practiced lovingkindness toward myself and compassion for her situation, reminding myself of the good in her even if I couldn't see it in the present moment. Working through those times was difficult but enormously helpful. I hope to continue to heal this relationship and transform it, at least within myself.

THE FULLY OPENED HEART

If you want to be happy, love everyone. This might sound pretty simplistic, but the happiest human beings I know are the spiritual teachers who make it their life's work to beam out love unconditionally. This is the kind of love we aspire to in the final category of lovingkindness recipients—all beings, human, animal, and beyond. When we cultivate lovingkindness for all beings, we replace the feeling of "other" with caring and connection. We include all without distinction: those who are suffering *and* those who in their ignorance cause suffering; those who are happy and those who cause happiness; people of all ages, ethnic groups, nations, and religious backgrounds, as well as all creatures and all forces seen and unseen. There is no limit to our love.

Buckminster Fuller came up with the phrase that famously defined our true situation: "We are all passengers on Spaceship Earth." And the fact that we're all on the same spaceship has become increasingly clear in recent times. What happens in Iraq influences what happens in Milwaukee. A downturn in the U.S. housing market has dramatic effects on the world economy. That in turn affects support for nonprofits doing charitable work, which has consequences for the poor in Bangladesh or kids wanting to participate in the Special Olympics. Burning fossil fuel with little regard for consequences can throw our climate system completely out of balance, melting polar ice caps, increasing the fury of hurricanes and other storm systems, and hastening the extinction of many species. In short, we are part of a vast, interconnected web of life. By realizing we're all in this together, it becomes clear that it's in our own interest to practice lovingkindness for the Earth and all of our shipmates.

A FREE JOY RIDE

We see a baby squeal with delight and we feel delighted. We watch a movie and feel satisfied when the good guy finally gets the gal. Someone we love succeeds at a project they were nervous about, and we feel happy for him or her. There is a Sanskrit word used in Buddhist practice for the feeling of happiness at the joy and good fortune of others: *mudita.* Mudita, translated as sympathetic joy, means resonating with the happiness of another. It's the joyful feeling we have when we're cheering for others or celebrating their success. Just as with lovingkindness practice, we can do "mudita practice" to develop and expand the natural uplifting we feel when others thrive.

When we focus on the good fortune and happiness of others, we are entertaining positive images in our mind, which makes us happy. The moment we think, *Oh, but I don't have that,* we drop into negative comparison, the mind tightens, and we're unhappy. If you're honest with yourself, you might have to admit that sometimes you do feel a little twinge of glee upon hearing of someone's misfortune. The French philosopher Montaigne wrote, "There is something altogether not too displeasing in the misfortune of our friends." The German language even has a term for this: *schadenfreude,* feeling happiness at the misery of others.

What is this feeling about? We probably can find the roots of this

Lovingkindness for All Beings

Begin by sending wishes for well-being to everyone in your home and immediate family. Gradually expand outward in your mind to include your neighborhood, your city, state, country, continent, and the entire planet. The traditional practice even includes beings beyond that. If you believe in angels, saints, nature spirits, and extraterrestrials, this is the point to include them in your lovingkindness practice. You might say: *As I want to be happy, so may all beings be happy. As I want to be peaceful, so may all beings have peace in their lives.* Notice how it feels in your body and mind to wish well to all without omitting anyone from your heart.

tendency in the way competition for survival is programmed into our brain. To me it suggests that we believe we are competing for happiness, as if there is a quota on the amount of happiness in the world. *If they have it, there's less for me.* But this is not true. For instance, it doesn't work that way with anger. Ever notice what happens when someone comes into a room who's very angry? Do you relax and think: *Oh, good. They're angry, so there's less for me!?* Probably not. We all know how being around a negative person rubs off on us. Fortunately the same happens with joy when we get our comparing mind out of the way and let ourselves rejoice in the happiness of others.

Jim knew how easily he could fall into envy and judgment with certain people in his life, especially those who loved their jobs and enjoyed their lives—quite a contrast to his own situation. He wrote me an email about this after the Awakening Joy session in which sympathetic joy was introduced.

"It's really hard to wish successful people even greater success. If they become happier, I'll feel even worse."

Joy in the Joy of Another

Imagine someone you are fond of smiling or laughing in happiness. What happens to you? Notice if a smile automatically arises. Take in those good feelings and send them out to that person: *May your happiness continue. May your happiness grow.* Think of others you would like to send this energy to, and notice how your own good feelings increase.

Now imagine all those people in a cheering section rooting for you. Direct the phrases of well-wishing toward yourself, taking in the feeling of support from them.

"Why don't you try it a few times," I wrote back. "See what happens, and let me know how it goes."

Much to his surprise, Jim found that the practice had the opposite effect. In his next email he said:

> Whenever I find myself being critical in my mind toward someone, I've started changing the thought to: *May your joy and happiness continue, and may good fortune follow you everywhere.* Once I've wished it for them, I find I really want them to have it.

I remember hitting a snag once when working on sympathetic joy. The practice traditionally begins with thinking of someone in a moment of triumph. For a while my mind was blank. I knew a lot of people who were pretty happy, but I wanted to root for someone who was in a moment of intense celebration. And then in a flash it came to me—Steve Young, the quarterback for the San Francisco 49ers, my all-time favorite athlete. For years, every time I'd thought about him, I would feel joy. So I imagined him right after winning the Superbowl, running around the stadium deliriously happy, going into the stands to high-five fans with a beautiful, goofy grin on his face. Bringing that image to mind was like opening the faucet of joy in my heart. My eyes welled up with tears. Once the valve opened, I was able to turn that thought toward other people in my life, sending them heartfelt wishes: *May your happiness grow.* Mine certainly did.

Keep your radar out for happiness around you. When you see or hear about others who are experiencing happiness in their lives, know that their joy is contributing a little more happiness to the world. Tune in to their reality and let their happiness rub off on you. Silently send them wishes that their happiness may continue and grow. Notice how you feel in your body and mind as you do this. If any thoughts of jealousy or envy arise, notice them without judgment, and return to your wishes for their continued happiness. As the Dalai Lama says, if we derive happiness from the happiness of others, we have at least six billion more opportunities to be happy.

PLAY IS LOVE

Play is one of the most immediate ways to access the joy of loving others. But we all too often turn down the opportunity because we must attend to those "matters of consequence" that the Little Prince lamented. Bruce was taking the course online from Connecticut and wrote to say that one snowy day he was outside with his two young boys building a snowman and fort. "I wasn't particularly enjoying the activity," he reported. "It was cold, I had stuff to do, and I was ready to go in." But his eight-year-old and four-year-old weren't. "In the Awakening Joy course we were talking about feeling joy at the joy of others, and I couldn't help but see how much fun they were having. I thought, 'This is a special moment. I need to let this soak in, not just get it over with.'" Instead of calling it quits, Bruce proposed huddling inside the fort and having hot cocoa. "We sat down together and shared a simple, precious cup of cocoa," he recalls. "The memory of that time of just being together still brings tears to my eyes, even a year later."

Playfulness and humor are actually ways of loving others, and they are a direct link to joy. Here are some of the ways course participants said they have let the love flow through playing:

- Laughing at unexpected situations instead of getting mad.
- Engaging in "time-wasting" activities such as Four-Square or Scrabble.
- Adopting a pet. "I named my dog 'Happy,' and she's really good at playing."
- Taking tango lessons and laughing instead of apologizing for all my mistakes.
- Skipping down the street with my kids.
- Singing conversations with my family, as if we were in an opera.
- Making music with friends.

Notice what happens inside you when you are engaged in play. The feeling is a lot like love, isn't it? Whatever we call it, this is the energy of life, endlessly changing, infinitely creative, and it is one of the easiest ways to love others. Play is not just an "extra" in our lives but essential for our well-being. David Elkind, Professor Emeritus of Child Development at Tufts University, says in his book *The Power of Play:* "Decades of research have shown that play is crucial to physical, intellectual, and social-emotional development at all ages." Play opens our heart and connects us with others in a joyful way. Instead of seeing it as a luxury, give yourself some playtime, not only for the fun of it, but as a way to open your heart.

LOVE IS ALL AROUND US

When Adam was a little boy, he would often have tantrums—usually meltdowns from being too wound up or overtired. When he quieted down enough to be able to hear me, we'd sometimes go through a little ritual. "Would you like me to tell you the people who love you?" I'd softly ask. He would quietly nod yes, and I would take him into my lap and wrap my arms lovingly around him. "Mommy loves you and Daddy loves you. Grandma loves you and Aunt Susan loves you. Gigi loves you and Linda loves you. Michelle loves you and Rose loves you. . . . " As I'd continue, I could feel Adam's body relax as he calmed down. Love is perhaps the best medicine around. When you're feeling down, recalling those who love you can be a comforting and healing balm. You can relax into that connection.

The more we allow our hearts to open, the more we see the truth that love is all around us. This is not just a pretty idea but a reality any of us can experience if we give ourselves a chance to let go into it. Kate, the young woman who teaches mindfulness to inner-city children, says she knows that "When all of the fear and sadness and feeling of separation falls away, the only thing left is love. That's the undercurrent." This unshakeable knowledge arose from something that happened to her one day quite spontaneously. Kate writes:

> I was sitting on the porch one beautiful sunny afternoon, feeling very happy. I'd closed my eyes for a moment, and when I opened them, the tree about ten yards in front of me had colors so vibrant it looked like it was glowing. I felt such a strong connection with it. I was part of that tree. Even the space between us was part of the connection. With no boundaries, I became part of the chair I was sitting in, part of the deck I was sitting on. The physical boundaries were still there in my mind, but on a deeper level there was no identifying *That's a tree, and this is me.* And I knew that the thing connecting us all was an energy of love.

Similar descriptions have occurred in cultures around the world and through millennia. Modern physics corroborates the fact that on the level of energy there are no boundaries. While science might not recognize the glue as "love," it's the word mystics most often use. Kate talks about her experience as "a feeling of coming home," and it has had a profound impact on her life.

I'd been horribly shy, with no confidence. That feeling of connection completely changed my life. I can feel connected with anybody now. All I have to do is love them. We're all part of this undercurrent. Though we all share suffering, we're also all linked by this love.

That underlying energy is love loving itself through you. Love moves in a circle. You take it in and send it out; you send it out and it comes back to you. You might notice that letting love flow through you happens quite naturally. And you can amplify its effect by engaging in the process consciously. Without resistance, receive the love that comes to you. The more you take it in, the more you can give it out. You are an instrument of love, and as your relationship to others becomes an expression of that, your capacity for joy grows. If your love rests on wishing happiness for everyone you meet and everyone you share this life with, your joy will be boundless.

Step 9

COMPASSION: THE NATURAL
EXPRESSION OF A JOYFUL HEART

*The only ones among you who will be truly happy are those
who have sought and found how to serve.*

—ALBERT SCHWEITZER
COMMENCEMENT ADDRESS, 1957

B Y THE TIME I reached my junior year in college, I was deeply dis-
illusioned by the world I saw around me. I had grown up believing
in Superman, in "truth, justice, and the American Way," but this was the
1960s. The assassination of President Kennedy three years earlier had put
an end to Camelot, for me and for many in my generation. The deaths of
innocent people in Vietnam had shattered my belief in the benevolence
of U.S. foreign policy. And here in the Land of the Free, thousands were
struggling for basic civil rights.

Majoring in psychology, which I thought would be an exploration of
what makes humans tick, turned out to mean listening to dry academic
lectures about the behavior of rats in mazes. I wondered what learning
standard deviations in statistics had to do with anything in my life. In
philosophy, Camus and Sartre began to make a lot of sense and were
swiftly leading me toward my very own existential crisis. I ended up deciding that life had no meaning at all and must be the bad joke of some
Higher Intelligence with a bizarre sense of humor.

I became more and more depressed. For several months I steered every
conversation toward my gloomy perspective. Friends began to keep their
distance, not wanting to be brought down by their brooding philosophical companion. The counterculture was increasingly attractive and offered

some hope—peace, love, and the Beatles—but inside I still couldn't find anything that made life seem worth living.

Then one day while eating my lunch in the Queens College cafeteria, something happened that steered me in a new direction. As I sat there alone, under my dark cloud, I started looking around at the crowd of people in the room, some talking earnestly together, some wandering around looking a bit lost. Instead of falling into my usual habits of comparing myself to them, or thinking about how isolated I felt from everyone, I began to just look at them as they were going about their business. Suddenly they all seemed to me to be basically decent human beings simply trying their best to find their way in the world. It was like the shifting of a kaleidoscope into a whole different configuration, and from that perspective, I understood that all they wanted was to be happy—and it seemed to me they all had that right. I don't know why, but in that instant a philosophical insight occurred to me. The one thing that could give life meaning for anyone would be to bring happiness to others. That would be a noble endeavor in an ignoble world.

As I contemplated the simplicity of my new theory, it gradually dawned on me that helping others in this way might be reason enough for *me* to be here and to live life fully. *Could that be? Might there be something that would make life worthwhile? What if I thought of myself and my own life in this way—about bringing happiness to others?* I felt a momentary rise of something inside as that little beam of light broke through my perpetual cloud. I left the cafeteria with a bounce in my step that had been missing for a long time.

Those thoughts followed me around over the next few weeks, and the rightness of them kept growing. Somewhere inside I think I knew that if I could help others find happiness, I would actually be happier myself—that would be a big leap for the cynic I'd become. It would take a while before I was living this new way of looking at myself and the world, but something changed that day that set me on the road to finding real happiness.

In a commencement speech he delivered in 1957, Albert Schweitzer said, "I don't know what your destiny will be, but one thing I do know: The only ones among you who will be truly happy are those who have sought and found how to serve." Over the years I began to discover this myself, first as a schoolteacher, then later as I came into contact with various spiritual practices. Throughout my search for my own happiness, the recognition I had in the college cafeteria—that everyone wants to be happy—has stayed with me. While we may find happiness and contentment for ourselves, we don't have to look very hard to see there's suffering in the world all around us. Rather than shielding ourselves from this all-pervasive reality, I've learned that responding to it with compassion and caring action leads to an even deeper level of well-being and a joyful, fulfilled life.

When we're motivated by a true spirit of generosity, we benefit as much as those on the receiving end. Jesuit priest Anthony de Mello says it this way: "Charity is really self-interest masquerading under the form of altruism. I give myself the pleasure of pleasing others." In the same vein, the Dalai Lama playfully speaks of working to benefit others as "selfish altruism." Step Nine focuses on this path to happiness: relieving the suffering of others and helping them find happiness.

The altruistic urge to serve others has been held up as an ideal throughout human history. We call those who act on it "heroes," "saints," "paragons of virtue," "humanitarians." We say they are courageous, great-hearted, compassionate, and noble. I saw these qualities in my childhood heroes, Fiorello LaGuardia, Lou Gehrig, and Gandhi. LaGuardia was a mayor of New York in the early 1940s, when I wasn't yet born, but I learned about him when I was a kid. One of my favorite stories was of a time when he was officiating in misdemeanor court in New York City. A man who had stolen bread to feed his family came before him charged as a thief. LaGuardia fined the man ten dollars, then turned to the courtroom and said, "I'm fining everyone in this courtroom fifty cents for living in a city where a man has to steal bread in order to eat." The defendant left with $47.50 in his pocket. LaGuardia's spirit so inspired me I knew *that's* the kind of person I wanted to be.

We have seen this same spirit in heroes like Martin Luther King, Jr., Nelson Mandela, and Mother Teresa. We saw it in the firefighters at the Twin Towers of the World Trade Center on 9/11. The acts of such individuals can move us to tears and also inspire us to act on behalf of others.

In Buddhist teachings I was introduced to a term that encompasses all these qualities and folds them into a spiritual aspiration I find deeply meaningful—*Bodhisattva*.

This word in ancient Sanskrit means a being who is headed for enlightenment, and specifically refers to those who aspire to that lofty goal for the purpose of liberating all beings from suffering. The term is now commonly used to describe one who selflessly works to relieve suffering whenever possible. Although this term may be unfamiliar to some readers, I am going to introduce it here since it so well names the ideal and the qualities that are the point of this chapter.

The idea of liberating all beings from suffering sounds like a stretch. But working to benefit others is something any of us can do. So I like to call those of us who are inspired by this vision of relieving suffering and increasing happiness "Bodhisattvas-in-Training." We do the best we can and in the process learn how rewarding and beneficial it is to express our caring heart.

For centuries students of Buddhism have affirmed their aspiration to serve others by formally taking Bodhisattva vows. Thirty years after my existential crisis and epiphany in college, I had the opportunity to do this in a ceremony led by His Holiness, the Dalai Lama. In an auditorium surrounded by thousands of others, I repeated these words, formulated in the eighth century, that would induct me into this high caliber club:

> For boundless multitudes of living beings, may I be their ground and sustenance. For everything that lives, as far as are the limits of the sky, may I provide their livelihood and nourishment until they pass beyond the bonds of suffering.

Most Buddhist vows, like this one, typically push the envelope of possibility. I assume it is a way to keep us aspiring to our highest abilities. But as I spoke those words, meaning them as fully as I could, I realized that I had taken my own version of this vow years before in that college cafeteria when I had that insight about helping others find happiness. Since then I had come to know the vow not as a heavy burden but as a reminder of what gives meaning and fulfillment to life.

Creating Your Own Bodhisattva Vow

You can make up your own version of a vow to relieve suffering in the world. The basic principle is seeing your own happiness in the context of how it can benefit others. Take a few moments to ask yourself what words would sincerely convey that wish in a way that uplifts your heart. For instance you might say something along the lines of *May my happiness lead to the happiness of others.* When you've found the phrase that resonates with you, silently state those words as a promise to yourself, connecting with the sincerity of intention they express. Notice how your body and mind feel as you do this.

Making a conscious pledge to yourself in this way can focus your aspiration to serve others. It is not necessary to be a Buddhist or get involved in formal ceremonies. You can do it your own way and create your own vows. However you may decide to do it, taking this step is a powerful prescription for an ever-deepening joy.

THE HEART OF COMPASSION

The quality of heart that moves and supports the Bodhisattva is compassion. In English the word means "to suffer with," but a beautiful and perhaps more meaningful definition of compassion in Buddhist teachings is "the quivering of the heart in response to suffering." It is the sincere wish that others be free of suffering. At its core, compassion is a recognition that we are all interconnected, that your suffering is my suffering, that when I see you in pain, my heart trembles.

Compassion is not the same as pity, although they are sometimes spoken of interchangeably. Pity carries a subtle quality of distancing and aversion: *Too bad about you. (I'm glad it's not me!)* Though pity may lead us to respond to another's suffering with a good intention to help, the heart is

The Mirror of Compassion

Neuroscience is revealing that we literally "feel with" others through what are called "mirror neurons" in our brain. In his book *Field Notes on the Compassionate Life*, Marc Barasch describes this process:

"Mirror neurons . . . are a kind of brain mechanism dedicated to empathy's motto: *I feel you in me* . . . One study showed that the same cells that light up when a person's finger is jabbed with a pin also light up when someone *else's* finger is pricked. We wince when we see someone stub her toe and hop painfully on one foot. We know how it feels. Just as our brain is said to have a 'grammar nugget' that enables us to acquire complexities of language, perhaps we have a 'Golden Rule nugget' containing the neurological ground rules for compassion itself."

holding back, not opening to the joy that is potential in the response. Compassion is a profound softening of the heart when it encounters suffering. When our hearts are moved this way, the wall of protection that might separate us from another dissolves. Tibetan lama Chogyam Trungpa says that with compassion, it is as if "your heart is completely exposed. There is no skin or tissue covering it. . . ." There is something sweet in the tenderness we feel when we reach out in compassion. To feel that tender is to feel alive.

When asked what compassion feels like, some participants in the Awakening Joy course responded:

- I feel uplifted and fulfilled as I give, a peaceful warmth.
- I feel very present and softer in my mind.
- I feel "soft" and a bit teary.
- My heart hurts in a good way, and I am pleased to be feeling that connection to another.

The deep caring that suffering evokes in us, the greatness of heart, is actually an uplifting state. It feels good to care. This capacity to care about others and about life is the essence of the compassionate heart.

CULTIVATING COMPASSION

Keeping our hearts open in the face of suffering takes patience and practice. The Dalai Lama himself had to learn how to develop compassion. In *Worlds in Harmony: Compassionate Action for a Better World*, he says:

> Whenever I speak about the importance of compassion and love, people ask me: What is the method for developing them? This is not easy. You cannot just press a button and wait for them to appear. When I was fifteen or twenty, I was quite short-tempered, but through Buddhist training and through difficult experiences, I have been able to improve my mental stability. Difficult experiences are very good training for the mind. They help us develop a kind of inner determination. . . . Through training, we can change.

The Buddha, who so profoundly understood suffering, was known as The Compassionate One, and one of the main aspects of his teachings is how to develop our caring heart. While our own suffering can open us to empathize with the suffering of others, we can also systematically deepen our compassion through formal practices. As with other practices you've learned in this Awakening Joy program, an effective way to begin is by training the mind through meditation.

Modern neuroscience corroborates the fact that focused meditation is one of the most direct ways to activate and strengthen those areas in the brain that increase empathy. In his laboratory at the University of Wisconsin, Richard Davidson did extensive research on the effect of compassion meditation on the brains of student volunteers who had done the practice for one week, as well as Buddhist monks who had done thousands of hours of such meditation. In this particular kind of practice, the meditator becomes completely focused on experiencing lovingkindness and compassion for all beings. In her book *Train Your Mind, Change Your Brain*, Sharon Begley reports the results of the functional MRI scans Davidson took of participants in one of his investigations:

> During the generation of pure compassion, the brains of all the subjects, both adept meditators and novices, showed activity in regions responsible for monitoring one's emotions, planning movements, and positive emotions such as happiness. Regions that keep track of what is "self" and what is "other" became quieter, as if, during compassion meditation, the subjects . . . opened their minds and hearts to others.

Stephanie has been studying a particular Tibetan Buddhist practice that teaches how to tune in to another person's experience. Even after a short time, she has begun to see the difference in her daily life. The meditation, she says, has begun to change her perspective, like switching the figure-to-ground focus. She writes:

> Instead of getting so caught up in *What about me?* you do a little more of *What about you?* and that changes everything. You can tune in to another person's pain and find out what might be needed. We all share the human condition. When you practice shifting your focus to others, you're able to get outside yourself enough to really be there when you're with them.

As has been pointed out throughout this book, this doesn't mean forgetting to pay attention to your own needs or collapsing into another's pain. As Stephanie has discovered:

> When you tune in to another's suffering and send out compassionate thoughts to them, rather than draining you, it actually fills you up with more energy. You seem to clear out the confusion of your small mind and replace it with something much more vast and vibrant. Under all the chatter in your mind, there's a basic goodness you touch that's deeper and

more profound. When you let down the fear, you get filled up with that basic goodness and sweetness of your caring heart.

Compassion practice does not have to be limited to formal meditation. Throughout your day whenever you see someone having a hard time, you can tap in to that place of caring inside you and send out thoughts of compassion.

AWAKENING THE COMPASSIONATE HEART

By the time she was thirteen, Spring was well on her way to trouble. With her father out of the picture, things were hard at home and school wasn't much better. One day she was caught stealing. It was her good fortune that she was only ordered to do community service. Her mother sent her to volunteer at a local church that is well-known for its generous and successful social service programs. There Spring found herself in a new world, in more ways than one. She was serving meals to the homeless, side by side with former addicts and prostitutes who were now clean and sober. To her surprise, she says, "I felt all this love, and it was beautiful." The very first lunch she served to the destitute and homeless turned out to be a transformative experience for her:

> I went to the refrigerator and saw packs and packs of hot dogs, stacks and stacks of bread that looked really old, and these giant cans of pork and beans. I remember thinking, *This is lunch?*

It was a cold day and Spring started wondering if anyone would show up. In fact, when it came time to serve, she looked out the door and there were hundreds of people in a line that seemed endless. As they came through the line, "I noticed that everyone looked so sad," Spring said. "They all had their heads down." At first the cook told her to give each person two hot dogs, two pieces of bread, and two scoops of beans. After a while as people kept arriving and the line still went on as far as could be seen, the cook announced, "One hot dog, one piece of bread, one scoop of beans."

I started to feel a sense of desperation as people kept coming through, holding their kids, with tattered clothes, hair uncombed, and hoping for some food. Before long the cook came out again and said, "Half a hot dog, half a piece of bread." And then we ran out of food, and there were still more people in line.

Spring watched for a long time as people drifted away, still hungry. Later, after she'd helped clean up, she went outside and sat down on the curb in front of the church. She says:

> I started sobbing, thinking *This is not right.* What struck me most of all was how much I cared. I cared about all these people I didn't even know. I cared about the kids. I cared that they didn't get food, that it was cold, and where would they would go? I just sobbed and sobbed. I'd never felt like that before.

Even though she was used to seeing homeless people in her neighborhood, being face-to-face with so many in such need had a profound effect. Spring says she was changed after that. "Something deep within me was affected by it all."

What Spring went through was a deep encounter with suffering that is a kind of initiation onto the path of compassionate action. Keeping your heart open in the face of suffering is not easy. We often want to run away from such pain. I think even that impulse proves the point that we care. We feel the suffering of others, and it is often painful because we don't know what to do. Sometimes what we encounter can be so overwhelming that remaining present with it can seem impossible. But when you can't close your eyes anymore to the pain, and you recognize how deeply you care, that is the awakening of the compassionate heart.

Spring, now in her twenties, is considered a pioneer in bringing mindfulness-based meditation practices to youth and communities of color at the East Bay Meditation Center in Oakland, California, which she cofounded and where she teaches. She has also taught yoga and meditation to young people in juvenile hall. Having once been a troubled teen

Developing the Compassionate Heart

While you are sitting quietly, bring to mind someone you care about who is perhaps going through a hard time. Feel the connection you share and your love for that person. Then, staying in touch with the meaning of the words, silently direct these phrases toward him or her: *May you be free of suffering.* Or, *I care about your suffering.*

You might also direct these phrases toward yourself, as well as toward those categories of others discussed in lovingkindness practice—those close to you, those you have difficulty with, those you may never know. Ultimately you might include in compassion all the people and creatures on the planet.

As you do this practice, pay attention to what happens in your body and mind. You might notice a softening of your heart or perhaps a feeling of expansion in your chest. Let yourself fully welcome these feelings. By being present with them, you are deepening your capacity for empathy and developing your compassionate heart.

herself, she understands the experiences of those who end up there, and she can respond without judgment and without distancing herself from their suffering. The need and pain she saw that day serving lunch to the homeless and destitute opened her to the rich rewards of compassionate action.

COMPASSION IS A VERB

Thich Nhat Hahn, Buddhist teacher and activist, makes the point that compassion does not stop with letting our hearts feel the suffering of others. "Compassion is a verb," he stresses. Compassion and action go hand in hand. In those same MRI scans of monks meditating on compassion, neuroscience researcher Richard Davidson discovered that the areas of the brain responsible for planning action also lit up. In *Train Your Mind, Change Your Brain,* Sharon Begley quotes Davidson conveying his report to the Dalai Lama:

> This was a novel and unexpected finding . . . There's no physical activity; they're [the meditating monks] sitting still. One interpretation of this is that it may reflect the generation of a disposition to act in the face of suffering. It gives real meaning to the phrase "moved by compassion."

Not only are we wired for compassion, we appear to be wired for compassionate *action.* When we see suffering and feel compassion, it is natural to want to do something in response.

In his book *Field Notes on the Compassionate Life,* Marc Barasch quotes a young boy who understands exactly how this works. This eight-year-old was asked, "If you knew how someone else felt, would you be more likely to help them than if you didn't?" He replied, "Oh yes. What you do is, you forget everything else that's in your head, and then you make your mind into their mind. Then you know how they're feeling, so you know how to help them." From the mouth of babes . . .

When we remain present with our own aching heart at the suffering of another, we "make our mind into their mind," and that helps us know what to do. While Nyla was taking the Awakening Joy course, a friend of hers gave birth to a baby who lived for only three days. "I wanted to do something for her," Nyla wrote, "but I noticed that my first instinct was to run away from the hard feelings and uncertainty, and my fear that I might do something wrong." Learning about the practice of pausing to sit with her feelings, she decided to try it. What happened gave both Nyla and her friend deep comfort. She writes:

> I got in touch with my heart and realized I wanted to send my friend something to remember her baby with. I sent her a journal, a candle, and a tree to plant. The email she sent me in thanks still gives me goose bumps. She said the gift was exactly

what she needed. Sitting with those difficult feelings allowed me to get to the other side of my fear and make a real connection with someone having such a hard time. And when I saw her again, I also had the courage to ask to see a picture and talk about her baby. She was so grateful and said it was hard when people pretended like nothing had happened. Without the tools to face my own fear, I could have been one of those people.

COMPASSIONATE PRESENCE

When we don't know what to say in response to the suffering of another, sometimes just being present is enough. A story submitted for Canfield and Hansen's *A 3rd Serving of Chicken Soup for the Soul* has since become a popular example of the value of this response. The writer Leo Buscaglia was asked to be a judge for a "most compassionate child" contest. The winner was a four-year-old boy whose mother told the following story. Her son noticed that his next-door neighbor—an elderly man whose wife had just died—was sitting outside in his yard crying. The boy went over and climbed into the man's lap. When he returned home, the mother

In the Field of Compassion

When others you know are going through a difficult time, instead of rushing into action, pause for a moment to imagine what it would be like to be in their situation. From a wise and centered place, sense what kind of action would be appropriate. Perhaps it is to simply sit with them, or listen without trying to take away their pain. If it seems that they want to open up but can't, you might ask a question that helps reveal their feelings. Stay connected to your heart, both the ache and the sweetness of your caring response, and hold their suffering in that field of compassion.

asked, "What did you say to him?" Her child replied, "Nothing. I just helped him cry."

Offering our compassionate presence not only helps another but deeply nourishes us as we do it. And we don't need to know how to do anything other than be present. Jennifer is a hospice volunteer in Canada. One day she was asked to spend some time with a frail woman in her mid-eighties. "She tends to speak mostly in Dutch," Jennifer was told. When she found Louisa, she was talking to herself quietly and picking at the belt holding her into her chair. Jennifer introduced herself, and Louisa looked up and began speaking to her in Dutch. It didn't matter to Jennifer that she couldn't understand. Instead, she says:

> I just let go into her big beautiful eyes and rested fully in whatever feeling or emotion she was communicating. It was an astonishing experience. At times I'd be sharing in a quiet happiness, and at other times I'd be awash in deep sadness. Sometimes both our eyes were full of tears, and sometimes we smiled and laughed together. For almost two hours, there was a sense of open-hearted connectedness that I found intensely nourishing.

When Jennifer was leaving, Louisa pulled her toward her and gently kissed the top of her head. Jennifer says:

> On reflection, joy seemed to be the absolutely appropriate word to apply. While on one level I experienced a whole myriad of emotions, behind that shifting panoply was this steady sense of connection, of wholeness, of joy.

FROM RIPPLES INTO WAVES

Sometimes our compassion ripples out into the world in ways we can't even imagine. The ripple my sister Susan created when she lost a dear friend would unexpectedly become a great wave that now alleviates the suffering of thousands around the world. Susan is a gifted artist who was trained in fashion design. At school she studied alongside a brilliant Puerto Rican student, Antonio Lopez, whose creative genius set a new standard in the fashion industry.

Susan and Antonio had immediately recognized something in each other. In class they would work side by side, and Antonio would tease her: "I don't know why you're bothering to draw when you're going to be my model." Susan says, "I used to laugh when he'd say it, but secretly I knew I would have been glad to be his pencil sharpener. He exuded a positive energy that was just magical."

Susan did become Antonio's model—his first and favorite. And over the next two decades she would be his confidant as well as a close friend to both Antonio and his partner, Juan. In 1987, struggling with complications from AIDS, Antonio moved into Susan's Los Angeles home to spend his final few months. With no health insurance or money left to pay his medical bills, Antonio was essentially wasting away with no treatment to ease his suffering. Moved to take action, Susan decided to put on a show of Antonio's work as a fund-raiser. "In those days people were scared to even mention the word 'AIDS,'" she says, but Susan managed to convince a friend who owned an art gallery to host the event. To his amazement, 2,500 people came to Antonio's show.

Having watched helplessly as her friend died, Susan turned her personal sorrow at losing him into compassionate action to benefit all those who suffered from this epidemic. "I was devastated," she says, "but putting my energy into that idea provided an outlet." As a memorial tribute to Antonio, she and a couple of friends asked photographers they knew to donate their work for a silent auction and benefit to raise awareness of AIDS. Now, over two decades later, the organization she and Hossein Farmani started and still run—Focus on AIDS—regularly presents a benefit auction of works donated by world-class photographers. It has raised over $3 million for AIDS projects, including establishing the first children's AIDS hospital in India, which treats four thousand children each month; an orphanage and women's organization in Cambodia; and various AIDS projects in Africa.

Acting from her heart for the sake of others actually helped Susan discover not only her life's calling but also her career. Because of Focus on AIDS, she now plays an extensive role in the world of professional photography. And year after year her sorrow for the suffering of others continues to turn into the abundant joy of working to do something to help. Reflecting on what has happened, Susan says:

> It's funny, I was doing something to honor Antonio from my heart, and it not only made a big difference in others' lives, but it completely changed my life too. It's the most meaningful thing I do. And what's interesting is that I could never have imagined it would lead me to who I am now.

Whether what you do to alleviate suffering is small or large, compassionate action is one of the most fulfilling ways you can live your life. Angelina Jolie, who could choose to live in the lap of ease and luxury, has instead become a UN ambassador, traveling the world to speak about the poverty of children around the globe. Her dedication began when she was filming on location in Cambodia and saw the plight of children there. I saw a television program with Jolie in which the interviewer remarked on how generous she was to devote so much time to humanitarian activities when she could be more fully enjoying the life of a Hollywood celebrity. I

Caring for the World

The next time you read or hear a news story that reveals yet more suffering in the world, pause and notice how you feel. It may be outrage or helplessness. Go beneath those feelings and get in touch with how much you care. How might you respond? Whatever action you take—volunteering, writing a letter, sending funds—do it as a conscious compassion practice. You might speak the phrases silently as you carry out your action: *May you be free of suffering* or *I care about your suffering.*

remember Jolie looking at the woman and replying, "You don't understand. This is what really brings me joy, and my celebrity status is what allows me to do it."

Although it is wholesome and virtuous in itself to feel compassion, acting on it is what leads to your greatest happiness and hopefully to the greater well-being of those you seek to help. When you feel compassion rise in your heart, listen to hear what it motivates you to do. Julia Butterfly Hill is known for her work saving the old-growth redwoods in California. At a lecture I heard her say that people often come up to her after a talk or presentation saying, "Oh, Julia, you've really inspired me!" Her response: "That's wonderful . . . inspired you *to do what?*"

THIS IS THE WAY IT IS

Rose, a physician and a meditation teacher, volunteered to go to Tibet for a month as part of a medical team setting up clinics in monasteries, schools, and orphanages. There she witnessed extreme poverty—people living without access to clean water, women with crippling arthritis whose job was repairing roads because their nomadic life was gone, orphans whose parents had died of tuberculosis and who'd had little food and care since. As she encountered such suffering, Rose felt increasingly helpless. As she watched the women faithfully spinning their prayer wheels in hopes of improving their lot in life, their ritual looked so hopeless.

Her despair and dismay only intensified back at home when she was faced with all the luxuries and excesses of our culture. The great disparity between the two worlds was just too much to bear. In a crisis of faith, Rose went on a personal retreat to try to sort things out in her mind.

In the presence of a wise teacher, she allowed all the feelings of anguish to pour through her. Looking back, she says she felt like a child who was having a tantrum and screaming, "I don't want it to be this way, and it *is* this way. It has to stop! Somebody has to stop it! Why doesn't somebody stop it?!" Day after day, Rose's body and mind tightened with her futile desire for the terrible suffering in the world to end. On the other side of this debilitating anguish would be a profound and unexpected gift, but Rose would get there only when she accepted the truth of the suffering in the world and balanced her compassionate heart with a deep understanding.

Vowing to keep your heart open to suffering doesn't mean that you add to it by getting overwhelmed or burning yourself out. The point of the teachings is to create balance and well-being in your life, not overwhelming chaos. You are one of the most important recipients of your compassion. This can be hard to remember, but it is essential.

What helps with this is the practice of equanimity, the ability to remain composed and balanced, even in the face of challenges. Equanimity means neither getting caught up in the desire for circumstances to be a certain way nor pulling away from them in disgust or annoyance. While it can sometimes look like indifference, equanimity is actually based in a deep and compassionate understanding of the nature of life—that all things change, and that reacting from frustration or anger rather than responding with wisdom only creates more suffering. President Obama is sometimes criticized for his equanimous disposition, especially by some

Inviting Equanimity

Take a few deep and mindful breaths. Now let your awareness move slowly through your body, inviting each area to relax. Silently say to yourself: *May I have balance and equanimity in this moment* or *May I be centered in this moment.* Imagine what you would look like, what you would do and feel, if you were in easeful balance, and let yourself step into that.

This is especially useful if you notice that you are in a situation that is upsetting. As you do this practice, notice when thoughts arise wishing for things to be different from how they are at the moment. Allow even the confusion and agitation in your mind to just be, instead of trying to overcome it or push it away. Breathe, and let yourself relax into equanimity, leaning neither into desire nor aversion.

who want more bluster and bravado in his reactions. But in my eyes he is a good example of equanimity in action.

Like the tool of mindfulness, equanimity is a quality of mind that lets us simply acknowledge, as American monk Ajahn Sumedho puts it, this is "the way it is." In fact, so essential is this teaching in developing a balanced state of mind that that phrase became the title of one of his books. Energy spent feeling distressed and wishing things were different diminishes our capacity to respond. Suffering exists. Now what can effectively be done about it?

Compassion doesn't mean rescuing everyone we see from suffering. It means doing what we can, while also honoring our own limits. As the Serenity Prayer, used in the twelve-step program of Alcoholics Anonymous, says: "Grant me the courage to change the things I can, the serenity to accept the things I cannot change, and the wisdom to know the difference." Equanimity teaches us to care deeply but not be overwhelmed by our caring.

Thich Nhat Hanh, who was deeply involved in trying to alleviate the suffering in his country during the Vietnam war, often talks about the importance of equanimity for acting effectively in the face of danger. As an example, he refers to the boat people, refugees who risked the high seas and other dangers as they attempted to escape the war. Many were lost. Those boats that made it to safety, he reports, were the ones that had at least one calm person aboard. Their energy was enough to inspire others to find that place of courage, determination, and calm within themselves.

YOU NEVER KNOW . . .

Reading or hearing about suffering and cruelty, or about the destruction of the planet, awakens compassion and the desire to take action. But once you actually take that step, the task can seem so enormous that anything you do may seem to make little difference. Equanimity also allows us to not be rigidly attached to the outcome of our actions. Once we've done what we can, we don't really have control over what happens, nor can we ever accomplish everything that needs to be done.

Oren is a young activist who, like a lot of young people, has many different irons in the fire. Besides teaching meditation and Marshall Rosenberg's Nonviolent Communication skills, he works with people to heal trauma, is involved in sustainability efforts, participates in a nonprofit peace organization, and is a singer and musician. Engaged in so many ways, he has come to understand the value of equanimity. In a conversation about compassionate action, he told me:

> Thomas Merton says that an activist has to come to terms with the fact that what is done may ultimately be fruitless but that you're not doing it solely for the "hope of results." He says that as "you get used to this idea, you start more and more to concentrate . . . on the value, the rightness, the truth of what you do for itself." A Talmudic story similarly says that if the world were ending and you knew that nothing would make a difference, you'd still do what's most aligned with the heart's deepest values. Beyond the effect any action may have, living with integrity and responding to the circumstances in the best way I know brings the possibility of joy.

Aline is another dedicated young person who has learned to live and work with equanimity. She has been engaged in environmental protection and community development in countries like Senegal, Peru, Romania, and Ukraine. Yet despite all her work, she still witnesses heartbreaking destruction. "In Siberia, 60 percent of the logging in the formerly pristine region where I lived is illegal. I would see trucks and trucks of logs going to China. It was really painful."

We might think it could actually be too painful for her to continue doing the work. Aline could quit in disappointment and with a sense of failure. Instead, her response is a model of equanimity:

> I think it's important to take the long-range view. It's not about getting immediate results. It's like planting seeds. If you plant a seed and come the next day and think, "Oh nothing's come yet," you can get really frustrated. But if you plant the seed and think, "Okay, now is the time to water it and nourish it

and be patient," it will grow. There's something about trusting when you don't necessarily know what the results will be that comes back twofold. You may not see something concrete, but there's a feeling of belonging to the world, being part of the larger community. Something good comes back that you never would have expected.

As Joseph Goldstein likes to say, "You never know." When taking action comes from your heart rather than from the desire to see results, you can continue working without getting depleted, and you can derive joy rather than disappointment from the part you are playing. Gandhi said, "Whatever you do may seem insignificant to you, but it is most important that you do it." Why? Because as we do even the smallest compassionate action, we ourselves grow and unfold as noble beings.

DEVELOPING EQUANIMITY

Some of us may be temperamentally more equanimous than others, but like any other quality, equanimity can be developed. Each moment of mindfulness, nonjudgmental awareness, strengthens equanimity. As with lovingkindness, there is also a practice to develop this facility. The phrase traditionally used is: "Your happiness or unhappiness depends on your actions, not only on my wishes for you." Once again, this practice is intended to help us accept the way things are. But when I first heard that phrase, it felt to me rather cool and detached and seemed to be lacking in compassion. Even the variations I tried felt like they had an edge of not caring. But over time I began to understand that I can't prevent people from suffering, even those I love most deeply.

The first time I participated in a retreat dedicated to developing equanimity, I collided with that truth. I'd begun doing the practice by imagining various friends and saying the equanimity phrase. Suddenly my son Adam, then ten years old, came to mind. As I tried to direct those words toward him, something in me snagged. It was much harder to accept someone's suffering with equanimity when the someone was my own son. Could I really do that?

What followed for the next hour I refer to as my "Clockwork Orange" meditation. In the famously wrenching film by that name, there is a scene in which the protagonist is being programmed through forcibly viewing a string of ugly and horrifying scenes. As I sat in the meditation hall trying to practice equanimity, one scene after another of every parent's nightmare passed through my mind—drug addiction, car accidents, terminal diseases, self-destructive habits. As each horrible thing that could happen to Adam came into my mind, I would try to say that traditional phrase. Over and over I found myself recoiling in horror, silently crying out *No, No!* After some time I began to realize that as my son grew older, there would be little I could do to protect him from whatever suffering he was to meet in his life.

At some point the horror gave way to acceptance and finally relief in giving up the idea that my vigilance could protect my son. Of course he would face challenges, and the equanimity phrase I was using eventually morphed into *I honor your life's journey.* The entire process was tremendously

Equanimity Practice for a Loved One

Bring to mind someone you care about, preferably someone you love deeply. Hold an image of that person in your mind's eye and repeat these words as if they were a blessing: *Your happiness or unhappiness depends upon your actions, not only on my wishes for you.* Or you might want to say: *I care for you but I cannot keep you from suffering.* Just notice any feelings that arise and continue to repeat the phrase while taking in the meaning. When you can see and accept that the actions of that loved one have more effect on his or her life than whatever you might want, take in that feeling. Find where the sense of balance and release is expressed in your body and mind. You may at this point want to change your phrase to: *I honor your life's journey.*

freeing and has since allowed me to trust Adam's wisdom to find his own way. I'm happy to say, he's an amazing young man who is now in his twenties. None of my worst fears have come to pass, and although I have little control over how his life unfolds, I'm confident that he is going in the right direction.

BREAKING OPEN TO LOVE

Tibetan Buddhism teaches that equanimity allows for compassion without limits. It is the ability to feel compassion for the good and the bad, your allies and your enemies, the environmental activists and the polluters. Even if this is understandable as a concept, it might be hard to truly feel this. Perhaps the only way to really allow ourselves this degree of equanimity is to fully acknowledge and accept the depth of suffering in the world.

Rose knew that being on a retreat would not protect her from the overwhelming feelings she had in response to the suffering she'd seen in Tibet. In fact, it was the opposite; there would be no way to avoid that pain. So when she came face-to-face with its deepest expression, she didn't pull away. One day as she was meditating, all the feelings came to the surface, and letting go into them entirely, she found what was on the other side:

> I was crying and sobbing, "My heart is breaking. My heart is breaking." And I just kept allowing that experience. All of a sudden it became, "Ah, my heart is broken. My heart is broken open!" It felt as though something I was holding on to had shattered inside. I'd broken completely wide open. And all of this love began pouring through. It was like I broke open into universal compassion.

The grief and the pain continued, but Rose now felt like she was in the depths of a vast and caring universe:

> There was no one to hold and no one being held. Just the deep recognition: This is how it is in the world. There *is* this much

pain. Beings *are* doing this to each other. It's true *and* there's this much compassion and care, this much love.

What arose then was that profound understanding that arises when equanimity and compassion are in balance. Rose writes:

> I felt a deep love for all beings—all beings without exception. I saw behind the suffering to the beauty of each being. I could see the divinity in all the people I'd seen in suffering—the shining of who they were was untouched by the suffering. And the beings who were causing the suffering had that same shining.

For Rose this was an utterly transforming insight. She adds, "I know the potential for any one of us to cause harm through our suffering, and I felt great compassion for that." That experience lifted the despair that had paralyzed Rose. Now when her work leads her into the midst of so much suffering, she is able to respond with an open heart, yet hold the clear and balanced perspective that is the basis of effective action.

NURTURING THE SEEDS OF A NEW GENERATION

In 1975, when I was a young man still searching for my place in life, I was fortunate to get to know Robert Hall, a well-known and inspiring Gestalt therapist who was teaching at Naropa Institute. One day he asked me what I thought my destiny was. I replied I didn't know, but I thought I was supposed to do something that would contribute to other people's lives. He looked at me directly and said with great kindness and conviction, "I think you will. I think you'll touch people and make a difference in the world." His words had a huge impact on me. I sensed that perhaps he saw something that I didn't quite know. And I started to believe he could be right.

We don't have to be famous or charismatic leaders to have a similar effect. Each of us can empower others to find and fulfill their destiny. Every young person is a good candidate to invest in, even those who might be confused or seem to be lost. In fact, these are the very ones who need us, but it takes courage to respond when the challenge is great. Jan was on the verge of surrendering to failure when she came to a weekend workshop I was leading. While there, she found the inspiration to go on and ended up learning the value of never giving up.

Jan told me she had been teaching elementary school for fifteen years, and loving it—until a child appeared in her third-grade class who actually caused her to consider leaving her job. I'll call the girl Teresa, but her real name, aptly enough, translates into English as "Warrior Princess." Teresa was loud, disruptive, pushy, and she fought—with the other children, with the rules, with everything. Nothing Jan tried had affected that behavior.

When she asked if I had any advice, I told her I was a former school-teacher and shared with her my practice of looking for the key to each child's heart. I suggested that she give herself the same challenge by spending some private time discovering who this girl really was. When the workshop was over, Jan returned home eager to give this idea a try.

A few weeks later I heard from her. When Jan arrived at school on the Monday after the workshop, Teresa was peeking around the corner waiting for her. "I felt a certain sadness at the sight of her darting eyes—like an animal that doesn't know if she's going to be punished or welcomed with open arms," Jan wrote. "In that moment I realized what a large stick we wield as adults over the mental state of children. I had been so focused on punishing and making her as miserable as she was making me that I had almost lost her, this strong, strange, feisty girl."

To the child's surprise, Jan gave her a hug and told her they were going to work at understanding each other and find ways to make their day joyful. Even more surprising to Teresa, Jan invited her to have lunch, just the two of them, each day that week. Usually a student had to earn that privilege through good behavior. Teresa showed up for lunch that day and each day after, eagerly offering Jan "a week's worth of eye- and mind-opening conversations." She learned that there was a lot of trouble at home, and she began to understand some of what her Warrior Princess was dealing with every day.

By the end of the week, the two were laughing together, "looking for the joy in each other," as Jan put it. There were a few relapses into noisy and loud, pushy behavior, but the change in the child seemed hopeful. Then, on the first day when Jan didn't have lunch with her, Teresa didn't show up for class that afternoon. "The other children told me a boy had hurt her on the playground, and she got in a fight with him." When Jan saw her Warrior Princess in the school office, she says, "I wanted to cry with her. We had made such progress, but the scars in this child's life run deep." Jan's final words in that note held some promise. "I won't give up . . . and at least I now see her as a fellow human being who is trying to find a path that makes some sense in this confusing world."

Jan had found a balance of compassion and equanimity in her relationship with Teresa that was helping her ride the waves and continue trying, even when things looked hopeless. Being willing to be present for a young person, and to remain loyal when the rewards are not immediate, is true compassionate action. The same power that Jan recognized as "the large stick we wield as adults," can be transformed into having a tremendously positive impact when we believe in children and see their potential.

Four months after that first message, Jan sent me an update on her Warrior Princess. Recently the principal had to adjust class sizes, which meant moving one of Jan's students to another teacher. Teresa might have been the logical choice. But Jan wrote:

> I realized then that I didn't want to lose this amazing person who had been a thorn but is becoming something else in our evolution together. That's when it hit me—she would be the last student I would want to part with!

Jan may never know what her caring has meant for Teresa's life. As a schoolteacher myself, rarely have I found out the results of my efforts to support young people in discovering their true beauty. But a few years ago, I received an email that said: "Are you the Mr. Baraz who was my teacher and changed my life?" There at the end of the message was the name of Suzanna, who had been in one of my sixth-grade classes decades before.

I remembered that she was always trying to be helpful and make others happy. But there was a sadness about her that used to make me wonder what else was happening in her life. Although I would not learn the inner landscape of her world until years later, the intensity of her pain revealed itself one dramatic afternoon. During lunch Suzanna tried to put an end to her life by swallowing a bottle of aspirin. She returned to class, but when she began feeling sick, she started having second thoughts. She says, "I remember thinking, 'No, I do not want to die. Not like this.'" Suzanna passed a note to one of her friends. Terrified, the girl showed it to me. Within minutes an ambulance had arrived. After the school day ended, I spent the next few hours at the hospital until I could see that Suzanna was out of danger.

For the rest of the year I made sure that she received all the love and attention I could give her. At the end of the school year, I signed her autograph book with a sincere message that said, in part: "The sooner you become aware of the *real* you, like I have, the sooner you'll be able to appreciate yourself as I do."

In these last years since reconnecting, we've become friends. Suzanna's good heart is as radiant as ever, and what's more, she's at peace with herself. In a letter she wrote to me recently, I was surprised to find out

Being a Mentor

If you don't know how to begin offering your time to work with young people, contact a social service organization, such as the United Way or the Big Brother/Big Sister organizations or refer to serve.gov. If you belong to a church or other spiritual group, you will likely find there are many places you are needed and valued. The young people you have the opportunity to spend time with will teach you what works for them. Be present. Be absolutely trustworthy. Be genuinely encouraging. Help them fulfill their dreams. Let your connection be a practice of compassion and equanimity. And don't miss the joy.

that our year together and the words I wrote in her book were major factors in contributing to her shift toward well-being. Suzanna wrote:

> Though it took some time and, of course, life experiences, you gave me strength in believing that there must be more to me. . . . You helped open me up to a different perspective, and for that I thank you more than you could ever know. Every time I looked at your page in my autograph book, I felt happy. It was those very words that helped make me aware of the "real me." Not only did I begin to like myself, but I found that I love and respect myself.

You will find that there is hardly a better way to awaken joy than helping young people blossom. If your work doesn't put you in direct touch with young people, there are many volunteer mentoring opportunities available in your community, in your nation, in the world. In the process of responding to the call, you may find you have many opportunities to experience compassion—and equanimity! You may never know, but you can be sure that the good you've awakened will ripple out and make the world just that little bit better.

CALLING ALL BODHISATTVAS

When we become Bodhisattvas-in-Training, we set ourselves on a path toward a life that is meaningful and fulfilling. Expressing your caring by lessening the suffering around you is deeply rewarding. No matter how many challenges my young friend Aline has faced in her work around the world, she knows she'll continue doing this kind of service for the rest of her life. She writes:

> I think it's a very human thing to want to serve. It feeds something in the soul. If people look honestly, living their values counts more than money. If you're not aligned with your values it eats at you. When you are, something in you grows and comes alive. Each one of us has our own hidden purpose

inside, and needs to uncover it and give it wings. Service is one of the things that gets us in touch with that most natural and true part of ourselves.

According to Buddhist teachings, when the mind is clear and not preoccupied with *what's in it for me,* our inherent compassion is revealed. As Richard Davidson's neuroscientific research on compassion meditation has suggested, the natural response to seeing someone in distress is the impulse to help. We care about the suffering of others. And we feel good when that suffering is relieved. Whether we're involved in compassionate action ourselves, witnessing heroic actions in a movie, or reading about noble actions, a caring response to the suffering of others lifts us up. As Aline puts it, knowing that she's making a positive difference in people's lives is "one of the best feelings I've ever known."

Oren, the multitalented young activist, agrees that making a positive difference in the world has given him "some of the most deeply satisfying and meaningful moments in life." He continues:

> When I'm engaged in my work, at its best I'm stepping out of the way and life is moving through me. Whether teaching someone about Nonviolent Communication or working with someone in trauma or performing a song in front of an audience, the sense of self is not in the foreground. Life is moving through this mind and body and expressing what needs to happen in the moment, and that is a joyful experience. I am a part of life, not separate from it. That's what we're here for.

These young people love what they're doing, and they're doing what they love. As they demonstrate, sharing their talents and abilities for the well-being of others is the key to happiness.

You may think, "Yes, but those young people are doing things that are exciting and interesting, and I have to be stuck here in this little cubicle all day, or waiting on all these impatient people, or doing the same thing every day." Of course if you hate your job or are getting burned out, it's harder to access the joy of service. If your current livelihood or daily activities don't in themselves allow you that opening to joy of service, you could do compassionate action through simple acts of kindness—offering a sincere smile to coworkers, or taking an interest in the well-being of customers, or imagining how your job benefits people you'll never see.

Finding ways to lift up your heart changes your own life, which undoubtedly makes a difference for others. Shoshana's son Elias discovered this when he came home from college for the summer and found a job as a checkout clerk at a grocery store. Very soon he came up against the challenge it can be "to serve the public." Elias realized he could either spend the next couple of months gritting his teeth and getting through his shift, or he could reframe what he was doing in his job. He says:

> As a cashier it's really easy to get frustrated. Often people who come through the line are disrespectful or rude. You've been standing up all day, and you just want to be rude right back. I decided to make it a meditation practice to remember the human goodness of each person coming through, and to let that remembrance, and my love for humanity, shine out in the way I interacted with them—a kind of spiritual *namaste*, or bow to their spirit. It turned the job into a practice that made a visible difference in my life.

And it probably also did in the lives of those who came through Elias's checkout line. I certainly know how much a kind greeting did for me in a similar situation. I regularly cross a toll bridge on my way to the Spirit Rock Center where I teach. Several years ago there was a toll-taker whose presence was so uplifting that I'd try to guess which lane he was in, just so I could receive his "blessing." As I'd hand over my fee, he'd give me a radiant smile and a heartfelt, "I hope you have a great day!" I'm sure he did that with every single person crossing the bridge. It's easy to imagine the sense of satisfaction that he'd go home with each night. Years later I still remember him for how he brightened my day with his joyful spirit. We can't all be Albert Schweitzers, but we

Giving Is Good for You

Numerous studies have shown that giving in various ways has a beneficial effect on the giver.

- According to the measures of a Social Capital Community Benchmark survey, those who gave contributions of time or money were "forty-two percent more likely to be happy" than those who didn't give.
- Psychologists have identified a typical state of euphoria reported by those engaged in charitable activity. They call it "helper's high," and it's based on the theory that giving produces endorphins in the brain that provide a mild version of a morphine high.
- Research at the National Institutes of Health showed that the same area of the brain that is activated in response to food or sex (namely, pleasure) lit up when the participants in the study thought about giving money to a charity.
- At Emory University a study revealed that helping others lit up the same part of the brain as receiving rewards or experiencing pleasure.

can be ourselves, doing whatever we do and recognizing the tremendous power we have to bring a little more happiness into the world.

If your job can't be transformed in some way, consider getting involved in volunteer activities outside of work—helping out in a senior center or at a food bank, reading to children in library programs, assisting those with special needs. You never know what kind of change might come about in your life as you get you in touch with your spirit of compassion and make a difference in the lives of others.

Perhaps you have been moved and experienced a warm and uplifting feeling as you read some of the stories of kindness and compassion in this chapter. Maybe you've been inspired to reach out to help others yourself in some way. If so, you know the feeling psychology professor Jonathan Haidt has called the "elevation" response, the feeling of uplift and inspiration we experience on witnessing selfless acts and good deeds. Haidt writes: "Elevation is elicited by acts of virtue or moral beauty; it causes warm, open feelings . . . in the chest; and it motivates people to behave more virtuously themselves." Those "warm, open feelings" sound a lot like the way participants in the Awakening Joy course describe happiness.

Awakening joy in ourselves is also a way to serve others. By remaining in touch with your own aliveness and appreciation for life, you remind those around you of their own capacity to do the same. Rather than being self-indulgent or frivolous, to be joyful is a gift we give to those we meet and to the world. Joy awakens our love for life, and it's contagious. This is what the planet needs in order to heal and thrive. This is what we all need in order to blossom and to live fulfilling lives. For the sake of all of us, be happy.

Step 10

THE JOY OF SIMPLY BEING

Happiness cannot be found through great effort and willpower
but is already there in relaxation and letting go.
—LAMA GENDUN RINPOCHE

I WAS LYING ON the white sands of a spectacular beach on the Greek island of Sifnos. The Mediterranean Sea was a deep blue. The delicious smell of spanikopita from the nearby taverna filled the air. I was surrounded by a group of wonderful friends I had recently met while we were all gazing at the wonder of the Acropolis. And to top it off, we all loved singing together. I was in Paradise. Or could have been.

It was my annual European holiday, something I treated myself to each summer after a year of teaching elementary school in New York. I was right where I'd planned and hoped to be. But instead of really being there, immersed in that idyllic setting, I was caught up in my usual worries: *What am I going to do next? Something feels missing in my life. Will I ever really be happy?* I'd carried into Paradise the same agitated thoughts that ran my mind at home. They'd followed me as I drove to school in the morning. They'd been with me as I tried to fall asleep at night. And they made it so that I was everywhere but *here.*

On that island of Sifnos, if I had just let myself settle into where I was at that moment, I would have found exactly what I was looking for—the joy of simply being. It would take a few weeks in the magic of Greece, but eventually I did experience what it was like to stop looking for the next thing and just let myself *be.* I have to admit that being in Paradise definitely helped in the process, but the point is still the same. When I finally allowed myself to relax, let go of all my concerns about the past and the future, and just settled back into the moment, I discovered that the happiness I longed for was right under my nose. And for the first time in my life, it occurred to me that it might be there anytime, anywhere.

As I've been saying throughout this book, the joy we're looking for is inside us. Each step in the Awakening Joy program has focused on cultivating positive mind states, such as gratitude or compassion, that allow our inherent capacity for joy and well-being to arise. But there is another way to access joy—letting go of trying to make any particular state of mind happen, and connecting with your innate joy and aliveness.

The key to this deeper level of joy is learning how to relax, body *and* mind. As you do, your natural capacity for well-being and happiness emerges. I once heard a great Tibetan master say that the whole of spiritual practice could be summed up in two words: Be spacious. That is what the joy of being is about—entering into a spacious relationship with the moment. You let go of agendas and let your mind settle into a sense of presence. This state of ease and openness—this place inside I like to call our true home—is waiting for you all the time.

Allowing yourself to just relax and simply *be* might be so foreign that it takes a little time to get used to, as I found that first week or two I spent in Greece. We *think* we want more intensity, perhaps because it seems to make us feel more alive. But when we take a break from the adrenaline rush of stimulating activities and learn to rest in the moment, we meet a dimension of well-being that is full of vitality and renewal.

If you've ever undertaken a cleansing fast, you know that there's an initial period when all the food you can't have looks so good and you feel deprived. But as your body starts to detoxify, you begin to feel light and energized, and you don't miss all the potato chips, pizza, and fudge brownies. When you return to eating, you're attuned to the subtleties of taste and texture, and everything seems more flavorful. In the same way, there's a period of adjustment as you slow down or take a break from the momentum of a busy life. When you've learned how to take a time-out for *non-doing,* everything in your "doing" life becomes more alive and fulfilling.

Such moments of renewal can happen even when you're involved in daily activities. A martial arts student begins by slowly practicing movements of defense, and after a while he or she has the ability to fend off three attackers at once. In the same way, as you become more familiar with this quality of non-doing in quiet times, you can also find it in the midst of a busy life.

What I'm primarily encouraging, however, is consciously taking regular time-outs to be right here, right now. Eckhart Tolle says, "[L]ife is inseparable from the Now; it can unfold only Now." Most of our "Nows" are filled up with planning, fixing, producing, and all the other necessary actions of daily life, but there is a great joy in getting out of the fast lane to simply *be*. You can do this for an instant or for a day. Whatever length of time you find, it will renew your spirit and connect you with life in a profound way. Relaxing is the healthy complement to doing. Even God rested on the seventh day of creation.

You might think, "Great! This is the kind of road to happiness I like. I'm going to flop down on the couch and just *be* there in front of the TV for a while." Sorry, but *being* is not the same as spacing out and doing nothing. Although it might look like kicking back or vegging out, in the state of being I'm referring to, you are alert and relaxed at the same time. So turn off the TV, put down the remote, and see what happens when you discover *this* moment.

All of the other steps in this program support this final step. You started with setting the intention to awaken joy, deciding to do your part to find where true happiness lies. Mindfulness is what gets you here in the present and helps you wake up to life. Gratitude expands the heart so that you can meet the moment with appreciation and wonder. The capacity to work with difficulties as they arise gives you confidence to know that you can be present for whatever hand life deals you. Living with integrity aligns you with your highest values and frees you of remorse, creating the conditions for inner peace. Developing the ability to let go allows you to flow with the changes of life, rather than trying to hang on to something you think will make you happy. Learning to love yourself helps you stop the self-judgment, access the goodness inside, and settle into being who you are. Connecting with others is about letting your love shine through naturally. Compassion arises as your heart meets suffering and responds. All these qualities and actions are ingredients in our recipe for happiness, and they continue to support you, functioning like a hologram in which they interactively strengthen each other. In this step you rest on what you have derived from them and enter into a connection with life that is effortless and joyful.

WHAT IS *BEING?*

Most of you reading this book in some way or another know the experience of *being* I'm talking about. You may recall moments as a child when you sank into a deliciously relaxed state of ease and happiness. You may find yourself accessing this state in a yoga class, during moments of quiet reflection, or while out running. It can happen when you're dancing, playing an instrument, or looking at microorganisms in a biology lab. There are different "flavors" of being and different ways of accessing them.

Being "in the zone" is an experience common among athletes or performers when they are so engaged with the game, the music, or the drama that they forget themselves. Time slows down, and they often find themselves executing brilliant moves. Karlene Sugarman, a sports psychology consultant, lists a number of qualities that characterize the zone: relaxed, confident, focused, effortless, automatic (the thinking mind is not in the way), and fun (deeply enjoyable). These qualities also define the state that I'm talking about. However, there is another quality Sugarman includes to describe the zone for performers and those engaged in a certain task—being in control. This is different from the state of *being* addressed in this chapter. The only task here is to let go of effort and settle into a state of relaxed presence.

In describing the state of *being,* course participants most commonly use words such as: aware, spacious, peaceful, smooth, restful, and light. They say that during the experience:

- A calmness falls over me, I "quiet" and feel my physical body loosen.
- I feel open and ready, no thought.

- I feel a fullness in my chest and a feeling in my throat as if I'm about to sing or cry out in joy, and sometimes there are tears of joy.
- My mind becomes more available to a deeper sense of order.
- My body posture comes more into alignment.
- I feel whole and at ease, unjudged, unjudging, loving and able to love myself as I am and circumstances as they are.

Being Aware

In the midst of any activity in your day, stop for a moment of being. Become mindfully aware of your experience. Notice that you are thinking, that thoughts come and go. Notice whatever emotions that might be arising. Feel the sensations in various parts of your body. Feel your breath coming in and going out. Notice that you are not making awareness happen. It happens by itself effortlessly. You are simply aware. Feel the spaciousness and peace.

BOREDOM AND BREAKTHROUGH

You might wonder: If you're not busy doing something, where's the joy in that? We're so used to stimulation and entertainment that the idea of quieting down enough to tune in to stillness and silence can sound pretty boring. It might even seem scary. When I was younger, the thought of not having something planned in my calendar for a Friday night was terrifying. "What will I do with myself?" I'd wonder. A weekend with nothing going on can feel to us like a terrible emptiness. So we persist in perpetual motion. But what exactly are we afraid of?

There are some good reasons for being afraid to stop filling up your life with action. When you're not distracted, you're alone with your mind.

Having nothing to immediately chew on, it can dredge up a little frightening "entertainment" from the past, or create a horror movie of the future. This is where meditation or some other reflective or introspective practice is such a valuable support. In seeing how the mind works and learning to be at ease with all of its contents, you develop the faculty of equanimity. As Rick Hanson pointed out in Step Nine, equanimity is deeper than calm, because even when our thoughts are bouncing off the walls, with equanimity we can remain balanced and aware, not collapsing into the chaos. We can abide in the awareness of the swirl, rather than in the swirl itself.

There is a huge reward in learning to make friends with your mind: You discover the exquisite experience of just being present. Drawing upon the practices you have learned throughout this book, you build the foundation for a mind that needs no entertainment to enjoy the moment. This allows it to relax into a state of ease. I once attended a lecture by a Tibetan master who started his talk with the enticing line, "Tonight I will talk about the real breakthrough in spiritual practice." The huge crowd in the auditorium was abuzz with excitement, thinking that they would be the fortunate ones to receive these special teachings. The master then proceeded to ramble on for the next two hours in a rather uninspired manner. As the crowd grew increasingly disappointed and restless, he suddenly stopped midsentence, leaned forward, and whispered, "The real breakthrough is boredom!"

Smiling, he sat back to explain to his puzzled audience what he meant. As long as we're looking for the next experience to delight or entertain us, we miss the big secret: When we learn to disconnect from constant stimulation and distraction, we begin the work of freeing our mind from the restlessness of wanting and not wanting. And we also arrive at the doorway to the peace and well-being that come with completely resting in this moment. The flip side of boredom turns out to be peace.

DOORWAYS TO BEING

When I was a child, I was enthralled by astronomy. But growing up in New York City, I couldn't see many stars in the sky, so I would beg my

When I stop to appreciate a flower, the weight drops from my shoulders. I settle and get quiet, and I feel spacious and expanded inside.

—A COURSE PARTICIPANT

parents to take me to my favorite spot in the world: the Hayden Planetarium. When the day would arrive for the new monthly show, I could hardly contain my excitement. Gazing up at that magic star-filled sky dome, all I could say, over and over, was "Wow!" The vast expanse seemed limitless. The Earth, and everything on it including me, was just a tiny speck. I somehow felt both infinitely small and mysteriously connected with something infinitely great. Those moments in the darkness of the planetarium, with my parents on either side of me, I was led by wonder into the present moment. Nowhere else existed.

We're all born with the capacity for wonder and awe, and these are doorways for us into being. Jesus said, "Truly I tell you, unless you change and become like children, you will never enter the kingdom of heaven" (Matthew 18:3). When we pause in childlike wonder and appreciation, we enter the kingdom of heaven, for in those moments we are profoundly connected to life.

As a child I regularly fell into this state of wonder by experiencing what I came to call the Big Giggle. I'd ask myself certain questions that would stop my mind and turn me inside out: *What does it mean to be alive? How did I get into this body and end up being this person other people call "Jamie" and I call "me"?* Then I'd wait as the questions carried me deep into a place where I could no longer tell who was asking the question. The boundaries between me and the rest of life would dissolve. In that moment there was just presence, with no distracting thoughts or feelings. It was an experience of life moving through me, and it was profoundly joyful. This could happen to me anywhere—in the middle of school, walking down the street, or lying in my bed at night. When I let myself go into it, I would often start to laugh to myself—sometimes right out loud. It was like a button I could press at any time, and the Big Giggle would follow.

In the right frame of mind, we can be in awe of just about anything and be transported through our attention into the moment of being. This is essentially an attitude of deep appreciation. We might find it in viewing a painting, washing dishes, or watching a superb actor at work. While there are endless things to appreciate, poets and scientists would agree that being in the natural world rivets us to the moment in a special way, and we find ourselves in a profound state of being. Sally Clough Armstrong, one of my teaching colleagues at Spirit Rock, puts it this way:

> When I let my mind really appreciate what is right in front of me—the clouds or a rainbow or a bird flying by—there is a sense of wonder and amazement at the richness of life. To truly open to that, the mind has to be still. There's a sense of aliveness relating to the outside, but the internal experience is one of stillness, of stopping and connecting with life. It's just stillness and aliveness without a lot of mental content to it.

Nature has no agenda for us. When we're present with the sights and sounds in any natural setting, we are free to not-do. We can be simply present for the soft breeze touching our face. We can open our senses to receive the images of trees and flowers, and take in the sounds of crickets and the rustle of wind in the leaves. And we enter the "stillness and aliveness" Sally describes.

Wonder and appreciation are in themselves relaxed and receptive states, a receiving rather than reaching out. We are awake and attentive, and the door opens to a delightful state of being. This is the way Guy Armstrong, another of my teaching colleagues, puts it:

> It's not that we have to do anything special, but rather when we stop striving, natural happiness is there to be touched. Our basic nature is peaceful, and that peace brings a kind of joy. All we have to do to find it is to stop disturbing it. When the body calms down and the mind can just relax and rest, there's a joy and delight in that experience which is very pleasurable in itself and very renewing. There's a feeling of the batteries being recharged: aliveness refreshing itself.

You can drop into this relaxed, effortless presence at any time—while listening to music, soaking in a hot bath, meditating, or sipping a cup of tea. It can also happen in the midst of energetic activities, like swimming or hiking or singing. It happens when we invite it and stand in awe at the miracle of being alive. It happens when we set aside the judging mind that separates us from the moment. And it arises when we realize we have nowhere to go but here.

WEEDING THE MIND

The state of being is not only delightful and renewing, it has a very practical benefit as well. Deeper than conflicting thoughts, it is the source of wisdom. When we find ourselves confused or pulled apart by indecision, tapping in to what some call our "peaceful center" can align us with what will bring our life into harmony.

For my wife, Jane, gardening is a way to drop into that feeling of wholeness and experience its benefits. She says:

> Gardening helps me relax and connect with an inner peace. I love taking a break from the emails, phone calls, and never-ending to-do lists to step outside into the world of dogs, birds, and squirrels, into the changing weather patterns, and feel the anchoring of big trees, which have been around longer than I have. The interesting thing is that even though I'm not trying to solve any problems, clarity comes and things just seem to fall into place. While I'm weeding the garden, it's like I'm weeding my mind as well.

When we give ourselves the time to relax and let our minds be "weeded," we can better listen to those inner promptings that keep us on track with our deeper life purpose. We're all familiar with what happens when we don't listen or can't hear because the chaotic thoughts in our mind are taking the driver's seat. We're likely to plunge over a cliff. That's what happened to Allison when, in confusion, she gave up the love of her life.

I met Allison on her first meditation retreat at Spirit Rock and, although it was clear she had some major struggles going on in her life, I was struck by her sincerity and deep longing for peace. She'd come to the retreat looking for a lifeline, she said, and told me about how she'd been through several destructive relationships, and in and out of substance abuse, often occasioned by or in response to bouts of depression. Finding a way to pay the bills was one of her main preoccupations. Now she was ready for a change, a big change, and she was ready to do whatever would help.

Over the next two years, Allison regularly attended my weekly meditation group in Berkeley, and I got to know more of her story. A couple of decades before, when she was in her twenties, Allison met David. She had been leading a wild life, many boyfriends, lots of partying. "I was out of control," she told me. In hope of finding some balance, she'd made an appointment with an acupuncturist—David. Right from the start there was a special chemistry between them. When the strong attraction became apparent to both of them, David stopped seeing her professionally, and they began a loving relationship. "I had been living a lie with many of my friends until then. David said to me, 'You have to tell the truth.' And somehow that stuck."

Allison did start telling the truth—to everyone but herself. The voice of fear told her that what she and David shared couldn't possibly last. After a few months, Allison broke off the relationship. Although something within her was begging to stay with David, doubt and fear, disguised as the lure of fun and adventure, had won out. "I knew he was a healthy partner who would love me, but I didn't love myself," Allison recently reflected. "I felt awkward being in a 'wholesome' relationship. It was too foreign for someone with my background. And I just wasn't mature enough to listen to what I really needed. He was like a saint and I wanted excitement. I ended my relationship with him because I was not done 'being bad.'"

David was devastated, and his grief led him further into the spiritual practice he'd been doing for a couple of years with a Kriya Yoga teacher from India. He soon found himself managing his guru's ashram in the United States. A few years later David became a monk himself and took a vow of celibacy. The title of swami, a master of yoga and Hindu philosophy, was conferred upon him. David brought his big heart, his guitar, and his storytelling ability to his work as a spiritual teacher, and in time he became known as the Storytelling Monk. As the number of his followers increased, he was able to establish a network of orphanages, schools, and shelters throughout India and South America, dedicated to providing refuge and support to street children and the poor in the villages he visited. He never forgot Allison and would often explain, when people asked how he became a swami, that a woman in Berkeley had unwittingly pushed him into the arms of the Divine by breaking his heart at the perfect time.

Meanwhile Allison floundered. For the next seventeen years, she was led down dead-end alleys by those confusing voices inside saying: "This way to happiness; no, that way." The unexpected catalyst that began to turn her life around was a class in physiology taught by an inspiring teacher at a community college. "Wow, we are just amazing beings," Allison remembers thinking. "I was learning that there are over a trillion cells in the human body, and each little cell's only job is to work for my well-being. I began to wonder how could I do anything to harm this body that is nothing less than a miracle."

That was the beginning. Allison stopped drinking, started letting go of unhealthy relationships, and soon found her way to Spirit Rock and that meditation retreat I was leading. "I felt like I'd found everything I'd been looking for my whole life," she told me. "Part of me literally woke up." It would take her a while to climb out of the disorder in her life, but Allison knew she was on the right track and steadily moved in a new and positive direction.

THE STILL, SMALL VOICE WITHIN

The voice of wisdom, that inner guide, is hard to hear when the mind is filled with distractions, conflicting desires, and self-doubts. Throughout this book we've seen many instances of people's lives descending into chaos when they believed a particular "story" they were telling themselves. And we've also seen that although these stories are programmed into us, they are not our only guide. A deeper wisdom is always available. It might be covered by a lot of static, but it's there, and we hear it when we drop into being present, when we get past all the noise, relax our grip, and tune in to the clarity that arises from the stillness within.

Each of us has our own way of accessing this wisdom. We might call it intuition or guidance or the "still, small voice within." The Third Zen Patriarch says: "Stop talking and thinking and there is nothing you'll not be able to know." For many, prayer is the way to contact this deeper level of truth. Mother Teresa said, "Prayer is putting oneself in the hands of God . . . and listening to His voice in the depth of our hearts." Buddhist monk Ajahn Chah spoke about "listening to the One Who Knows." In letting go of agendas and being at ease with this moment, the "figuring out mind" gets out of the way and we can hear the wisdom inside.

It's hard to connect with the receptivity of *being* and hear the truth inside when you're anxious or stirred up. How do we sort out the various voices when we must make a decision or choice in life? I sometimes find that taking a break from my mind and getting into my body—going for a walk or taking a bike ride—helps discharge agitated energy, gets me grounded, and clears my mind enough to discern the answer that feels right.

How do we know when an answer "feels right"? For me, the voice of wisdom usually has a tone of kindness, clarity, compassion, and understanding. I sense it won't steer me wrong. There's usually a feeling of relaxation in my body, a softening in my heart, a release in my gut, a drop in my shoulders.

When I ask course participants how they know when they've arrived at a good decision, responses have included these:

- I feel like everything in my body and mind is in alignment.
- There is a great feeling of calm and readiness to accept what is happening now and what may happen in the future.
- I feel solid, like I'm standing in my truth.
- The muscles in my body feel soft and released, as opposed to tense and holding on, and my monkey mind quiets down.
- I live inside my skin with greater ease.
- I feel a clarity in my mind and a sense of kindness in my heart.

It was challenging for Allison to break the habits that were driving her, and the voice of wisdom inside was still distant. But David had helped awaken something in her those many years before by seeing what was true and real, and now she was watering that seed by taking care of her body, meditating, and paying attention to what she really wanted. "I started reading a lot and spending time by myself. I had wanted inner peace, but I never thought it was possible before. I just hadn't known how to get there." Allison was finding her way toward happiness.

And then she slipped. Longing for love and connection, she struck up a friendship with a married man. Although she knew it would cause pain to everyone involved, the attraction was strong, and the confusion of voices inside drowned out the voice of wisdom she was just getting to know. Desperate, she talked to friend after friend. "When I contemplated having an affair, I told at least four people what I was planning to do, and not one of them said 'Don't do it.'" Allison sought out an old boyfriend who surprisingly provided exactly what she needed. "He said, 'Don't do it. It's not you. You aren't that person anymore.' There was this huge 'thank you' that arose inside me and a tremendous sense of relief when I heard the truth. It rang like a siren inside my soul and *woke me up*." We know the ring of truth when we hear it.

Allison heard another clear message as well: Contact David. This time when she searched for him on the Internet, she found him—as the Storytelling Monk. "I was looking for my anchor of truth to keep me on the path I had worked so damn hard to stay on." Allison mustered up her courage and sent the swami an email. Within minutes he replied. "He wrote me that he was just telling his students the week before that I was one of his first gurus, because when his life went into crisis after we parted, he found his true self. He said he'd been sending me blessings and prayers for the last twenty years."

Over the course of the next two months, they stayed in daily touch by email. It soon became obvious to both of them that their old love story was not finished. David invited Allison to join him in India for a meditation program and a pilgrimage to various holy places he had organized for a group of his students. This time when Allison met David, she was able to hear what she had known to be true all along—he was the perfect partner for her.

With the blessings of his fellow swamis in the order, David has made the decision to forego being a monk, marry Allison, and continue doing his spiritual work as a lay person. As Allison looks back on her life and the lessons she's learned, one of the most important among them is knowing how to listen carefully to her deepest self and act on that. Now she knows the signs that point the way. She says:

> When I stay grounded in my truth, my heart feels light and open and expansive. When I am living outside the truth and out of alignment with my integrity, I feel a weight on my chest, on my heart. This pressure disconnects me from others. And it doesn't leave until I make peace with whatever the problem is.

TRUSTING LIFE

When you know how to listen to that voice inside, you begin to live in a way that aligns you with life. You find yourself increasingly in the right place at the right time. You can call it listening to your intuition or to the voice of God in your heart, but it lets you live in trust instead of fear.

Part of trusting life is knowing that what you need in order to live in harmony with yourself and with life is always available. As Ram Dass says in *Be Here Now*, "Whenever you're ready, you'll hear the next message." You might not always hear it inside you. Sometimes the message we recognize as the truth comes from someone else. Your best friend or your grandmother offers some sage advice, or you get an astrology reading, or you open up a fortune cookie, and you immediately have a sense that what you are hearing is just for you. You are brought back from a confusion of thoughts and into the moment. Once again you realize that you can trust in life.

This became clear to me one memorable time long before I'd learned how to listen for the wisdom inside me. At a major turning point in my life, I consulted a psychic, and the message I received still remains a guide. Reverend Miller looked a lot like Colonel Sanders, but instead of dispensing Kentucky Fried, he served up his own brand of wise guidance.

Setting Up a New Ring Tone

The more we practice quieting down and listening to the truth inside, the more easily we access our wisdom. Think back to a good decision you've made in your life. Try to remember the moment when your course of action became clear to you. How did you know it was the right thing to do? What was the feeling in your body? What was the tone of voice in your mind? Each time you make a good decision, pay attention to your experience, that sense of rightness and ease in your heart. Get to know how it feels. Whenever you are facing a decision, see if you can quiet down enough to access it and listen to what it is trying to tell you.

Overwhelmed by indecision, and a little desperate for some good advice, I made an appointment. At five dollars a reading, what was there to lose?

I made my way past the clutter of books in his living room and sat down before him to lay out my problem. There were several directions I could go in my life, and I didn't know which one to choose. Every one of them seemed good, I told him, but what if I blew it by choosing the wrong way?

Reverend Miller listened intently as I poured out my confusion, then closed his eyes and sat there for what felt like an eternity. I imagined he was consulting with the spirit guides he often spoke about. Finally, he opened his eyes and looked straight at me.

"Well, I'm not going to tell you what to do," he pronounced. My disappointment must have been obvious as I sighed. Just as I began wondering if this was worth the five dollars after all, he spoke again: "But I will tell you one thing."

"Yes?" I replied eagerly. Reverend Miller looked at me with great kindness and a clarity that came from years of being a keen student of life. "It doesn't matter," he said.

"What do you mean it doesn't matter? That's my life you're talking about," I shot back, incredulous and somewhat annoyed. At that, the Reverend proceeded to give me my money's worth.

"Fear blocks any movement on your journey," he began. "But once you get past that and take the first step, life opens up and shows you what to do next." He went on to say that we might find that a choice clearly leads us to the goal we wanted, or we may discover after a while that another option is better. But either way we learn valuable lessons. Or we might start out thinking we know where a certain choice is leading us, and in the process, other possibilities and opportunities we never could have imagined turn up. "Any way you choose, it doesn't matter," he said. "If you listen carefully and you're patient, life will lead you where you need to go as you continue on your journey."

It was the best five dollars I ever spent. And over time I saw that Reverend Miller was right. When I listen to fear, things only get more confusing. But if I let go of the fear and just move forward, the way becomes clear.

Einstein is reported to have said that the most important question we can ask ourselves is: "Is the Universe friendly?" That's a question that comes up when we talk about trusting life. One could make a good a case for the Universe being unfriendly. Life is filled with suffering and the good times don't last. We lose people we love and at any moment something terrible could happen. Maybe the only answer to the question is: It depends upon how we choose to look at it. And that choice affects our experience of life.

I choose to answer Einstein's question with a resounding *Yes!* When life is hard, we learn to deepen our compassion and understanding. When it's wonderful, we can enjoy our good fortune gratefully. The more I see that each moment of my life, good or bad, is a gift, the more I trust that I can let go into life.

Learning to trust life is a lot like learning to swim. The first time you're on your own in the water, you flail around, sure you're going to drown. Then as you relax a bit, you see that treading water is possible. Finally, when you let go completely and just relax, you find that you are magically held up by the water. It was ready to support you all the time. You just needed to trust enough to relax and let it do that.

When you stop flailing around and let yourself relax in trust, you begin to see that life is not out to get you but is instead a beautiful ocean in which you are swimming. The more you tune in to your peaceful center, the more confidence you develop in your ability to "stay afloat" no matter what is happening. The more you rest in being, the more you trust life. And the more you trust life, the more you can let yourself be guided by the wisdom available to you in that profound relaxation.

I had a glimpse of knowing what it would be like to so profoundly trust life that I would have no fear. It has been a guiding aspiration ever since. On one of my trips to India, I traveled to Lucknow to spend some time with a remarkable teacher, H. W. L. Poonja, called Poonjaji or Papaji by his students. Earlier in life he had been in the British Army, and he and his wife had raised a family. By the time I met him he was eighty years old, yet one of the most vital human beings I'd ever encountered. His electric smile alone made me feel more alive.

As a student of Ramana Maharshi, a great Indian sage who taught the philosophy of nondualism, Poonjaji was committed to getting his students beyond simply developing a meditation practice. He wanted them to have the direct realization that their true nature is much vaster than the limited idea they had of themselves. The route to his goal was simply relaxing the mind and letting go deeply into their *beingness.* By that time I had been a teacher of mindfulness meditation for a dozen years. In my experience, training the mind took a lot of effort, which seemed necessary in order to reap the many benefits I'd seen in myself and count-less others. And here he was telling me to stop all effort and let go of any doing as the method to free the mind. I was intrigued by Poonjaji's approach but skeptical. Yet little by little I found myself putting aside my thoughts and questions and simply melting into the incredibly delicious and powerful energy of Poonjaji's presence and love.

At one point he asked me a question, and as I searched inside for the answer, I went deeper and deeper, as if being pulled into a vortex. I'm not sure exactly what happened next, but it seemed that my mind short-circuited and stopped. When I came back, it was like I'd taken a trip into Eternity. I found myself looking at Poonjaji with deep love and appreciation. As our eyes met I sensed a strong energy flowing between us, along with the feeling that both of us were connected to one big ocean of *being*—the same ocean of being that I sensed as the source of all life. Whether it's called love, awareness, God, Self, or the Divine, I knew I was always held by it, that I could trust it, and that the way to knowing it was through simply relaxing into being.

WITHIN YOU AND WITHOUT YOU

We are part of life. How could we not be? We breathe in what the trees and plants breathe out and vice versa. We live in an entirely interconnected Universe. Thich Nhat Hanh talks about seeing that the paper you are reading these words on contains "the cloud, the forest, the logger." The fact that all things are connected in this way he calls "interbeing." In this complex web of interdependence, every living being is part of and affects everything else. The "butterfly effect" in chaos theory holds that a butterfly flapping its wings in Asia contributes to conditions that can result in a tornado in Oklahoma. A mutating virus in one part of the world causes ripples of fear across the entire globe. Just as we are not separate from our environment, we are also continually "interbeing" with all the other humans who make up our lives, from our ancestors to musicians on the other side of the ocean. A scruffy band from Liverpool, writing songs about love, can transform a global culture. As John Lennon put it: "I am he as you are he as you are me and we are all together."

We can understand interconnectedness as a concept, but knowing it through experience is what helps us to live in accordance with this reality. Alexa, the young woman who did her masters thesis on her journey from self-hatred to self-love, wrote:

> I can listen to myriad eco-psychologists tell me that I need to envision a world in which I know that I am a bit of the walking skin of the Earth. I can listen to the story of the Universe and be intellectually inspired, but it is not until I can integrate the concept of interconnection into a whole body, mind, heart experience that I truly know I am connected to all else.

For Alexa that experience comes through her spiritual practice, and through connecting with others through their personal stories. She says, "Through various spiritual paths, we begin to see our interdependence throughout the Earth community. Through sharing our stories, we can begin to *feel* connection." Through the many stories in this book you may have identified with, you have experienced interbeing with others. You have found yourself in them.

Knowing our interconnection changes our sense of who we are. Biologist Lewis Thomas reveals in a fascinating way how the cells of our body are "ecosystems more complex than Jamaica Bay." In *Lives of a Cell* he writes:

> A good case can be made for our non-existence as entities … We are shared, rented, occupied. At the interior of our own cells, driving them, providing the oxidative energy that sends us out for the improvement of each shining day, are mitochondria, and in a strict sense they are not ours. They turn out to be little separate creatures … replicating in their own fashion, privately, with their own DNA and RNA quite different from ours. Without them, we would not move a muscle, drum a finger, think a thought …

Thomas's recognition of "our non-existence as entities" is echoed in modern psychology, neuroscience, and Buddhist philosophy, all of which say we do not have a self separate from the complex process that sustains our existence. Buckminster Fuller said we are not nouns, we are verbs—fields of activity happening with thoughts and moods coming and going, countless sensations happening simultaneously, blood flowing, nervous system firing, hormones shooting through. We are a mind-body process that gives rise to a sense of a continuous, cohesive identity.

In an interview with Steve Donoso in *The Sun* magazine, Eckhart Tolle said:

> If I am not who I think I am; and I am not who everybody I know has been telling me I am; and I am not the story in my

head; and I am not the beliefs, the accumulated experiences, the memory traces—then who am I? Every answer to that question is dangerous, because every word that one might use will create another concept. The reality of who you are can never be expressed in words. Words are only signposts that point the way.

Tolle's words point toward that aware presence that observes and knows that we are thinking, feeling, loving, living. When we go beyond the illusion of separation, we see that on a deeper level we are connected to everything else in a way that sounds like what mystics throughout the ages have talked about. It's that ocean of being I felt with Poonjaji. From that awake and aware presence arises the love that consciously links us to all creation, from the mitochondria to the stars.

As you become increasingly familiar with the stillness and contentment of being, you lay the ground for a deep, abiding happiness. The last time I saw Ram Dass, he told me he was writing a book on contentment. When I asked him if he could sum up the secret of contentment, he looked at me with a smile and slowly said, "Plumb the depths of this moment." When you do that, you may find not only a new aliveness and wakefulness but an avenue to "the peace that surpasses all understanding."

In doing this program, you've developed various states of well-being and probably taken some significant steps in your life. You've seen that there are many ways to find happiness. This is a lifelong process, and as you continue this journey, you will deepen your connection to joy and allow it more and more to shine through. The great Sufi poet Rumi said, "Keep knocking, and the joy inside will eventually open a window and look out to see who's there."

May you be happy.

Acknowledgments

We are both deeply grateful to Toni Burbank, our acquiring editor at Bantam and one of the publishing industry's all-time greats, who welcomed this book with her hallmark enthusiasm and warmth. Beyond offering feedback on our initial drafts that significantly strengthened the material, she was a friend who offered heartfelt support. Danielle Perez carried the manuscript onward to completion, asking intelligent and insightful questions with a perspective that opened the door to a broad readership. She went beyond the norm in including us in the process, willingly responding to our ongoing requests and suggestions. Her vision and careful attention to detail at every point allowed the book to become all we had hoped it might be. We also appreciate and share Danielle's love of canine companions. Stephanie Tade, our agent, had unwavering faith in our proposal and landed it swiftly and expertly in the hands of our dream publisher. She embodies what this book is about—joy, compassion, caring, and integrity.

We are deeply grateful to Danna Faulds, who graced this book with her beautiful and profound poetry. Wise and heartful, her poems capture the essence of the teachings and elucidate the steps that awaken joy. We also thank Dr. Rick Hanson for his brilliant intellect and kind heart. Even in the midst of his own book deadlines, he offered careful feedback on our neuroscience references and was always forthcoming with an impressive mental index of resources. Jack Kornfield read an early draft of the manuscript and offered feedback that steered the book in the right direction. Joseph Goldstein answered some critical questions as we grappled with fine points about the nature of reality that ultimately went the way of non-being in the text. Fred Goldsmith and Ed Gerstenhaber did meticulous readings of the manuscript and offered insightful comments from welcome and needed perspectives. Jane Baraz read every chapter, sometimes in several drafts, always making useful suggestions, even at the eleventh hour.

JAMES:

It gives me great happiness to express my appreciation to everyone who made this book possible. I want to begin by saying that from the start this book has been a collaborative effort—a fruition of thirty-three years of friendship and ongoing conversation into the nature of true happiness. I first met Shoshana on my second meditation retreat in 1976. Overwhelmed and feeling not a little self-pity with a mountain of lunch pots to clean, this fellow retreatant came up to me whispering in an angelic voice, "Would you like some help?" I gratefully said yes and I've been benefiting from her help and support ever since. It was Shoshana who first encouraged me to write this book. In working together, she not only skillfully helped me clarify my ideas every step of the way, but also contributed her decades of spiritual wisdom and writing expertise. Although writing a book is not easy, the process for me included many moments of true joy and deep gratitude for our co-creation.

The Awakening Joy course, which the book is based on, has come about through the amazing grace and dedication of an extraordinary team, starting with Gretchen Thomas, whose technical know-how and incredible generosity helped take it from a small group of participants to an online course that has reached thousands. "Thank you" doesn't begin to cover it. Deep bows to Mary Helen Fein, who created a fabulous website that's both engaging and easy to navigate. Jane Baraz's wisdom, judgment, and hard work have consistently steered the course in the right direction. Kate Janke, course coordinator, has brought dedication and her natural radiance to make the participants feel welcome and part of something special. Gratitude to all the other behind-the-scenes people who've made the course a success: Deborah Todd, Andy McGuire, Nathan Friedkin, Jill Goodfriend, Deborah Henry, and Shoshana Cole. Northbrae

Community Church and especially Bob Davis gave us our home.

A big thank you to my special Joy Buddy Patricia Ellsberg, whose Big Love comes through her guided meditations, inviting participants to directly experience the various course themes. Musicians Eve Decker, Betsy Rose, Jennifer Berezan, and Melanie DeMore bring wisdom and inspiration to their music and allow everyone to experience the joy of song. I'm grateful to the stellar lineup of speakers—happiness experts, neuroscientists, and wisdom teachers—who bring to life the points I'm trying to convey. Special thanks to Rick Foster and Greg Hicks whose book *How We Choose to Be Happy* originally inspired me to create the course and was a valuable resource for the earlier courses. Deep appreciation to Rick and Greg, as well as all the other presenters at the Awakening Joy course in Berkeley, many of whose words are included in this book: Sylvia Boorstein, Rick Hanson, M. J. Ryan, Dacher Keltner, Marci Shimoff, Catherine Ingram, Anam Thubten Rinpoche, Jack Kornfield, Paul Ekman, Carolyn Hobbs, Guy Armstrong, and Dan Clurman.

I feel tremendous appreciation to all the people who have participated in the Awakening Joy course these last six years, and a special debt of gratitude to those who so generously shared their words and stories.

I am so blessed to have the friendship, wisdom, encouragement, and support of my teaching colleagues at Spirit Rock Meditation Center and am grateful to Spirit Rock, including the staff and Board, for being the beacon of consciousness that it is.

My main spiritual teachers and benefactors, Joseph Goldstein and Ram Dass, put me on the road to real happiness and have inspired and guided me since 1974. I pay homage to the Buddha for showing a way to end suffering and to the highest happiness. My undying gratitude to Neem Karoli Baba, who has guided this project from the beginning.

The sincerity and support of the Insight Meditation Community of Berkeley inspires me to find something useful to say every Thursday night. Special appreciation to Giedra Gershman, Joyce Rybandt, Nancy Benson-Smith, Ross Smith, Gay Gale, Joyce Kelley, Suzy Sloka, Jim French, Ernie Isaacs, Janet Keyes, Linda Gallagher-Brown, Steven Napoli, Jennifer Braun, John Porter, Jenya Zellerbach, Isabella Wilk, Mac Lingo, Dave Seabury, and Hime Levine for their incredible support. Also, great thanks to the Berkeley Buddhist Monastery and Reverend Heng Sure, for their gracious hospitality all these years.

I'm so grateful to the Dedicated Practitioner Program groups I lead for their ongoing wisdom, encouragement, and support as well as to all the Community Dharma Leaders who help me feel a part of a large network of people who have taught so many to discover deep peace and freedom for themselves. A big thank you to the group of young dharma mentors I have the privilege to guide—Alexa Ouellett, Anthony Rodgers, Kate Janke, Erin Hill, Oren Sofer, Aline Prentice, and Will Henry—part of the next generation who will share these principles so skillfully and touch so many people in the coming years.

Thanks to Daveen and Alan Fox and Lynn and Henry Moody, who generously provided me space to write. Sylvia Bell-Tull spent many hours transcribing and Janet Keyes organized my earlier writings, which were the foundation for much of this book and the Awakening Joy course. Thanks to Adi Bemak, Steven Newmark, and Toni Burbank for encouraging me to find my own voice. Special thanks to Catherine Ingram, Tara Brach, and Anna Grete Mazziotta for being there during some hard times.

Selma Baraz, Susan Baraz, Tony Baraz, Adam Baraz, and my beloved Pal gave me all the support and love I could want. And finally, to the love of my life, Jane Baraz, who, through thick and thin, has been with me every step of the way: Thank you, thank you, thank you.

SHOSHANA:

I am deeply grateful to James for the joys and challenges we have shared in creating this book, which has been a rite of passage for both of us. Through thousands of hours on the phone, hundreds of emails, and dozens of hours side by side, we have shared not only the work but the ongoing story of our lives. Thank you for climbing the mountain together and for your sincere dedication to living with an open heart, and inspiring me to do the same. It has been an honor and a gift to help make the Awakening Joy course available as a book, and to discover that it absolutely works. During the course of this work, James's "other half," Jane Baraz, has in so many ways offered her understanding, wisdom, and insight. I am grateful for her mind and heart, and for our deepening friendship.

The love of friends and family has been my support and fall-net throughout this process. Elias Alexander willingly shared his mother with yet another book as he passed through his final years of childhood and emerged as an amazing young man. I am deeply grateful to Laurinda Gilmore Graves for her steady friendship and fierce support and for always returning my calls. Sypko Andreae and Carolyn Shaffer conspired to feed me nutritious meals at critical times and in so many ways were there, including mini-celebrations along the way. If not for Carolyn, our dear dog would have spent many more endless hours lying in my office while I worked, only dreaming of running through meadows. My heart is filled with gratitude for the joy and constant love of that beautiful creature, Buddy-gi, and for her profound teaching as she graciously let go into death. Stephanie Phillips and Av Yitz supported us both with such care during her long passage out of life.

Deedie and David Runkel rescued me and the book by putting us up in one of Anne Hathaway's cottages during a very tricky time. Deedie's waffles at the finish line also helped a lot. Kay Lynne Sherman opened her home, her garden, and her heart, and has been a perfect Findhorn housemate. My "sister" Lolly Roy has, as always, understood at the most profound levels. A special thanks to all the rest of Elias's godparents, including my godbrother Jerry Roy, my godsister Amy Fates, Sypko and Carolyn, G. and R., Ted and Laurinda, Max Lan, Jim Wiley, and Barbara and Arnie Meyer, for carrying my son while I carried this book. Enduring thanks to Janet King for her enormous wisdom and constancy, right up to the end, to Daidie Donnelly for her friendship and superb coaching skills, and to Norma Burton who walked me through the valley to the light. And to my mother, Carol Susan Berry, who is an inspiration and guide.

Special thanks to the members of my fiction and nonfiction writing groups, who understood and supported all those cancellations, listened with such gentle care, and brought food and chocolate when most needed. My soul-sisters of the word: Susan DuMond, Lori Henriksen, Carol Hwoschinsky, Alissa Lukara, Maggie McLaughlin, Deedie Runkel,

Carolyn Shaffer, and Jodine Turner. I am also grateful to the Rogue Valley Peace Choir, the beloved Ensemble, and the late, great Dave Marston for the nourishment and remembrance of song. So many others deserve gratitude, including Nancy Bloom, Linda and Manny Cohen, Ted Graves, Connie Toth-Berindei, and special mention goes to Carly Newfeld's son Joss Mulligan who passed a sleepless night on the couch while the final chapter was being hammered out over the phone in the next room.

Finally, I owe a debt of gratitude to those who have offered the clarity and wisdom of Buddhist philosophy and practice, including that triple gem many years ago—Jack, Joseph, and Sharon—and especially S. N. Goenka, who untied the boat and set it moving. What a joyous gift to be alive.

BIBLIOGRAPHY

Barasch, Marc Ian. *Field Notes on the Compassionate Life: A Search for the Soul of Kindness.* Emmaus, PA: Rodale Press, 2006.

Bayda, Ezra. *Being Zen: Bringing Meditation to Life.* Boston: Shambhala Publications, 2002.

Begley, Sharon. *Train Your Mind, Change Your Brain: How a New Science Reveals Our Extraordinary Potential to Transform Ourselves.* New York: Ballantine Books, 2007.

Ben-Shahar, Tal. *Happier.* New York: McGraw-Hill, 2007.

Boorstein, Sylvia. *Happiness Is an Inside Job.* New York: Ballantine Books, 2007.

Byron, Thomas. *The Dhammapada.* New York: Alfred A. Knopf, 1976.

Camus, Albert. "Return to Tipasa" in *The Myth of Sisyphus: and Other Essays.* New York: Vintage Books, 1955.

Canfield, Jack and Mark Victor Hansen. *A 3rd Serving of Chicken Soup for the Soul.* Deerfield Beach, FL.: HCI, 1996.

Chodron, Pema. *No Time to Lose: A Timely Guide to the Way of the Bodhisattva.* Boston: Shambhala Publications, 2007.

Dalai Lama and Howard Cutler. *The Art of Happiness.* New York: Riverhead Books, 1998.

Dalai Lama and Howard Cutler. *Worlds in Harmony: Compassionate Action for a Better World.* Berkeley, CA: Parallax Press, 2008.

Elkind, David. *The Power of Play: Learning What Comes Naturally,* New York: Da Capo Lifelong Books, 2008.

Ekman, Paul and the Dalai Lama. *Emotional Awareness: Overcoming the Obstacles to Psychological Balance and Compassion.* New York: Times Books, 2008.

Emmons, Robert. *Thanks.* New York: Houghton Mifflin, 2007.

Faulds, Danna. *Go In and In: Poems from the Heart of Yoga.* Greenville, NC: Peaceable Kingdom Books, 2002.

Faulds, Danna. *One Soul: More Poems from the Heart of Yoga.* Greenville, NC: Peaceable Kingdom Books, 2003.

Faulds, Danna. *Prayers to the Infinite: New Yoga Poems.* Greenville, NC: Peaceable Kingdom Books, 2004.

Faulds, Danna. *From Root to Bloom: New Yoga Poems and Other Writings.* Greenville, NC: Peaceable Kingdom Books, 2006.

Foster, Rick and Greg Hicks. *How We Choose to Be Happy: The 9 Choices of Extremely Happy People—Their Secrets, Their Stories.* New York: G.P. Putnam's Sons, 1999.

Golas, Thaddeus. *The Lazy Man's Guide to Enlightenment.* New York: Bantam, 1980.

Goleman, Daniel. *Destructive Emotions: A Scientific Dialogue with the Dalai Lama.* New York: Bantam, 2003.

Haidt, Jonathan. "Elevation and the Positive Psychology of Morality" in *Flourishing: Positive Psychology and the Life Well-Lived.* Corey L. M. Keyes and Jonathan Haidt, Eds. Washington, DC: American Psychological Association, 2003.

Hanson, Rick. *Buddha's Brain: The Practical Neuroscience of Happiness, Love and Wisdom.* Oakland, CA: New Harbinger Publications, Inc., 2009.

Harvey, Andrew. *Light Upon Light: Inspirations from Rumi.* Berkeley, CA: North Atlantic Books, 1996.

Hobbs, Carolyn. *Joy, No Matter What.* Boston: Conari Press, 2005.

Kabat-Zinn, Jon. *Full Catastrophe Living: Using the Wisdom of Your Body and Mind to Face Stress, Pain, and Illness.* New York: Delacorte Press, 1990.

Kaza, Stephanie, ed. *Hooked: Buddhist Writings on Greed, Desire, and the Urge to Consume.* Boston: Shambhala Publications, 2005.

Keltner, Dacher. *Born to Be Good: The Science of a Meaningful Life.* New York: W.W. Norton & Company, Inc., 2009.

Kornfield, Jack. *The Art of Forgiveness, Lovingkindness, and Peace.* New York: Bantam, 2002.

Kornfield, Jack and Paul Breiter. *A Still Forest Pool: The Insight Meditation of Achaan Cha.* Wheaton, IL: Quest Books, 1985.

Levine, Stephen. *Who Dies? An Investigation of Conscious Living and Conscious Dying.* New York: Anchor Books, 1982.

Luskin, Fred. *Forgive for Good: A Proven Prescription for Health and Happiness.* New York: HarperCollins, 2002.

Lyubomirsky, Sonja. *The How of Happiness: A Scientific Approach to Getting the Life You Want.* New York: Penguin Group, 2007.

Makransky, John. *Awakening Through Love.* Somerville, MA: Wisdom Publications, 2007.

Maslow, Abraham. *The Farther Reaches of Human Nature.* New York: Viking, 1971.

McKibben, Bill. *Deep Economy: The Wealth of Communities and the Durable Future.* New York: Henry Holt & Company, 2008.

Muller, Wayne. *Sabbath: Finding Rest, Renewal, and Delight in Our Busy Lives.* New York: Bantam Books, 2000.

Myers, David. *The Pursuit of Happiness: Who Is Happy and Why?* New York: Harper Paperbacks, 1993.

Nisargadatta, Maharaj. *I Am That.* Durham, NC: Acorn Press, 1990.

Peace Pilgrim. *Peace Pilgrim: Her Life and Work in Her Own Words.* Santa Fe, NM: Ocean Tree Books, 1992.

Ram Dass. *Be Here Now*. New York: Three Rivers Press (CA), 1971.

Ram Dass. *Still Here: Embracing Aging, Changing, and Dying*. New York: Riverhead Books, 2001.

Rea, Rashani. *Beyond Brokenness*. Xlibris Publishing, IN 2009.

Riera, Michael. *Uncommon Sense for Parents with Teenagers*. Berkeley, CA: Celestial Arts, 2004.

Ryan, M.J. *Attitudes of Gratitude*. San Francisco: Conari Press, 2009.

de Saint-Exupery, Antoine. *The Little Prince*. Translated by Richard Howard. New York: Harcourt, Inc., 2000. [First published New York: Reynal & Hitchcock, 1943.]

Salinger, J.D. "Teddy" in *Nine Stories*. New York: Bantam Books, 1964.

Seligman, Martin. *Authentic Happiness: Using the New Positive Psychology to Realize Your Potential for Lasting Fulfillment*. New York: Free Press, 2002.

Sengtsan, Chien Chih (The Third Zen Patriarch of China). *Verses on the Faith Mind* (Hsin Hsin Ming). Translated by Richard B. Clarke. Toronto: Coach House Press, 1973.

Shah, Idries. *The Exploits of the Incomparable Mulla Nasrudin / The Subtleties of the Inimitable Mulla*. London: Octagon Press Ltd., 1983.

Shimoff, Marci with Carol Kline. *Happy for No Reason*. New York: Free Press, 2008.

Siegel, Daniel J. *The Mindful Brain: Reflection and Attunement in the Cultivation of Well-Being*. New York: W. W. Norton and Company, 2007.

Steindl-Rast, Brother David. *Gratefulness, the Heart of Prayer*. Ramsey, NJ: Paulist Press, 1984.

Swimme, Brian. *The Universe Is a Green Dragon: A Cosmic Creation Story*. Santa Fe, NM: Bear & Company, 1984.

Thomas, Lewis. *The Lives of a Cell*. New York: Penguin Books, 1978.

Thubten, Anam Rinpoche. *No Self, No Problem*. Ithaca, NY: Snow Lion Publications, 2009.

Tolle, Eckhart. *A New Earth: Awakening to Your Life's Purpose*. New York: Dutton, 2005.

Watts, Alan. *The Wisdom of Insecurity*. New York: Pantheon Books, 1951.

Williamson, Marianne. *A Return to Love*. New York: HarperCollins, 1992.

Wolcott, Harry F. *Sneaky Kid and Its Aftermath: Ethics and Intimacy in Fieldwork*. Walnut Creek, CA: Altamira Press, 2002.

James Baraz's Reading List

Brach, Tara. *Radical Acceptance: Embracing Your Life with the Heart of a Buddha.* New York: Bantam Books, 2003.

Boorstein, Sylvia. *It's Easier Than You Think.* New York: HarperCollins, 1995.

Coleman, Mark. *Awake in the Wild: Mindfulness in Nature as a Path of Self-Discovery.* Maui, HI: Inner Ocean Publishing, 2006.

Das, Lama Surya. *Awakening the Buddha Within.* New York: Broadway Books, 1997.

Goldstein, Joseph. *The Experience of Insight.* Boston: Shambhala Publications, 1976.

Goldstein, Joseph. *One Dharma.* San Francisco: HarperSanFrancisco, 2002.

Goldstein, Joseph and Jack Kornfield. *Seeking the Heart of Wisdom.* Boston: Shambhala Publications, 1987.

Goleman, Daniel. *Emotional Intelligence.* New York: Bantam, 1995.

Kabat-Zinn, Jon. *Full Catastrophe Living: Using the Wisdom of Your Body and Mind to Face Stress, Pain, and Illness.* New York: Delta, 1990.

Kornfield, Jack. *A Path with Heart.* New York: Bantam, 1993.

Kornfield, Jack. *The Wise Heart: A Guide to the Universal Teachings of Buddhist Psychology.* New York: Bantam Books, 2009.

Macy, Joanna. *World as Lover, World as Self.* Berkeley, CA: Parallax Press, 1991.

Moffitt, Phillip. *Dancing with Life: Buddhist Insights for Finding Meaning and Joy in the Face of Suffering.* New York: Rodale Inc., 2008.

Ricard, Matthieu. *Happiness: A Guide to Developing Life's Most Important Skill.* New York: Little, Brown and Company, 2007.

Rothberg, Donald. *The Engaged Spiritual Life: The Buddhist Approach to Transforming Ourselves and the World.* Boston: Beacon Press, 2008.

Ryan, M.J. *The Happiness Makeover: How to Teach Yourself to Be Happy and Enjoy Every Day.* New York: Broadway Books, 2005.

Salzberg, Sharon. *Lovingkindness: The Revolutionary Art of Happiness.* Boston: Shambhala, 1995.

Salzberg, Sharon. *Faith: Trusting Your Deepest Experience.* New York: Riverhead Books, 2002.

Tolle, Eckhart. *The Power of Now.* Novato, CA: New World Library, 1999.

Weisman, Arinna and Jean Smith. *The Beginner's Guide to Insight Meditation*. New York: Bell Tower, 2001.

Winston, Diana. *Wide Awake: A Buddhist Guide for Teens*. New York: Berkley Books, 2003.

WEBSITES FOR JAMES BARAZ

jamesbaraz.com. For all of James Baraz's retreats, classes, workshops, and articles, and a link to his recorded talks.

awakeningjoy.info. For information and to sign up for the Awakening Joy course.

insightberkeley.org. For schedule and information on James Baraz's Berkeley meditation community, and an archive of recordings of all weekly lectures.

ADDITIONAL RESOURCES

accesstoinsight.org. A comprehensive collection of the Buddha's translated discourses and commentaries by Buddhist teachers and scholars.

authentichappiness.org. The website of Positive Psychologist Martin Seligman. Includes questionnaires to measure your happiness level and archived copies of newletters on topics related to happiness.

dharma.org. For a schedule of retreats at the Insight Meditation Center in Barre, Massachusetts.

dharmaseed.org. For talks and lectures by well-known Western teachers of Theravada Buddhism.

focusonaids.com. For information on Focus on AIDS, its periodic fund-raisers, and to learn about its humanitarian projects around the world.

greatergoodmag.org. For cutting-edge research on the science of well-being, from the Greater Good Science Center at the University of California at Berkeley. Edited by Dacher Keltner, Ph.D., and Jason Marsh.

mindfulschools.org. For information and research on teaching mindfulness techniques to children in all education settings.

PatriciaEllsberg.com. For free downloads of Patricia Ellsberg's guided meditations for each step of the Awakening Joy course.

ramdass.org. For Ram Dass's teachings and schedule.

spiritrock.org. For the schedule of retreats and workshops at Spirit Rock Meditation Center in Woodacre, California.

wisebrain.org. The website of Rick Hanson, Ph.D., and Rick Mendius, M.D., focusing on the connections between psychology, neurology, and contemplative practices. Archived articles and copies of the Wise Brain Bulletin.

About the Authors

James Baraz has been teaching meditation for more than thirty years and the Awakening Joy course, both on-site and online, since 2003. He is a cofounder of Spirit Rock Meditation Center in Woodacre, California, where he regularly teaches, and he leads retreats and workshops around the United States and abroad. He lives with his wife, Jane, in Berkeley, California. Learn more about the course at www.awakeningjoy.info and James's other activities at jamesbaraz.com.

Shoshana Tembeck Alexander has studied Buddhism since 1970 and is the author of *In Praise of Single Parents* and *Women's Ventures, Women's Visions,* and, with the Findhorn Community, *The Findhorn Garden.* She has guided various works of several prominent Buddhist authors, including Tara Brach, Sharon Salzberg, and Wes Nisker. She lives in Ashland, Oregon.

Parallax Press, a nonprofit organization, publishes books on engaged Buddhism and the practice of mindfulness by Thich Nhat Hanh and other authors. For a copy of the catalog, please contact:

Parallax Press
P.O. Box 7355
Berkeley, CA 94707
Tel: (510) 525-0101
www.parallax.org

RELATED TITLES FROM PARALLAX PRESS

Happiness by Thich Nhat Hanh

Ten Breaths to Happiness by Glen Schneider

Present Moment, Wonderful Moment
by Thich Nhat Hanh

Pass it On by Joanna Macy

Not Quite Nirvana by Rachel Neumann

Wonderland by Daniel Doen Silberberg

Cultivating the Mind of Love
by Thich Nhat Hanh

BOOK GROUP ENDORSEMENTS:

Our group meets once a month in a phone conference, to share how the month's chapter has worked for us. People report unexpected changes in their approach to life, and a deepening in their understanding of themselves. *Awakening Joy* has helped all of us be pro-active in inviting positive qualities into our daily lives. Some in our group have expressed gratitude because it has helped them transform their despair at how things are in the world. Still others have also said that *Awakening Joy* has been a vehicle for deep enquiry, because of the self-honesty that has been awakened in practicing it. This book has been an immeasurable support. Thanks so much.
— CHRISTOPHER MCLEAN, Sydney Australia

The word "joy" has in the Finnish language many meanings; it can be everything from calmness to elation. But what it means deep inside you is the most important. Our meetings give us really good, challenging ways of sharing thoughts about joy in life. They broaden the understanding of joy, as you have so many nice people around you. After half a year with Awakening Joy, I feel really the everyday joy in my life, and I'm really often stopping and thinking about different situations, why am I feeling joy now, and in other situations reflecting on why I'm not feeling joy right now. You really start feeling joy just by reading the book. They group enhances the experience even more because you have others to share your thoughts and reflections with. By participating in this *Awakening Joy* course I have really started to create a good life with joy included in my everyday doings. This awakened joy has been noticed both in my private life, as well as among my working colleagues.
— PETER HOLMBERG, Finland Awakening Joy group

The *Awakening Joy* book and principles have been the soil from which our beautiful group has blossomed. The path of practice outlined in the book provides a guiding map for us each to follow and it acts as the meeting place for us all to come together in reflection. It offers us an opportunity to connect across departments in our organization around practices that contribute to our well-being.
— RAE HOUSEMAN, group facilitator, Insight Meditation Society staff Awakening Joy group, Barre, MA

I've taken the Awakening Joy course three times in a group and keep the book beside my bed to remind me to wake up and remember that even in suffering there can be relief and release. There are twenty people in our current group in Saskatoon using *Awakening Joy* with its many options to deepen our community and to find more ways to cultivate well-being. What a gift! Many, many thanks from Saskatoon!

—JENNIFER KEANE, Saskatoon, SK, Canada